Federalism in India

Federalism in India

Towards a Fresh Balance of Power

(With a Foreword by Lord Bhikhu Parekh)

Edited by

Lancy Lobo

Mrutuyanjaya Sahu

Jayesh Shah

RAWAT PUBLICATIONS

Jaipur • New Delhi • Bangalore • Hyderabad • Guwahati • Kolkata

ISBN 978-81-316-0659-9

Published by
Prem Rawat for **Rawat Publications**
Satyam Apts, Sector 3, Jawahar Nagar, Jaipur 302 004 (India)
Phone: 0141 265 1748/7006 Fax: 0141 265 1748
E-mail: info@rawatbooks.com
Website: www.rawatbooks.com

New Delhi Office
4858/24, Ansari Road, Daryaganj, New Delhi 110 002
Phone: 011 2326 3290

Also at *Bangalore, Hyderabad, Guwahati* and *Kolkata*

Typeset by Rawat Computers, Jaipur

Printed at Chaman Enterprises, New Delhi

Contents

Foreword

Lord Bhikhu Parekh

For the architects of the Indian Constitution labouring on the design of the new state, one of the important questions was how to meet the apparently conflicting demands of diversity and unity. India's diversity was wide and deep, and rooted in the differences of religion, language, culture and ethnicity. It had existed for centuries, demanded public recognition and could neither be exorcised out of existence nor privatized. Like many of their countrymen, the architects of the Constitution also thought that the diversity was a source of the country's vitality and creativity, and hence not just a brute fact to be accepted, but a value to be cherished and promoted by the state.

Diversity was important, so was the unity of the country. The fact that a weak and divided India had repeatedly fallen prey to foreign invasions and recently broken up under the pressure of the Muslim separatist demand added urgency to the goal of national unity, and gave it a particular orientation. For the founding fathers and mothers, India should be not only united but unified, but also remove all potential sources of division and fragmentation, enjoy the undivided loyalty of its people, insist on its territorial inviolability and be strong enough to meet internal and external threats. Its unity obviously could not be based on language, ethnicity, religion or culture – on one or all of which European states had relied. Since India had no pre-existing nation to sustain its state, the latter had to find its source of unity within itself, and that could only be politico-legal in nature. India was to be united in terms of common subscription to a unified and hierarchical structure of authority committed to the realization of certain constitutionally prescribed goals. The state was to be centralized, that is run from a single centre which alone spoke and acted in the name of all its citizens, and controlled and when necessary overrode such other centres of power as were allowed to exist at regional and local levels.

The Indian federation as designed by the Constitution was a product of these two guiding principles and had several unique features. It showed great respect for cultural and religious diversity. Almost unique in the history of modern federations, religious minorities are free to be governed by their own personal laws, and with state assistance, religious and cultural minorities enjoy a near absolute right to set up and maintain their own educational and cultural institutions, and so on, thereby making India almost a federation of cultures. The same right is not extended to the states, they do not enjoy the kind of autonomy or parity of status with the central government that their counterparts do in United States, Australia and other federations. The central government can unilaterally alter their boundaries, dismiss their governments and appoint their governors who are answerable to it alone. It also controls the major sources of revenue, amounting to nearly two-thirds of the total revenues of all the states put together, and is able to exert considerable financial pressure on the heavily dependent states.

Unlike almost all other federations that are symmetrical and whose constituent units enjoy identical rights and powers, the Indian federation is asymmetrical. Article 370 grants the state of Jammu & Kashmir a degree of autonomy and protections not available to others. Under Article 371 A, no act of Parliament is to apply to Nagaland and Mizoram without the resolution of their Legislative Assemblies in matters relating to their religious and social practices, ownership and transfer of land and its resources, and the administration of civil and criminal justice. The asymmetry is largely bound up with culture and involves states with distinct cultural identities.

The Indian state as designed by the Constitution then has a complex structure. Politically and fiscally, it has a strong unitary orientation; legally and administratively, it is quasi-federal and culturally, it grants considerable autonomy to religious and cultural communities and is highly decentralized. Since the Indian state comes out differently on different dimensions, and these are incommensurable, the frequently asked question whether it is 'fully', 'truly', 'semi' or 'quasi' federal makes little sense. And even if we limit it to the distribution of powers between the central and state governments, it is not very helpful because the distribution can take several different forms, none of which can be held up as the 'essential' or defining feature of a 'truly' federal state.

During the 60 odd years of its existence, the Indian federation has undergone important changes, some as a result of the tension inherent in its design and others because of factors external to it. The states could not remain mere territorial units as the Constitution imagined. They had their dominant languages and demanded linguistic reorganization, first conceded in 1956 and then extended to other states in 1960, 1963, 1966, 1968 and 2003. Language could not be separated from culture, and over time the states became cultural, even ethnocultural units, with their distinct assertive identities. Since the Constitution showed great sensitivity to culture, the demands of culturally articulated states for autonomy could not be ignored. In the course of forging their cultural identities, the states met with inevitable resistance from long existing local and subregional identities, which they flattened, marginalized or suitably incorporated. While demanding decentralization from the centre, the states were not prepared to extend it further, and the principle of federalism stopped at their boundaries.

Economic, political, constitutional and other factors also played and continue to play an important role in shaping the federal structure. As different states developed along different lines and at different paces, they made different demands on the central government and sought greater economic autonomy. Liberalization of the economy facilitated the free movement of capital, and led to greater competition between them to attract foreign or national capital, and a demand for a greater freedom to pursue their own policies. Globalization respects no boundaries between or within countries, and it too has reinforced the federalizing trends.

Misuse of the central government's constitutional power to dismiss democratically elected state governments for ideological or narrow partisan purposes under Article 356 led to a widespread demand to limit it, endorsed by the Supreme Court in its Bommai Judgement in 1994. The absence of a single dominant party at the centre and the ensuing need for coalition strengthened the hands of regional parties and their demand for greater autonomy for states. The movement of leaders from the regional level to the national and back again gave the states political salience and dignity. Being a chief minister of a state was now equal in importance to and sometimes even more important than being a cabinet minister in the central government. Moving to the centre was no longer the height of political ambition. In these and other ways state politics acquired a new dignity, a new status and weakened the earlier centralist ethos of the Indian federation.

Due to the above-mentioned factors and other related factors, the tightly structured Indian state has been considerably loosened, and the states enjoy considerable political visibility and potency. Since we have long been accustomed to thinking of national unity in terms of centralization, the weakening of the centre and the emergence of a polycentric India fills many with unease. Some fear that it reduces the country to a sum of its fractious parts, each pursuing its narrow interests in disregard of those of the others and the whole. Others even think that such a weak India lacking a sense of collective purpose could once again become a prey to foreign powers, be the states or more likely multinationals, and lose its independence for all practical purposes.

Such fears are misplaced, at least as of now. The Constitution's assumption that strong states mean weak India has been proven wrong and that gives us the vitally necessary space to rethink the design of the Indian federation. A federal state necessarily implies at least two identities, the national and the regional, and its success depends on balancing the two and using each to check the excesses of the other. The regional or state-based identity gives cultural depth and emotional immediacy to the national identity, and the latter in turn gives it historical depth, wider context, and security and self-confidence. One does not have to cease being a proud Bengali or Gujarati to be a proud Indian. Rather one is likely to be more committed to one's Indian identity if it recognizes and respects one's Bengali or Gujarati identity.

Like all federal states, the Indian federation has a psychological and moral basis, an important point that is often ignored and is sustained not only by appropriate policies, practices and institutions but also by the way in which its citizens integrate and feel at ease with their regional and national identities. The two might get into conflict when each is defined in narrow and exclusive terms. We have learned from experience that the earlier attempt to privilege the national identity and marginalize and even frown upon the regional was misguided and counterproductive. The regional identity or self-consciousness is restoring the balance without going to the other extreme of marginalizing or denigrating the national. Indeed powerful pan-Indian forces at several crucial levels ensure that this is unlikely to happen. So long as the Indian state respects and nurtures both identities and designs of its federal structure appropriately, its decentring need not pose a threat to its unity.

Fifteen excellent chapters assembled in this volume trace the biography of the Indian federation and analyse the challenges it faced in the past and is likely to face in the future. Written by distinguished experts from different disciplinary perspectives, they locate the federal structure within the wider economic and political framework and show how its internal logic is shaped by the latter. The volume has the further advantage of being policy oriented and includes valuable recommendations on how new challenges can be best met. It is informed by the belief that federation is the only way to unite a country as diverse as India and to give its democracy firm roots. Democracy and federation share a common impulse, to bring power closer to the people and give them a sense of control over their lives. Their destinies are therefore interlocked, and each can be strong and vibrant only if the other is. This salutary message as well as its perceptive analysis and well-considered policy recommendations make this volume a most welcome addition to the growing literature on the subject and of considerable interest to scholars, policy makers and the general public alike.

Bhikhu Parekh
University of Westminster and House of Lords

Acknowledgements

Centre–state relations have been changing their character over the decades particularly after two main national parties lost their dominance and had to cobble up alliances with regional parties who demanded their pounds of flesh. This volume contains select papers of a seminar held at the Centre for Culture and Development, Vadodara. We were fortunate to have a keynote address from the former Secretary to the Lok Sabha for many terms, Dr S. Kashyap, and the concluding address was given by the governor of Gujarat, Dr K. Beniwal. Professor (Lord) Bhikhu Parekh has been kind enough to provide a Foreword. We thank Professor A.M. Shah for his guidance in preparing this volume. Mr R.H. Ittagi needs to be thanked for his editorial assistance. The paper presenters have revised their papers after the comments from the seminar participants. We thank them for their prompt cooperation. We are grateful to Economic and Political Weekly for permitting us to take up the jointly authored essay, 'Resource Federalism in India: The Case of Minerals' by Ligia Noronha, Nidhi Srivastava, Divya Datt and P.V. Sridharan (Vol. XLIV. No. 8 pp. 51–59). Alka Srivastava deserves our thanks for facilitating the funding for the seminar from ICSSR – New Delhi. Amba Gamit and her team at CCD have assisted in the word processing. Finally, Pranit Rawat and his team deserve our kudos for efficiently bringing out this volume.

Abbreviations

ADB	Asian Development Bank
AGP	Asom Gana Parishad
AP	Andhra Pradesh
BCIM	Bangladesh, China, India and Myanmar
BJP	Bharatiya Janata Party
CMP	Common Minimum Programme
CR	Conflict Resolution
CR	Composite Ratio
CSS	Centrally Sponsored Schemes
DMK	Dravida Munnetra Kazhagam
DRDAs	District Rural Development Agencies
ER	Expenditure Ratio
FDI	Foreign Direct Investment
FSRII	Fiscal Self-reliance and Improvement Index
GDP	Gross Domestic Product
GS	Gram Sabha
GSDP	Gross State Domestic Product
GST	Goods and Services Tax

HDC	Hill Districts Councils
HDI	Human Development Index
IB	Intelligence Bureau
ILO	International Labour Organisation
IMF	International Monetary Fund
INC	Indian National Congress
ITPO	India Trade Promotion Organisation
J&K	Jammu & Kashmir
JNNURM	Jawaharlal Nehru National Urban Renewal Mission
KLLADS	Karnataka Legislator's Local Development Scheme
LGs	Local Governments
MEA	Ministry of External Affairs
MGNREGA	Mahatma Gandhi National Rural Employment Guarantee Act
MHA	Ministry of Home Affairs
MMDR	Mines and Mineral Development and Regulation
MOU	Memoranda of Understanding
MPLAD	Members of Parliament Local Area Development
NATGRID	National Information Grid
NCTC	National Counter Terrorism Centre
NDC	National Development Council
NEP	New Economic Policy
NIA	National Intelligence Agency
NRHM	National Rural Health Mission
NTRO	National Threat Reduction Organization
OBC	Other Backward Class
PCTV	Prevention of Communal and Targeted Violence
PDS	Public Distribution System
PESA	Panchayat Extension to Scheduled Areas
PPP	Public–Private Partnership

PR	Panchayat Raj
PRIs	Panchayati Raj Institutions
PSs	Panchayat Samitis
RAW	Research and Analysis Wing
RBI	Reserve Bank of India
RJD	Rashtriya Janata Dal
RLGs	Rural Local Governments
RR	Revenue Ratio
SC	Scheduled Caste
SDP	State Domestic Product
SERP	Society for Elimination of Rural Poverty
SEZ	Special Economic Zone
SNGs	Subnational Governments
SSUW	Social Security for Unorganized Workers
ST	Scheduled Tribe
TDP	Telugu Desam Party
TFC	Thirteenth Finance Commission
TORs	Terms of References
UCLG	United Cities and Local Government
ULGs	Urban Local Governments
UP	Uttar Pradesh
USA	United States of America
VAT	Value Added Tax
VMC	Vadodara Municipal Corporation
VPs	Village Panchayats
ZPs	Zilla Panchayats

1

Introduction

Lancy Lobo, Mrutuyanjaya Sahu and Jayesh Shah

The failure of the centralized state, both in economic and in political governance, has swung the pendulum in favour of decentralized systems in recent years across the globe. This phenomenon is not only confined to constitutionally declared federations but also seen in unitary systems, spanning countries with varying ideological spectrums and levels of development (Wheare 1953). Federalism is one of the most important, effective and greatest political institutions of the contemporary world. Federalism, as a system of intergovernmental relations between the federal centre and the regions, provinces and states, developed out of need to reconcile the goals of regional and national development in multinational countries. Federalism is also commonly understood as a theory of government that uses power to check power amid opposite and rival interests. The idea of federalism is rendered trivial when applied only to the coexistence of state and national governments. Rather, federalism offers no less than an enabling basis for development of self-organizing and self-governing capabilities under conditions of equal liberty and justice (Shvetsova et al. 2004).

Indian federalism serves the second largest population in the world, comprising an unparalleled multiplicity of cultures, religions, languages and ethnicities. The federal system has served extremely well for India in terms of promoting democracy, strengthening the national unity and achieving a fair level of economic progress. The basic essence of federalism lies in maintaining unity in the presence of diversity in terms of accommodating, preserving and promoting distinct identities within a larger political union. Though Indian federalism is not among the world's oldest federal political systems, it is, nevertheless, steadily emerging as a key feature of its political system, and also as an interesting example of the innovative potential of federalism.

The history of federalism and centre–state relations in India remains characterized by political mobilizations and intermittent struggles towards a more meaningful federal set-up (Roy 2011). Alarmed at the volatile turn of events preceding the birth of free India and the country's partition, the framers of the Indian Constitution opted for a 'Union of States' with a strong centre, keeping aside the idea of a loose federation that had engaged their attention initially. Our founding fathers decided on a federation with a strong central government for holding together the diverse economic, linguistic and cultural entities as a way of avoiding fissiparous tendencies (Pal and Aggarwal 2010: 69ff). Whether India is a federation at all, has long been debated by scholars and experts who hold different views while interpreting the federal nature of the Indian Constitution. For instance, some scholars describe federalism as 'administrative federalism', others argue for 'market preserving federalism' and some others describe it as 'coming together federalism' versus 'holding together federalism'. Countries such as United States are considered examples of 'coming together' federalism, while India is considered an example of 'holding together' federalism. Paul H. Appleby (1957) observes that India is 'most federal' insofar as the centre is weak and depends upon its units for the execution of several developmental programs and plan projects. Others call it 'cooperative federalism', an 'amicable union' (Austin 1966). K.C. Wheare (1953) characterizes it as 'quasi-federal'.

Acknowledging the democratic deficit, the Constitution was amended in 1992, paving the way for the introduction of a third-tier system of governance at the level of panchayats and municipalities, which in turn not only revolutionized the decentralized governance in the country but also brought in a fresh equation with respect to centre–state relations. The late 1990s witnessed a weakening of national political parties, emergence of coalition politics and a shift in the centre–state power balance. Politically, however, with the rise of regional parties and coalitions, states seem to have gained an upper hand of late in many spheres of governance, whereas the centre finds itself restricted even when there are serious problems regarding law and order issues or foreign policy matters. Provisions and articles narrated in the Constitution of India needs revisit as the country needs fresh balance of power looking to the new 'low' in centre–state relations.

The Constitution of India and Centre–State Relations

The Constitutional scheme of governance at the centre and in the states is provided in Part XI (Articles 245 to 263) and Part XII (Articles 264 to 298), with few related provisions on trade and commerce in Part XIII and on All India Services in Part XIV. Broadly it deals with three types of relations, namely, (a) Legislative Relations (Articles 245–255); (b) Administrative Relations (Articles 256–263) and (c) Financial Relations (Articles 264–293).

The scheme on legislative relations is largely based on the federal principle of 'subsidiarity' under which what can best be administered from the centre are kept with the Union (Union List), those which are more of regional or local interest are assigned to the Units (State List) and those with some items of common concern in the Concurrent List. Part XI distributes the legislative powers between the Union and the states. The subject matter of legislation is listed rather exhaustively in the three lists given in the Seventh Schedule. The Constitution gives autonomy to centre and states within their respective fields. Parliament may make laws for the whole or any part of the territory of India and the state legislature for the whole or any part of that state. However, after applying the doctrine of territorial nexus, state laws, which have extraterritorial operation have been held valid by the court. There are several judicial doctrines evolved by the Supreme Court to interpret possible overlapping of jurisdictions in the matter of legislative powers of Centre and states.

Article 356 of the Constitution of India has always been the focal point of a wider debate of the federal structure of government in Indian polity. Article 356 deals with imposition of President's rule over a state of India. When a state is under President's rule, the elected state government (led by the Chief Minister and the Council of Ministers) is suspended, and administration is conducted directly by the Governor of the state. The Governor is an appointee of the President and thus, effectively, a functionary of the Union government (the central or federal government). Thus, imposition of

President's rule negates the federal character of the Indian political system, where administration usually is shared between the Union and state governments. It also militates against the democratic doctrine of popular sovereignty, since an elected government is suspended. These reasons have made Article 356 a controversial one. Nevertheless, it was used repeatedly by the central government to suspend state governments (of opposite political parties) based on genuine reasons or trumped-up excuses (Arora 1990).

In the 1970s and 1980s, it almost became common practice for the central government to dismiss state governments led by opposition parties. The Indira Gandhi regime and post-Emergency Janata Party were noted for this practice. Indira Gandhi's government between 1966 and 1977 is known to have imposed President's rule 39 times in different states. Similarly, Janata Party, which came to power after the Emergency, had issued President's rule in nine states which were ruled by Congress. It is only after the landmark judgment in 1994, in the *S.R. Bommai vs Union of India* case, that the misuse of Article 356 was curtailed. In this case, the Supreme Court established strict guidelines for imposing President's rule. Subsequent pronouncements by the Supreme Court in Jharkhand and other states have further whetted down the scope for misuse of Article 356. Hence since 1995, the number of cases of imposition of President's rule has come down drastically (19 cases between 1994 and 2014). The judgment delivered by the Supreme Court put a check on arbitrary dismissal of state governments in future and strengthen the federal structure of Indian polity which had hitherto been damaged on several occasions particularly when different political parties were in power at the centre and the state.

Another issue with respect to legislative relations, which caused friction between centre and states, is the power of the governor to reserve any Bill passed by the State Assembly for consideration of the President, sometimes for an indefinite period. A law adopted, sometimes more than once, by the assembly can therefore become a law in the state only after the assent by the President (Articles 200 and 201 of the Constitution of India). Today, the situation is that different political parties are in power in different states. In other words, between 1952 and 1967, single party controlled both the Parliament and state legislatures. However, this situation does not exist anymore. Since the governor owes his appointment and his continuation in the office to the Union Council of Ministers, he is more likely to act in accordance with the instructions, if any, received from the Union Council of Ministers rather than act on the advice of the state Council of Ministers in the matters in which the central government and the state government do not see eye to eye. Indeed, the governors today are being pejoratively called the 'agents of the Centre' (http://lawmin.nic.in/ncrwc/finalreport/v2b2-4.htm). It is true that the central government is not expected to give any instructions that compromise the status and position of the governor, nor is it expected to remove him for not implementing the instructions given by the central government. The experience for the last several years belies this hope.

The Constitution does not furnish much guidance to the governor – in which matters he should accord his assent and in which matters he should withhold assent. In such a situation, the legitimacy of this power, which empowers him to undo the will of the legislature by just declaring that he is withholding his assent, is open to question. In the absence of much guidance provided by the Constitution, in cases where this power can be exercised and in view of the further fact that no court is entitled to go into the justification of such withholding, conferment of such power is bound to be inherently arbitrary and discriminatory. Here again no time limit is fixed within which the President should take a decision.

There have been instances where many Bills have been pending with the President for periods of up to six years or more and some Bills for more than twelve years (http://lawmin.nic.in/ncrwc/finalreport/v2b2-4.htm). Another feature of Article 201 is that the President directs the Governor to return the Bill to the legislature and the legislature passes the Bill again (with or without amendments) and when it is again presented to the President for consideration, the Article does not say that the President is bound to grant his assent, as it is said in the case of the Governor by the first proviso to Article 201. 'It is rather surprising that even after the Legislature reconsiders the Bill, passes it again and presents it to the President for consideration, it can be stalled, if he so chooses, by not assenting to it and by cold storaging it' (http://lawmin.nic.in/ncrwc/finalreport/v2b2-4.htm).

As the President would be guided by the Union Council of Ministers in this behalf, it may quite happen (indeed, as it has already happened) that when a different party or group is in power at the centre, it can easily neutralize and nullify the will of the state legislature by advising the President to withhold his assent or cold-storage it even after the Bill is presented to the President after the reconsideration of the Bill.

Another issue that opened up a set of administrative problems is regarding the role of centre in accomplishing effective decentralization under the 73rd and 74th Amendments to the Constitution. The states which are supposed to make law in this regard have been slow in the matter of empowering panchayats with functions, funds and functionaries. Meanwhile through court interventions and otherwise, *panchayats* have elected representatives who are not able to organize governance at local levels as expected. There is a feeling that the existing arrangements need a fresh look to put the third level of governance back on rails to make democracy function.

Given the degree of permanency of the federal structure, the questions that arise for consideration are as follows:

- How does the scheme manage to resolve intergovernmental conflicts and how effectively?
- How satisfactory is the mechanism available to overcome backwardness in some regions towards a more equitable distribution of socio-economic goods and services?
- What kind of relationship is built between village governments and the state government and how it strengthened or weakened the federal scheme of governance?

Impact of Rise of Regional Parties in Centre–State Relations

Regional parties have grown perhaps the most potent force in Indian politics ever since independence. It has remained the main basis of many regional political parties, which have been governing many states since the late 1960s. The year 1967, however, proved to be a watershed in the history of independent India when, perhaps, for the first time the centre–state relations were put to a test. Simultaneously, it was also the beginning of a period when coalition politics started at state level.

The coalition governments were formed in many states, including Bihar, Haryana, Kerala, Madhya Pradesh, Orissa, Uttar Pradesh and West Bengal. This was the time when certain issues of importance pertaining to centre–state relations came into the fore, both in the form of criticism of the functioning of existing mechanisms and processes, because the regional political parties wanted to create their own niche in their respective regions. There were widespread demands for providing greater autonomy for the states in their functioning particularly from regional party led governments. Governments led by the regional parties in the states also started putting up a united front, demanding more administrative and fiscal autonomy. The de-institutionalization of the Congress Party's federal structure contributed immensely to the erosion of India's federal system. The Dravida Munnetra Kazhagam (DMK) led government in Tamil Nadu, Left Front in West Bengal and other regional parties raised the bogey of 'fiscal imbalance', 'central misrule', 'politics of planning', 'impartial governor' and 'fair deal to the states'.

With a prolonged period of coalition governments at the centre, the economic crisis and decentralization of power, the new era in the history of federalization of Indian politics started at the beginning of the 1990s. With the liberalization of the economy in the early 1990s, came the de-licensing of industrial sector and the restoration of powers to the states over industrial policy. The states have felt that the power of raising resources is not commensurate with the development responsibilities given to them. In addition, over the course of years, a feeling has been generated that the distribution of fiscal resources has not always been fair. Political biases have influenced the amounts distributed and many states felt deprived and blamed the centre for their lack of development. After neoliberal economic reforms, states also gained more room to pursue their own social and economic priorities. Similarly, more space in economic policy making was sought to be provided to the states. Controls prevailing in many areas were removed and the operation of the market largely restored. On the other hand, inadequacy of public services in critical areas, such as health care and education, led to the demand for a greater decentralization to bring governance closer to people with a view to ensuring greater degree of accountability (Bagchi 2003: 21ff).

Regional parties have started becoming part of the Union government by providing strategic support or by being a part of coalition partner in the late 1990s. Many states ruled by regional parties, that have generated their political importance since late 1990s, have started demanding special packages for their respective states in return of their strategic support to the coalition Union government. Around the same time, there are fissiparous forces at play in different parts of the country, seeking establishment of their own autonomous entities and demanding for creation of new small states and delegation of more powers to the elected bodies at the district and lower levels. All these political processes and demands generate a debate that this is really a high time to look into fresh balance of power in centre–state relations. On the whole, an analysis of rise of regional parties in India witnessed a further weakening of national political parties, emergence of coalition politics and a shift in the centre–state power balance. Politically, however, with the rise of regional parties and coalitions, states seem to have gained an upper hand of late in many spheres of governance.

Issues and Challenges for Indian Federalism

Along with survival and progress, the working and operation of the centre–state relations for more than six decades have shown its strength and weaknesses. There are certain trends that have come to disturb the balance of power and cooperative spirit in the working of the centre–state relations. The growing centralization of power within the Indian federal system has gone so far in order to make the states more as a set of subordinates than equals. There are some problems that have generated conflicts and tensions between centre and states on a number of occasions. Thus, Indian federalism has to face manifold challenges in the emerging environment in terms of changing policies and institutions even as it faces severe constraints. There has been a fundamental transformation of the operative principles of federalism since the 1990s. The transition from plan to market necessarily envisages a greater role for decentralized levels of government. Despite the adoption of a planned development strategy, there are significant differences in the level of development, market penetration and governance capacity.

There are also significant interstate variations in the capacity to generate revenues and standards of physical and social infrastructures provided. Political elements have intervened in significant ways to influence the transfer system. The different parties in power, at the centre and in the states, make it difficult to create a coordinated policy environment at the two levels. At the same time, emergence of regional parties as ruling parties in states and their ability to leverage power at the central coalition has placed strain on both intergovernmental policies and institutions. While the dominance of single party in a government at central and state levels for over three decades provided stability, it did not allow mechanisms towards dispute resolution, or systems and institutions of government (Rao and Singh 2006: 26ff).

The rhythm and the beat of the political system, and the federal system within it, have undergone significant changes on account of a variety of socio-economic and political factors. The nation today is passing through critical times with 'federalism' in India being under a great stress. In the context of rapidly changing socio-political-economic conditions of today, the role of the centre and states as envisaged in the Constitution has come under a considerable strain with respect to the principles of federalism and functioning of the central government. The contemporary debates centred around foreign direct investment (FDI) in retail trading, the goods and services tax (GST), Right to Food Act, Prevention of Communal and Targeted Violence (PCTV) Bill, Tamil Nadu's stand on Sri Lanka, West Bengal's stand on River Teesta water-sharing treaty, the Lokpal Bill and the National Counter Terrorism Centre (NCTC) raise a number of disturbing questions regarding the very nature of Indian federalism or popularly called centre–state relations in India. However, legitimate questions arising in this context are as follows:

- Do we need to rethink federalism in the Indian context today?
- Are the existing arrangements governing Union–state relations – legislative, executive and financial – envisaged in the Constitution as they have evolved over the years, working in a manner that can meet the aspirations of the Indian society as also the requirements of an increasingly globalizing world?
- If not, what are the impediments and how can they be remedied without violating the basic structure of the Constitution?

About the Volume

Chapters in this volume address, under the structure of Indian federalism, a wide range of complex issues affecting the centre–state relations in the context of political, social and economic developments that have taken place over the years besides seeking to explain their implications in terms of their symbiosis with the projects of nation building and state formation in India. With India's political architecture, this volume is designed to begin with an account of the constitutional structure and evolution of Indian federalism. Indian federalism has been viewed through changing constitutional and judicial lenses, as the polity has evolved over the last six decades.

Some chapters narrate that there is no longer anything 'quasi' about India's centralized federalism, and that the ways in which it has adapted to the federal principle, its innovations and experimentations are now readily accepted by the judiciary as legitimate areas for judicial review and also analyses the interface between the local and higher level governments in the context of promoting national integration and inclusive growth. This volume critically brings to the fore the fact that the championing of federalism by the regional parties at the state level works against decentralization further down in reality. In the twenty-first century, the decentralization in India has become nobody's child. Fiscal federalism in India has always been deeply problematic with vertical and horizontal imbalances not only persisting till date but also getting further aggravated in many cases. To some extent, the issue is unavoidable. This volume gives a brief account of the fiscal system in India and of important fiscal discipline among the states in terms of ensuring a macroeconomic stability and efficient provision of infrastructure and pro-poor services in a least distortionary manner.

Chapters in the volume also argue about the failure of any single party in terms of gaining a majority in the central Parliament and the growing dependence of national parties on the support of regional parties to run the government at the centre, which have given a substantial elbow room for the federal units to bargain and influence important decisions at the centre. It also highlights the impact of India's economic liberalization in paving the way for a kind of new regionalism and different forms of assertion of states' rights and points out that the specific institutional arrangements of federation in India, which is both centralized and decentralized, administratively speaking, have added an additional strength to holding such a vast and diverse country together.

It also talks of the economic, political and cultural potential associated with paradiplomacy. States' paradiplomacy can also be arguably useful for the purpose of addressing some of the long-standing problems with our neighbouring countries such as water sharing, terrorism, illegal cross-border migration and environmental protection, among others. Does the functioning of the institutions of federalism in the context of resource development ensure the goals of economic efficiency, political participation and protection of rights? How can federalism be strengthened, given the current developments in the area of natural resource development? Some of these questions have been raised in this volume. While the centre and states are proactively engaged in creating investment opportunities for resource development, the local people in resource-bearing states are concerned that the authorities may overlook local environmental and social responsibilities. Internal security has always been a big critical issue for the Indian state, though never recognized officially as such. This volume deals with the issues related to internal security, while analyzing the perspective of centre and the counter arguments of states examines the wider questions related to Indian federalism.

About the Chapters in the Volume

All the 15 chapters in this volume, written by experts in the field, dwell on the new and emerging trends in federalism in particular and the Indian political system in general in a larger context of global and regional changes. This volume is interdisciplinary in its approach in terms of bringing together some of the finest scholars from political science, law, economics and history, with many of them drawing on their own extensive involvement in the public policy process.

As with India's political architecture, this volume is also designed to begin with an account of the constitutional structure and evolution of Indian federalism. Dr Kashyap, a constitutional expert, provides an historical review of the causes and results of shaping a federal democratic system in India in his chapter, *Inter-governmental Relations Revisited: Towards a Fresh Balance of Power*. He observes that India's Constitution has been variously described as quasi-federal, federal with a strong unitary or pro-centre bias, federal in normal times but with possibilities of being converted into a purely unitary one during the Emergency. Reasons for this unique unitary federal mix are found in the constitutional history of India, the sheer size of the country and the nature of her complex diversities based on religion, language, region, culture, etc. Highlighting a conflict resolution (CR) mechanism to build a new balance of power in intergovernmental relationship, he argues that the constantly evolving federal structures and innovative devices have proved to be very powerful. CR and power sharing mechanisms have been integral to national integration, democracy and good governance. As a way out, he concludes, a great deal needs to be reformed in our politics, but most of the desirable reforms can be brought about within the constitutional framework by exercising a strong political will – through an executive action or ordinary legislation. Only in the context of rare cases, constitutional amendments may be deemed necessary and can be accomplished without violating the basic structure of the Constitution.

Patel's chapter on *Indian Federalism: Semantics and Lessons from Practice* points out that in the last six decades, the changing nature of Indian politics has compelled scholars to employ a variety of frameworks while analysing and making a sense of it. Indian politics, of which federalism is an inalienable part and practice, is analysed by employing two dominant frameworks that had the longest run, namely, systemic and Marxian. These two major frameworks, dominant till the 1970s, lost their relevance and popularity thereafter to a great extent. However, they continue to be used in one or the other *avataar;* chief among them being postmodernist framework, 'Federation-Building' framework, social capital framework and psephology framework. He points out that the processes of economic reforms, in the wake of an increasing globalized external environment, have opened up new avenues for the states to take economic initiatives without depending on the Union. This is, he argues, a potentially dangerous trend as it can threaten the economic and political balance arduously forged and maintained by the Union.

The chapter, *Autonomy and States' Rights in the Indian Federal Union: Original Intent, Contemporary Content* by Arora, explains that Indian federalism has been viewed through changing constitutional and judicial lenses, as the polity has evolved over the last six decades. The polity has moved from being a federal structure initially dominated by a single party to a vibrant multi-party federal democracy marked by the federalization of the party system and the emergence in greater strength and numbers of single-state and multistate parties. He argues that there is no longer anything 'quasi' about India's centralized federalism, and that the ways in which it has adapted to the federal principle, its innovations and experimentations are now readily accepted by the judiciary as legitimate areas for judicial review. All through his argument, he attempts to examine the gradually evolving approach of the judiciary, from a quasi-denial of the federal nature of the Constitution to a growing recognition of the significance of federal principles underlying the basic structure of Indian democracy.

The local self-government plays a critical role in enhancing democracy in a federal system; it brings governance closer to the people through both representative and participatory democracy. Democratic decentralization, by making participation easier, makes empowerment of the local people more feasible at the local level than at the national level, especially for minorities and vulnerable groups. S.N. Sangita's chapter entitled, *Interface of Local and Higher Governments: Nation Building and Inclusive Development in India,* analyses the interface between the local and higher level governments in the context of promoting national integration and inclusive growth. It observes that although local governments enjoy a constitutional status, they remain ignored by the state governments and, hence, unable to function as units of self-government. Finally, it suggests that the effective functioning of local governments depends upon the central and state governments and the support of civil society organizations and movements as well.

The chapter by Anil Kumar Vaddiraju on *Whither Decentralization in India? The Interesting Story of a Nobody's Child* critically brings to the fore the fact that the championing of federalism by the regional parties at the state level works against decentralization further down in reality. However, a fresh perspective on federalism and decentralization would inform us that neither the regional parties nor the national parties are interested in decentralization, or strengthening of decentralization anymore. In the twenty-first century, decentralization in India has become nobody's child. By way of substantiation, he examines three states: Karnataka, which traditionally showed interest in decentralization, is not interested anymore; Andhra Pradesh, which, ruled by the Congress Party for the past ten years or so, has shown no enthusiasm to decentralize or strengthen local bodies; and in Tamil Nadu, the traditional disregard for decentralization continues. Kumar's main contention is that, in these three states, ruled by BJP, Congress and AIADMK respectively, going by the prevailing trends, at present and/or in the near future, no matter whether a national party or a regional party is at the helm, a complete disregard for decentralization is more likely to continue.

Fiscal federalism in India has always been deeply problematic with vertical and horizontal imbalances not only persisting till date but also getting further aggravated in many cases. To some extent, the issue is unavoidable. Sen in his chapter, *Fiscal Federalism in Operation: Case of India*, presents a brief account of the fiscal system in India and of important fiscal discipline among the states in terms of ensuring a macroeconomic stability and efficient provision of infrastructure and pro-poor services in a least distortionary manner. Most centrally, he argues that the transfer system as it has been operating so far has not been able to offset the fiscal disadvantage of the poorer states. There is a vertical imbalance and also a substantial 'horizontal imbalance' in India that refers to differences among individual states (units at the same level) in their ability to meet the expenditure responsibilities, given the revenues at their disposal. Such an imbalance arises mainly because of varying levels of economic development across states. A more developed state has a higher revenue base to tap into and would normally raise higher revenues per capita, while greater economic activities and higher private incomes reduce its public expenditure obligations. The opposite would normally be true in the case of less developed states. For an effective balancing, he argues, the central government needs to rethink policies that tilt its own expenditures away from low-income states. It also needs to convert the taxation of interstate trade from an origin-based system to a destination-based one. In the area of intergovernmental transfers, the primary mechanism for equalization, the thrust must be on a system based on normative assessments.

During the last two decades, fiscal decentralization has been a critical component of economic reforms in India. The decentralization includes fiscal arrangements, which not only involves the devolution of government authority from the central government to the lower-tier governments, but also fiscal incentives to the local governments. The chapter *Fiscal Decentralization to Subnational Governments (SNGs) in Indian Federalism,* by Barik, analyses the aspect of fiscal decentralization to subnational governments (SNGs), such as state governments and the units below them, known as local governments (rural and urban local governments) in India. He provides a bird's eye view of the evolution of Indian federalism and a description of the prevailing system, and then brings out anomalies in the assignment of fiscal responsibility between the centre and states and the states and local governments. Finally, it highlights the major shortcomings of intergovernmental policies and institutions in India, which had planning as a cornerstone of development strategy.

Taking the case of one of the most developed states, Gujarat, Nayak and Agrawal, in their chapter, *An Analysis of Fiscal Relation and Adjustment with the Centre: A Case of Gujarat,* attempt to examine the issues related to the devolution of resources from the centre to the states, with a special focus on the role of the centre in determining the fiscal performance of Gujarat. They argue that over the years, the transfer of resources from the centre to Gujarat has happened in such a way that the state indebtedness to the centre has gone up in terms of widening fiscal gaps and mounting repayment liabilities. This gap has further gained momentum postliberalization and economic reforms. The paradox of positive discrimination, that is, to reduce the regional disparities has continued with each Finance Commission. All the features of sharing such as tax effort, economic progress, salt cess and economic distance have been put before the successive Finance Commissions but unfortunately nothing concrete has come out.

Indian federalism has become less centralized of late as a result of popular pressures, the breakdown of the Congress Party dominance, and the fragmentation of political parties. India's changing federalism has come about less through the adaptation of formal institutions and more through the proliferation of state-based political parties, aggregating varied interests based on region, language, caste, class or views on secularism. Today, Indian federalism remains gravely endangered by populist imperatives originating in the states that ingress so far into the Union's jurisdiction as to enervate Parliament and the Union Executive. This issue has been addressed at length by Sanghavi in his chapter, *Federalism and Regionalism in India.* He argues about the failure of any single party in terms of gaining a majority in the central Parliament and the growing dependence of national parties on the support of regional parties to run the government at the centre, which have given a substantial elbow room for the federal units to bargain and influence important decisions at the centre.

Regionalism has remained perhaps the most potent force in Indian politics ever since independence, if not before. Adopting a constructivist view of regionalism, Bhattacharyya's chapter on *Federalism and Regionalism in India in the Age of Globalization* highlights the impact of India's economic liberalization in paving the way for a kind of new regionalism, and different forms of assertion of states' rights. He argues that there is no necessary conflict between federalism and regionalism as far as India is concerned. Federalism in India, which is born of disaggregating a once centralized colonial state, has more or less successfully provided for the institutional space for the accommodation of varied political expressions of regionalism. The relation has been complementary as well as conflictual, depending on the concerned contexts. Since independence, in most cases, an appropriate accommodation of the regional concerns through allowing for autonomy, constitutional recognition of identity at various levels and the devolution of powers amount to the regions serving as the building blocks of nation formation. He points out that the specific institutional arrangements of federation in India, which is both centralized and decentralized, administratively speaking, have added an additional strength to holding such a vast and diverse country together.

In continuation, Nag, in his chapter entitled *Regions in Nation or Nation in Regions: Regionalist Aspirations and Federalist Dilemma in Postcolonial India,* traces the development of regionalism in India in its various manifestations, while highlighting the cultural, political and economic contexts of these regionalist movements. He observes that regions have formed the essence of Indian political evolution. Regions are, therefore, a political reality in India and unlike many other countries, it is the existence of these diverse regions and their political aspirations that have forced India into constituting itself as a federal polity and not the other way around. It is not to be construed as a concession to regions. Indeed, it is this federal polity that has seen India through many crises besides saving from getting disintegrated. But neither federalism as a principle can be absolute nor regional aspirations curbed to a limit. Hence, he argues regional movements counterpoised with the federal structure of the Constitution and the nature of pressure it exerts upon the latter resulting in certain crucial dilemma, questions and challenges for the polity.

Mohapatra's chapter on *Cooperative Federalism, Competitive Regionalism and Regional Parties-Led Coalition Governments: Roles, Rights and Responsibilities* attempts to present some important aspects of the relationship between the federal structure of Indian politics and coalition politics. He argues that over the years, with the regional parties having gained due to a gradual decline of the Congress Party and its dominance over our body politic, the relationship between the centre and state governments has come under severe challenges, not merely due to the fact that the political parties remain accountable to people with respect to various issues that they are entrusted to govern at their respective levels of administration, but more so when two different parties or coalitions are leading governments at the centre and at states. Coalition politics has now become a dominant feature in Indian politics, especially at the national level. For over a decade, no single party has been able to gain an electoral majority.

The impact of economic globalization and regionalization has made it possible for the states of India to interact with foreign investors in a *de facto* sense if not *de jure*. Jha, in his chapter, *Federalism, Regionalism and States' Paradiplomacy in India,* addresses the factors responsible for the development of paradiplomacy in India. He argues that there are two factors that can be attributed to the rise of paradiplomacy in India. First, it is the dominance of coalition governments at the national level in India; second, it is the initiation of economic liberalization in the early 1990s, which in turn has given the Indian states unforeseen opportunities to engage in activities that fall under paradiplomacy. He talks of the economic, political and cultural potential associated with paradiplomacy. States' paradiplomacy can also be arguably useful for the purpose of addressing some of the long-standing problems with our neighbouring countries such as water sharing, terrorism, illegal cross-border migration and environmental protection, among others.

Does the functioning of the institutions of federalism in the context of resource development ensure the goals of economic efficiency, political participation and protection of rights? How can federalism be strengthened, given the current developments in the area of natural resource development? Some of these questions have been raised by Noronha, Srivastava, Datt and Sridharan in their chapter, *Resource Federalism in India: The Case of Minerals.* While examining the federal structure of India in the context of minerals, they suggest ways in which this can be strengthened through expanding the space and institutional capacity for local governance and by improving compensation and the sharing of resource revenues. The contributors argue that liberalized investment rules are attracting foreign and Indian capital to resource-rich states in India. Given their financial and development problems, these states see the resources – minerals, oil, natural gas and hydropower – as key revenue and development handles, and are demanding a greater share in the economic benefits of their development. While the centre and states are proactively engaged in creating investment opportunities for resource development, the local people in resource-bearing states are concerned that the authorities may overlook local environmental and social responsibilities. States are demanding a more 'fair' distribution of resource rents, as also the local people in terms of a better recognition of rights and compensation in view of the adverse effects of resource development. Finally, they conclude that resource federalism can be further strengthened through the creation of more independent bodies to determine issues related to centre–state interests, expanding the space for local governance; improved compensation and the sharing of resource revenues and enhanced local institutional capacity.

Internal security has always been a big critical issue for the Indian state, though never recognized officially as such. Tripathi, in his chapter, *Internal Security; Pretext for More Central Control or Genuine Urge to Counter Terror*, deals with the issues related to internal security. While analysing the perspective of centre and the counter-arguments of the states, he examines the wider questions related to Indian federalism. He argues that India, as a country, has faced several security threats, both from the external and internal sources. The unitary bias of Indian Constitution was defensible at the time of independence. Even now India is among the countries that have been witnessing several secessionist movements, while Naxalism as a threat is looming large. Hence, he makes a plea that persisting internal security complications cannot be solved only by a strict implementation of rules and procedures. The Government of India needs to go beyond the conventional thinking and that the role of the state should be duly recognized.

There can be no doubt that given the current debate on the topic, thorough probing is not only desirable but also very necessary. Crucial is the understanding of the dynamics of centre–state relations in the context of interplay of various factors. Not merely is this a question of constitution and its operation, it is also concerned with the entire gamut of relationship involving both the state and the society. In all the chapters, an attempt has been made to understand and explain the nature of centre–state relationship and federalism in

India with reference to various 'pulls and pressures', both indigenous and exogenous, which prove decisive in the shaping of intrastate relations in India.

References

Appleby, P.H. 1957. *Public Administration in India: Report of a Survey 1953*, New Delhi: Cabinet Secretariat, Government of India.

Arora, S. 1990. *President's Rule in Indian States: A Study of Punjab,* New Delhi: Mittal Publications.

Austin, G. 1966. *The Indian Constitution: Cornerstone of a Nation*, Oxford: Clarendon Press.

Bagchi, A. 2003. 'Rethinking Federalism: Changing Power Relations between the Center and the States', *Publius: The Journal of Federalism*, Vol. 33, No. 4, Emerging Federal Process in India (Autumn), pp. 21–42.

http://lawmin.nic.in/ncrwc/finalreport/v2b2-4.htm. Retrieved on February 20, 2014.

Pal, K. and Anita Aggarwal. 2010. 'Dialectics of Democracy and Federalism in India', *International Politics*, Vol. 3, No. 5, pp. 69–84.

Rao, M.G. and Navikar Singh. 2006. 'The Political Economy of India's Fiscal Federal System and its Reform', *Publius: The Journal of Federalism*, Vol. 37, No. 1, pp. 26–44.

Roy, M. 2011. 'Federalism, Party System, and Structural Changes in India', in Paul Wallace and Ramashray Roy (eds.), *India's 2009 Elections: Coalitions Politics, Party Competition and Congress Continuity*, New Delhi: Sage Publications.

Shvetsova, O., Mikhali Filippov and Peter C. Ordeshook. 2004. *Designing Federalism: A Theory of Self-Sustainable Federal Institutions*, Cambridge, UK: Cambridge University Press.

Wheare, K.C. 1953. *Federal Government*, London: Oxford University Press.

2

Intergovernmental Relations Revisited

Towards a Fresh Balance of Power

Subhash C. Kashyap

The nation today is passing through critical times. Our polity is under a severe strain. Faith of the people in the quality, integrity and efficiency of governmental institutions stands seriously eroded. Security, unity and integrity of the nation are threatened. Problems and conflicts abound. One of the most difficult areas of concern is the Union–state relations. The question is, to what extent the multifarious conflicts can be seen as emerging from the relationship between the Union and its constituent units and the tendency of the so-called centre to centralize powers in its hands? Can rebuilding federal structures and balancing power sharing mechanisms help resolve conflicts?

Some Conceptual Clarifications

Federal polity usually refers to the political system in a country with a rigid written Constitution defining and delimiting the powers and functions of both the federal legislature and government, on the one hand, and local or state legislatures and governments on the other hand. In a classic federation like that of the United States, sovereignty is divided between the federal and the state institutions, both partaking of sovereign powers in their respective spheres.

A classic federation, literally and historically, is the result of an agreement. It is when two or more sovereign states resolve to surrender part of their sovereignty and join hands to constitute a new union, a federal polity is born. It is a union without the constituent units losing their own identities. In fact, in a classic federation, the federal government enjoys only those powers that are, by agreement, surrendered to it by the units. However, there are also instances of some large countries where an existing unitary system may decide to share powers with the units under an agreed system of devolution or distribution of powers, for the sake of administrative convenience or for meeting linguistic or ethnic demands. Canada and India are examples of such polities. However, in every case of federalism – classical or otherwise – (i) the Constitution occupies the supreme position. It is written and relatively rigid, that is, not easily amendable; (ii) there are at least two levels at which government functions. In other words, two separate governments – federal and state – coexist; and (iii) as the arbiter of any disputes between the federation and the units as also between the units themselves, the highest judiciary – federal court or Supreme Court – enjoys a great authority and prestige.

Many countries that do not strictly fit in with the definition of a federal polity and yet have many of its features are variously described by scholars as some kind of a federation or a polity covered by some variant of federalism. Today, one hears of all kinds of 'innovative' federalisms – cooperative, executive, emergent, responsible, parliamentary, populist, legislative, competitive, fiscal, restructured, reluctant or quasi-federalism among others. 'Federations without federalism' is also mentioned.

The Western mind is anxious to reduce everything to a model or to fit every phenomenon into one of the models of its own conception. The tyranny of models and paradigms, however, may be dangerous.

Federalism today is basically an integrative device intended to keep different communities or divergent religious, linguistic, racial, tribal or other group identities together united under one nation–state. Problems of social pluralism are sought to be resolved by an arrangement or agreement to arrive at a balance in sharing political power. Irrespective of any variant of federal polity, federalism is relevant only in a situation where pluralism is territorially based, where particular groups are concentrated in separate territorial units or where the societal diversities are territorially identifiable, definable and separable. Federalism, as a political system, can be a meaningful performer only for a society faced with territorial diversities. It is an arrangement between separate territorial entities to come together or to avoid break-up and stay united by sharing power through a free democratic will. In a pluralist society, and in large nations with a multiplicity of diversities, federalism is the only way to genuine democracy.

India's Constitution has been variously described as quasi-federal – federal with a strong unitary or pro-centre bias, federal in structure but unitary in spirit, federal in normal times but with possibilities of being converted into a purely unitary one during the Emergency, etc. The fact is that it is difficult to put our Constitution in any strict mould of a federal or unitary type; it has features of both. It cannot be considered unitary because it provides, for example, the distribution of executive and legislative powers between the Union and the states and provisions affecting the powers of the states or Union–state relations cannot be amended without ratification by the states. It cannot be considered strictly federal both because the residuary powers vested in the Union and territorial identities of the states can be varied by Union Parliament through an ordinary legislation. The Supreme Court once called it amphibian.

Reasons for this unique unitary-federal mix are to be found in the constitutional history of India, the sheer size of the country and nature of her complex diversities based on religion, language, region, culture etc. There is perhaps no other comparable example of a classic plural society and a massive federal polity that is representative, republican and parliamentary, uniting and protecting under its umbrella numerous religious, linguistic, regional and other diverse identities. As has been well said, India is a continental federal polity constituted into a single territorial sovereignty as a result of historical forces.

The Constitution describes India as a 'Union of States'. A separate part is devoted to 'Union–state Relations' meaning that it is about relations between the whole and its constituent parts and not between the centre of authority and its peripheries. The Constitution makers avoided the use of words such as 'federation' or 'centre'. Actually 'central government', 'central legislature' and 'central laws' are an unfortunate hangover persisting from the days of the centralized government during the colonial rule. A great deal of mischief has been caused by the wrong use of these words.

Sources of conflicts in federal polities can be traced to differences based on ethnicity, religion, language, territory and culture. Single most important source of conflicts in federal societies is the tendency of the Union to dominate the units, to make them dependent and to treat them as subordinates, not as equal partners in government, and to work for the centralization of authority under a top-down model.

We glibly talk about the 'transfer of power to the people' or 'decentralization of power to the grassroots' as if the power legitimately belonged to the bosses in Delhi or the so-called 'centre' and now they were condescending to transfer some of the power to 'we, the people' at the grassroots. In a democracy, all the sovereign powers belong to the people and it is for them at the grassroots to hand over some of these to higher tiers in the wider interests of a larger society and national and individual security. Democracy must begin at the local levels and to be safe and lasting, it must be crowned with a federal polity.

Moving towards building a new balance of power in intergovernmental relationship requires a conflict resolution (CR) mechanism. In recent decades, CR has developed into a distinct discipline in the academia and policy studies discourses. In specific situations, the nature of conflicts may vary; strong disagreements may emerge on grounds of ideologies, principles or differences in perception. Also, there may be areas beset with a genuine conflict of material interests. The notion of CR may be distinguished from prevention aimed at creating an atmosphere as a preventive measure, management involving a gradual incremental change through continued efforts and settlement on an *ad hoc* basis. All these may be stages in CR or independent goals. CR involves dealing with the root causes of the conflict and eliminating them once for all through necessary systemic changes and restructuring institutions and relationships aimed at an honest balance of power between the union and the units.

In the context of Indian federalism, it is important to revisit the areas of conflict in intergovernmental relations and secure a proper balance of power sharing between the Union and the units. The constantly evolving federal structures and innovative devices have proved to be very powerful. CR and power sharing mechanisms have been integral to national integration, democracy and good governance. In fact, the Constitution of India itself has been the most potent CR mechanism – founded on the spirit of accommodation, adjustment and respect for diversity – ethnic, religious, linguistic and others.

Whatever conflicts arose – and there were many major ones – were all sought to be resolved under the Constitution, for example, Tamil, Punjabi and North-East movements for secession or independence or demands for new states. Geographic boundaries of the states have often been reorganized. In 1956, they were organized on linguistic basis. Several states were then created as needed. Later, more states were formed, for example, Haryana, Himachal Pradesh, Nagaland, Manipur, Mizoram, Arunachal Pradesh and Goa. The ease with which the map of India has been redrawn and reorganization of states effected during the last more than 60 years bears an eloquent testimony to the unique resilience and flexibility of the political system and efficacy of its CR mechanisms. In 2001, three large states were bifurcated to create three new states of Jharkhand, Uttarakhand and Chhattisgarh to respect and encourage the aspirations of the local people. Not all ethnic conflicts have been resolved. Movements continue for Vidarbha, Bodoland, Bundelkhand, and others. The process goes on. It is this dynamic process that is the source of the greatest strength to the system.

The number of states which was 14 has doubled. As at present, the Union consists of 28 states and 7 union territories. Some unique solutions of regional councils, development boards, etc., have been attempted with varying degrees of success. We experimented with Bodoland Autonomous Council, Darjeeling Gorkha Hill Council, Jharkhand Area Autonomous Council, Leh Autonomous Hill Development Council, Tribal Areas Autonomous District Councils in Tripura, etc.

India's Constitution is replete with CR and power sharing devices such as the Finance Commission, the Fifth and the Sixth Schedule, the Eighth Schedule, Reservations for SC/ST and Backward Classes. Also, we have the CEC, CVC, C & AG, CBI, CRPF and the like.

There are special provisions for adjudication of Inter-State Water Disputes, Inter State Council (Article 263), Article 370 for Jammu & Kashmir and Articles 371 to 371–I for Maharashtra, Gujarat, Nagaland, Assam, Arunachal and Goa.

Some scholars have suggested that India should be viewed as a civilizational state and not as a nation–state. Another suggestion is to call India a federal nation–state. We are, no doubt, a highly pluralistic society but our pluralism is not territory based. It is of a special kind. We have much diversity of various sorts, pulling us at once in the same or in opposite directions. The Indian society remains fragmented and segmented at every level on different grounds. Our basic problem has never been one of territorially based diversities or pluralisms. Our diversities are within and cut across territorial units. In a sense, our diversities in themselves are plural and our pluralism is diverse – both horizontally and vertically. However, what seems to divide also unites. In fact, our diversities are our greatest strength and a great cementing factor when it comes to national unity. Diversity is not division and unity does not mean uniformity or conformity. Also, unity of India and integrity of the nation as concepts are very different from national or political integration.

When India achieved independence or what is called transfer of power in the midnight of 14–15 August 1947, unfortunately only the masters changed. The people did not feel the glow of freedom or transfer of power to their hands. The Constitution also continued the colonial model. Some people felt that they had been more free in their daily lives before independence and that they were being interfered with more and their freedom being taken away. For example, in the North-East, that feeling seemed to dominate.

We can look this matter from a different angle: the people have to function through their representatives. The state leadership is the closest representative of the people. Each state leadership deserves to be respected by the Union government. If the leadership does not deliver, it is for the people of the state to wake up and act. If the people of the state allow themselves to be exploited by their leaders – whether they are tribal leaders or caste or community leaders – they can only blame themselves. If the caste, community and tribal leaders come to have a vested interest in not developing and in exploiting their own people, then they become greater enemies of their people than anyone else. And, the solution has to be found by the people themselves in their own area. Many of the problems of the people and of polity – whether in the east or west, north or south – have to be solved in the area itself. In the North-East, before India's independence, the traditional institutions gave them more freedom and power to take their own decisions at the grassroots level. Problems arise and a feeling is generated when somebody takes away their freedom and independent identity.

The question is, where do we go from here. What is the way ahead?

Time has now come for a review of the Union–state relations and local governance institutions. More innovative federal structures need to be devised. It is necessary to address the deep-rooted sources of conflicts. We have to go for a different variant of the parliamentary system that is compatible with the new federalism, one which should build a united nation of a large number of autonomies considered not just as subordinates or subsidiaries, but also as federal and more importantly as equal partners at various levels, rooted in our culture, ethos and genius, and taking into account our weaknesses and needs of making the federal union an ever-developing and lasting reality. The honest and the practical way ahead for the Union is to lose its extra weight and shed its tendency to be the centre with a monopoly of power to dominate over the units and the people. In short, the only way to preserve 'India, that is Bharat' as a 'Union of States', is to work towards building it as a 'federal Union' with multiple tiers of government and sharing of powers from the lowest grassroot levels of panchayats to the Parliament and the Government of the Union. Incidentally, this would be the most rational and practical way of operationalizing the Gandhian vision of a Constitution for India with the sovereign power vested within the people at the grassroots and building from below. Gandhi conceived of public life as a mission of sacrifice and service and not as a lucrative profession. He advocated a less expensive election system linked with watchdog councils and separate elected chief executives at each local level. In the Gandhian model, the village is at the centre and all the power is posited at the grassroots and in a bottom-up (instead of the present top-down) approach; it travels upwards to the next tier of governance. There may be three or four tiers of governance represented by successive concentric circles with power at the highest level being limited to the minimum essential areas such as national security and external affairs. This also represents the quintessence of the subsidiarity principle in the European Union and Germany where those work that cannot be done at the lowest level are entrusted to the next higher tier.

Governance means dignity, development and growth of the individual to one's highest potential. This calls for power being ultimately vested with the individual citizen. Struggles for separate identities or greater federalism in pluralist societies are often not a fight for social justice, for the promotion of interests of the disadvantaged sections of the society or for protecting the rights of the units as against the Union. The real issue is not even that of separate cultural or ethnic group interests. The entire conflictual situation revolves around the issue of sharing the fruits of political power. Ethnicity, language and religion are politicalized to be used merely as the means to legitimize one's claims in the struggle for political power. For any CR to succeed, we must transcend vote bank politics built on corruption, casteism, communalism, black money power, crime and cabal rule.

While there is no dichotomy between a strong Union and strong states, the way Union governments have operated during the last more than 60 years have misused their powers blatantly for political and partisan ends, particularly under Articles 352 and 356 – Proclamations of Emergency and imposition of President's rule in the states – has weakened the case of the Union beyond repair.

Of late, the role and functioning of our Council of States, which was conceived by the founding fathers as a federal house consisting of the representatives of the states, has been considerably compromised on political, party and personal interest considerations of the rulers.

The Constitution Commission (2002) recommended (a) greater consultation between the Union and the states through the Inter–state Council under Article 263; (b) establishment of an Inter–state Trade and Commerce Commission; (c) treating inter–state river waters as national assets and enacting legislation for dispute resolution; (d) appointing only persons of eminence with a detached outlook as Governors in consultation with the concerned chief ministers and respecting their five-year term; (e) using Article 356 only as a last resort after action under 256, 257, 355, etc., fails; (f) deciding questions of majority support only on the floor of the House and (g) in case of a hung house, election of the chief minister by the House.

The federal structure has come to stay and needs to be strengthened. The states are more and more asserting themselves through their political clout. They are demanding ever more space and extracting greater share of powers of governance and financial resources. However, the central problem today is not of Union–state relations. It is of greater decentralization of economic and political powers. And instead of bottom-up approach, top-down approach should be applied. It is heartening and nothing short of revolutionary that after the 73rd and 74th Amendments coming into operation, India has 3.20 million elected rulers – over a million of them women. However, the states by and large seem unwilling to transfer power lower down and the MPs and MLAs feel uncomfortable and threatened by the new grassroot leadership. The Union and the states should concentrate on essentials following the subsidiarity principle. Economic liberalization must come with decentralization of political power and of management, while income tax, corporate tax and indirect taxes could be moved to the Concurrent List. Government at each higher level may be chosen by and remain answerable to the lower level. Government at a higher level should have no power to remove or supersede a duly elected government at a lower tier. If we are serious about providing a multi-tier governance and taking power to the doorsteps of the people at the grassroots, the Constitution should clearly provide for the distribution of powers between the Union, the states and the local governments, making the 11th and 12th schedules mandatory. It would do no harm either to the basic structure of the Constitution or the parliamentary system.

When the basic units of the federal Union at the grassroots become small and autonomous, most of the conflicts related to ethnicity and quest for freedom may get resolved and it may be possible to involve various groups in governance more closely and this may make the Union stronger and the nation more integrated, emotionally and culturally. There is every case for another *States Reorganization Commission* (*SRC*) and creation of some 40–50 states of almost equal size and equal representation in one or both Houses of the Union Parliament. However, we should delink the ethnic aspirations from political demands for separate states. Apart from new states, substate and supra-state structures may be created to take care of common group concerns, which cannot be handled at the state level. Combined with strong zonal councils, this would lead to greater stability, more accountability, stronger Union and better administered and more developed or fast-developing states. Norms for governor's appointments need revamping. Sarkaria Commission recommendations should be examined and implemented. Problems regarding Article 356 are only due to improper operation and interpretation of Articles 256, 257, 355, 356 and 365. These need to be read together.

It would be worth considering whether there should be a provision for President's rule or national government at the Union level also. One alternative worthy of further examination may be of having Lok Sabha constituencies as administrative units and subdistricts and tehsils may similarly coincide with MLA constituencies. That way, in a multi-tier system, it may be possible to involve various groups in governance and thereby making the nation more integrated, emotionally and culturally. Some such innovative multi-tier federal structures may have the potential to resolve many of the conflicts in our polity and arrive at a proper power sharing arrangement in Union–state relationship.

Apart from restructuring the federal Union set-up, we need administrative reforms, parliamentary reforms and overall reforms for good and clean citizen-friendly governance. No single reform can provide a miracle cure. Ideally, a simultaneous action on all fronts is required.

A great deal needs to be reformed in our politics, but most of the desirable reforms can be brought about within the constitutional framework by mere political will, executive action or through ordinary legislation. In rare cases only, constitutional amendments may be deemed necessary. These can be enacted under the Constitution itself without violating its basic structure. And, in any case, Constitution is also only a means. The end is the freedom and the weal of the people.

The ultimate way ahead would be to revisit Indian democracy and rebuild our federal polity on the foundation of an honest relationship between the Union and the units with governments at all levels providing good people-centric governance.

Today, public opinion is anxious for urgent changes. The time to act is now. Vested interests should not be allowed to come in the way. An early initiative may be of immense help in transforming the present national climate of doom and despondency to one of hope and harmony.

3

Indian Federalism

Semantics and Lessons from Practice

Priyavadan Patel

> Personally, I do not attach any importance to the label which may be attached to it – whether you call it a Federal Constitution or a Unitary Constitution or by any other name. It makes no difference so long as the Constitution serves our purpose.
>
> —Rajendra Prasad
>
> (Quoted in Granville Austin, *The Indian Constitution*, 1999, p. 186)

Semantics and Architecture of Indian Federalism

The Indian Constitution from the very days of its making and then after its working has continued to be the most debated political text in the post independence period. A large part of this contentious nature and continuously evolving character of the Indian Constitution is due to the equally complex nature and character of diversities and pluralities of Indian society (Baxi 2002). In order to serve one and all sections of Indian society and all the regions of subcontinental sized polity, it went on to pile up structural and functional complexities.

What exactly is the meaning of Indian federalism and how best can it be conceptualized and described continues to be an ever engaging academic and political preoccupation till date. In the Constituent Assembly (Nigam 2008), the members had tried to grapple with this semantic challenge but only partially succeeded in meeting it as the above quoted words of Rajendra Prasad indicate. It is well known that the attempts were made to draw, though selectively, on other time-tested and successful federations, namely, the

United States of America, Canada, Switzerland and Australia. The existing pool of theoretical and empirical knowledge was modified to suit the socio-cultural and politico-geographic needs of the newly constituted Indian nation–state and its polity. The innovative modifications, 'in fact, produced a new kind of federalism to meet India's peculiar needs' (Austin 1999: 186).

If we examine the historical evidence and experience of federal constitution making, we find that the Indian case stands out as an exception on several counts. For instance, the Indian Constituent Assembly was singularly fortunate to be left alone in drafting the federal architectural design without facing any significant resistance from the federating entities. As Austin has succinctly observed 'the relative absence of conflict between the 'centralizers' and the 'provincialists' (1999: 186) made the Consembly's task comparatively easy'. This was not the case with the US Philadelphia Convention in 1784 and Canada's Ontario and Quebec question.

This is not to say that the draft federal provisions were not debated and that there was a near complete consensus in the Consembly. In fact, the fiercely contested debates occurred in the Consembly on such draft proposals as: (i) the scheme of distribution of power between the central federal structure and federating provinces; (ii) the logistics of the centralized revenue and tax collection and the scheme of its fair and just distribution among the federal units and (iii) the palpable suspicion and distrust about the (mis) use of provisions of emergency power on partisan, political party lines rather than constitutionally mandated and validated grounds. In spite of strong arguments made by the members on these issues, it is reasonably fair to state that the differences of opinion on these vital aspects of constitutional federal architecture were not so much over the substance as over the 'techniques'. Had it not been the case, the Consembly members would not have just stopped demanding the allocation of more financial resources to the federating states but also would not have left the task of collection and distribution of revenue solely in the hands of the central federal government. It seems the secondary role for the federating states was designed and agreed to in good federal faith and mutual interest of a nation–state surrounded as it was by daunting challenges to its survival.

The Indian federal architecture has altered and advanced the frontiers of conventional conceptualization of federal systems that the world has seen so far. Wheare's conceptualization of such a hitherto known federal system as autonomous of each other in already agreed domains of operation is one such instance (1956: 97). The post-World War II challenges of physical and emotional reconstruction of shattered societies of the West required increased cooperation between the federal and provincial governments. This, in turn, increased interdependence between the top and bottom components of a federal structure. Birch emerged as a major theorist of this novel form of federalism. He conceptualized it as 'cooperative federalism' (Birch 1955) while listing the following as its distinct features: (a) administrative cooperation between the two governments engaged in a federal set-up; (b) partial financial dependence of lower level on upper level of government and (c) upper level government's supportive developmental initiatives in the subjects constitutionally placed under the state list. The Indian federal architecture fits this characterization of 'cooperative federalism'.

However, the Indian federal architecture is not free from criticism and objections. Some of these critiques are 'text bookish' in nature but have historical parallels of sorts. As a result, some scholars have questioned the genuineness of the Indian federalism. Three criticisms as outlined and discussed by Chaube (1998) are taken up for discussion. First, despite 'federalism' being usually listed as one of the most salient features of the Indian Constitution, it is questioned as to why there is no mention of the term in the Indian Constitution. Interestingly, American Constitution is also no exception to this amiss. Instead, the word preferred and used is 'Union'. Indian and American Constitutions share a common ground so far as this question is concerned. The Indian federation is usually referred to as 'Union of States', although in general parlance and more due to linguistic convenience, the popular usage is 'centre–state' relations. This shows that the semantic essence of federalism is captured and encapsulated in the term 'Union', but colloquially expressed in the usage of the other related term.

Second criticism lies in the etymological meaning of the word 'federation', which actually means 'union by treaty'. Here, if we see the historical evidence, then this criticism too sounds unsustainable. American federation was a mixed bag. There was no crafting of a Union by the constituent units or 'states' on the basis of signing treaties to that effect. Originally, 13 British colonies got together as a confederation that covered about today's 10 per cent of the territory in 1776. The Philadelphia Convention was held in 1787 to frame the constitution without any such treaties. One very important aspect associated with federation making needs to be highlighted here. According to Chaube (1998: 37), 'the Philadelphia Convention had no mandate of the states beyond 'revising' the confederal constitution'. In this process, there was an element of coercive pressure tactics involved in making the small and reluctant states to fall in line. As is known, the rest of the American federation was forged by annexation, invasion, purchase and treaties. This part of the historic process was missing in Indian federation making. Kashyap (2004: 75) has succinctly summarized it in the following words:

> The emphasis on India being a 'Union' was to convey the fact that it was not the result of a contract or agreement between the constituent units but a forthright declaration by the Constituent Assembly which derived its power and authority from the sovereign people of India. No State could, therefore secede from the Union nor could it suo moto vary its territory as laid down in the First Schedule of the Constitution.

The Indian federation in this sense was singularly fortunate in terms of avoiding a massive future catastrophe that the United States had faced. Following words by Ambedkar are reassuring:

> The Americans had to wage a civil war to establish that the States have no right of secession and that their Federation was indestructible. The Drafting Committee thought that it was better to make it clear at the outset rather than leave it to speculation or to dispute. (Kashyap 2004: 75)

Hence, the question of any treaty between the two did not arise in the Indian case. Nevertheless, the emergence of a large and complex federation can rarely be free from the labour pains of a birth. In the case of Indian federation making, to some extent, coercive and invasive practices were employed and the process continued till the liberation of Goa in 1962 and 'inviting' Sikkim to join the Union of India. It seems federations rarely emerge on the basis of a democratically reached complete agreement and mutual consent. Historical circumstances and geopolitical contingencies as well as compulsions play a huge role in the creating and shaping of a given federal system.

The third criticism on federal genuineness emanates from the near complete and almost unilateral power of the Indian Parliament to make changes in the geographies of the federated states. Under the Indian federal system, the territory of a state is its 'rightless' possession. It can be changed and redrawn. State identity in the context of the Indian federal system is thus divisible to the extent of in-system alterations. It is well known as to how Abraham Lincoln's Presidency had to face a devastating civil war to keep the Union protected from a complete collapse and disintegration.

So far as the question of ethnocultural composition of the federation is concerned, the Indian federation is more akin to the Canadian rather than American case. No other federation is ethnoculturally as diverse as the Indian one. Federations should not be artificially created and if created cannot be held together for long. For instance, the United Arab Republic and Pakistan could not be held together. What keeps a good federation going and evolve as a strong system of bilateral governance of one people in two jurisdictionally divided territories. A certain commitment to the substance and spirit of a participatory and representative democracy, either under parliamentary or presidential form of government, is a prerequisite for the successful functioning of a federal system. A kind of an Elitist management of federal systems is a dangerous practice. Masses must participate in the processes of federal governance; lest it holds a negative potential to harm the interest of the common people.

Perils and Promises of Democratic Federal Practices

Over the last six decades, the changing nature of Indian politics has compelled scholars to employ a variety of frameworks for analysing and making a sense of it. Indian politics, of which federalism is an inalienable part and practice, is analysed by employing hitherto two dominant frameworks that had the longest run, namely systemic and Marxian. Systemic framework is also known as structural-functional, modernization or developmental framework. It was mainly used by Selig Harrison, Myron Weiner, Rajni Kothari, Rudolph & Rudolph, Paul Brass, Richard Sisson and Iqbal Narain. The Marxian framework too evolved into two variants – classical (Marx's own basic works) and neo-Marxian frameworks (Gramsci, Ralph Miliband, the Frankfurt School, Althusser, Poulantzas, Ranjit Guha, Achin Vanaik, etc). These two major analytical frameworks remained dominant till the 1970s, but thereafter their relevance and popularity have considerably declined. However, they continued to be used in one or the other *avatar* or reincarnated forms. Some of the newly emerged and employed frameworks are the off-shoots of these two dominant frameworks. Chief among them are postmodernist framework (Lyotard, Michel Foucault, Rajeev Bhargava, Paul Brass), 'Federation-Building' framework (Baruah 1999), social capital framework (Robert Putnam, Ashutosh Varshney, Dwaipayan Bhattacharyya, etc.) and psephology framework (Yogendra Yadav, Zoya Hasan, Sandeep Shastri, Suhas Palshikar, Christophe Jaffrelot, K.C. Suri, Sanjay Kumar). An excellent body of literature has emerged as a result of applying these frameworks over time. Our understanding of Indian politics has been truly enriched. Many of these works have dealt with the question of centre–state relations either directly or indirectly.

Indian democratic project was launched in the midst of the most testing internal and external circumstances. Overcoming the trauma of partition, integrating the hopelessly scattered princely and ex-colonial territories of Indian geography into a single cohesive political entity, framing and giving it a Constitution and commencing the historic political journey as an independent nation–state were some of the stiffest historic challenges faced by the newly forged Indian nation–state. Besides, the external environment was not very conducive either. The world was divided into two ideological camps with the super power rivalries getting expressed and played up as bloody puppet wars in Asia. The Chinese threat was growing and looming large till its invasive culmination in 1962. Thus, the whole focus then was on creating, managing and holding on to the Indian Union of states as one unifying system of governance without reducing the democratic contents, denying legitimate rights or causing any injustice of any kind to any grieving constituent federating unit on one or the other issue. In the absence of any credible alternative or sufficient time on hand, the Indian federation got ill-fated to be mechanically created and held together rather than organically integrated as in the cases of Canadian or Australian federations. Even if the federation like Canadian had to deal with the case of exit from the union by one of its constituents, it was done in a far more democratic and unrepressive manner than the similar comparable cases in Asia. Mitra and Pehl (2010: 45) have well stated that:

> The framers of Indian Constitution ... were keen on federalism as a functional instrument for the creation of an Indian nation and a strong cohesive state. The leading politicians ... were besieged by threats to India's security both from outside and inside ... Thus for both constitutional and political reasons, the institutionalization of a strong

> federalism in the Indian political system appears to have been seriously compromised from the outset. Nevertheless, the political process has been able to adapt to this design ...

Against the backdrop of this brief semantic, historical and comparative understanding of the processes of federation making and working, it is intended here to raise some important questions and attempt to argue as to what lessons can be drawn from such a fiercely contentious and tumultuous political journey of six decades of Indian federalism under the broader rubric of Indian politics. A few important aspects of federal practices are selectively taken up here for a critical assessment.

Politico-Territorial Identity Quest as a Democratic Aspiration

The question of nationhood or statehood needs to be understood primarily as a perfectly democratic aspiration of the people or region to acquire a politico-territorial identity. In other words, the right to self-determination is as much democratic as the 'right to other's determination' by a union or central authority about a people or a region to be its part. Internationally, if you see, the two extreme examples of this lesson are found in the form of (a) Quebec and Canada and (b) Pakistan-Bangladesh and Tibet-China. One is democratic, liberal and considerate, whereas the others were/are brutally suppressive, authoritarian and nonliberal.

In an age of communication and information technology revolution, keeping a people or region under a coercive military control and captivity amounts to actually pushing them away from the centre or union. Arab Spring, Jasmine Revolution, summer of discontent, questions of Chechnya nationhood in Russia or Catalonia and Basque demands for independence in Spain besides several others are the best examples in the contemporary history. These examples show that in the final analysis, it is futile to hold a region or a people by military force and authoritarian power. The greater the use of force on people, the more hurt people will be. In the case of India too, this has remained an equally sticky and complex question. Democratic means offering the least cost-free scope for dealing with such complex and fiercely contentious conflicts. Multi-pronged dialogues, face-to-face discussions, genuine debates and persuasive efforts offer a mutually beneficial opportunity for resolving many such deadlocks between the two parties. India has been faced with three major challenges of this nature from Jammu & Kashmir, Northeast and Punjab with all the three becoming complicated because of their transborder linkages and manipulations. Here I need to refer to Baruah's argument (1999). That is to say, national identities are an extremely serious business. They must be viewed and considered against 'concrete historical settings'. Both China and India fall under this category. Both have acquired their today's respective national identities through an enormous historical struggle stretching across decades and centuries. Although politically differently cast in democratic and authoritarian political systems, both tend to react to and deal with questions of secession with an equal degree of ruthlessness, force, violence and zero tolerance, a political fact that needs to be properly understood by the secession-seekers. If the centralized authority deliberately fails to serve the purpose and interests of the federated units through economic deprivation, exploitation and subjugation *a la* practices amounting to internal colonialism, the demand for autonomy may be viewed as democratically fair and just. But if it is otherwise, then secessionist claims must be dropped and the people and the region concerned must willingly try to get integrated into the Union. In either case, the onus for a responsible and accountable conduct is to be on the Union and national political elites.

Dynamics of Fiercely Competitive Electoral Politics

It must be recognized that the political dynamics of electorally guided and dominated minimalist/procedural democracy has its inevitable impact on the relationship between the two, especially when both the levels of government are ruled by different rival political parties. In a democratically organized federal political system, the chief objective of the political parties is to mobilize voters, compete and campaign hard, win elections and capture power, preferably at all the three levels of federal governance. During this process, often either the centre or a state tends to committee excesses. It is observed that political contests over the last two to three decades have witnessed tempers run high to the point of bursting. However, it must be realized that the objective of a substantive democracy as conceived in the Constitution should not be lost in the process. The play of electoral-mobilizational political dynamics by the regimes at both the levels of politics must not play to the galleries in terms of arousing the voters against the other. To some extent, it is the pressure of performance and governance and/or the impatience of waiting in the wings of power which is changing the rules of the game between the two levels of politics in India. Whether this is desirable and good or not can be gauged by the lessons of the past, which may have some relevance for the future.

The recent electoral campaign in Gujarat between the BJP and the Congress turned the centre–state relations into a battle cry of the poll war. During its campaign, the BJP led by Narendra Modi accused the Congress-led UPA government at the centre of being unfair and unjust to Gujarat state. The central government got poorly projected and severely criticized as if it was the sworn enemy of the state of Gujarat from time immemorial. If all the states keep on demeaning and demonizing the centre in this manner, then surely the so sown seeds of discontent will germinate faster than ever imagined before and cause the disintegration of the federal republic of India. This phenomenon is not unilateral. The centre too needs to relent and alter its hegemonic mindset of the 1950s when it was considered wise to be strong and all powerful. But the times have changed after 1989. The disintegration of the former USSR, Yugoslavia and Czechoslovakian federations indicates the increasing fragility of sustaining large, complex and ethnoculturally diverse federal systems. These global trends over the last three decades have made the Indian intellectuals and the national elites quite fearful of the growing prospects of the Indian Union getting weakened. Increasing demands for more autonomy in governance and a larger share in the revenues by states such as West Bengal, UP, Jharkhand, Chhattisgarh, Gujarat, Karnataka, Orissa and Madhya Pradesh (which are ruled by the rival parties) are leading to a new federal architecture.

The most important lesson, to be drawn for remoulding and reshaping this multifaceted relationship between the states and the Union, is to measure the confronting issues of grievances from the perspective of substantive democratic values and commitments made in the Constitution. An honest, nonpartisan, nonpolitical and credible mechanism may have to be now evolved to determine whether a demand made by any state on the Union and vice versa fits in with the requirement of the constitutionally established procedure or not. The foremost consideration should be to continuously monitor and judge as to from which end of the spectrum – the Indian Union or the

Indian states – democracy in India remains safe and sound. We have sufficient cases on either end of the spectrum showing that both are potentially capable of endangering the democratic political processes and the entire Republic.

Lessons from Linguistic Reorganization of the States

The most famous case is the springing up of demands for linguistic reorganization of Indian states immediately after independence. These were the times when the Union was intensely committed to creating a homogenized and inclusive but centralized nation–state. Rajendra Prasad's (CAD 1999, vol. I: xvii, cited in Mehta 2010: 24) following words give us a robust sense of mainstream thinking of that period:

> After all a constitution like machine is a lifeless thing. It acquires life because [of the] men who control it and operate it ... We have communal differences, caste differences, language differences, provincial differences and so forth. It requires men of strong character, men of vision, men who will not sacrifice the interest of the country at large for the sake of smaller groups and areas ...

Ambedkar's thinking on this question was clearer as the following quote suggests:

> The [Indian] federation is a Union because it is indestructible. Though the country and the people may be divided into different states for convenience of administration, the country is one integral whole, its people a single people, living under a single imperium, derived from a single source. (CAD 1999, vol. II: 42, cited in Mehta 2010: 26)

Nation building and national integration were its unrelenting and uncompromising pursuits. In the zeal for protecting the Union, it lost sight of a bigger picture of democracy. It failed to see these demands coming from the states, especially those ruled by own or rival political parties as being fundamentally and genuinely democratic. The Union had erred on this count. In hindsight, we can see that instead of the collapse or weakening of the Union, the linguistically organized states have strengthened it. It has clearly served the purposes of substantive democracy. In fact, a brief dark spell of Emergency did a great service to the federal cause. It woke up the states to the reality of these threats emanating from the centre. On the other hand, some of the demands made by the states have, on occasions, challenged the basic structure of the Union, while compelling it to act in an 'undemocratic' manner in the interests of a larger picture. Several examples of militant and secessionist movements can be cited.

Threats from the Top

Post-Emergency developments have thrown up some more lessons. For instance, the democratic establishment of the country cannot always be viewed and trusted as being in the safe custody of the Union. This in turn has resulted in distrust of the Union with many states suspecting the role of its institutions such as the army, central bureaucracy, election commission, the President and the Governor. The coming together of eight major non-Congress ruled states in the 1980s forced the centre to appoint the Sarkaria Commission to look into and recommend changes in the centre–state relations in India. At present, the Congress-led UPA regime is increasingly conducting itself in a manner that borders on authoritarianism. For instance, its high-handed responses to the recent pan-Indian civil society demand that a strong Lokpal Bill be passed by the Parliament and also the demands for a severe action against the accused in a Delhi bus gang rape case are recent evidences of the regime's intolerance towards democratic dissent and protests against the wrongdoings. It is utterly undemocratic, to say the least. Stronger and well-governed states can check such authoritarian tendencies of the Union government by providing a better legal framework to deal with corruption and women's security issues. But most states seem to be more interested in extracting pounds of political flesh from such happenings rather than contributing to the cause of overall governance. This has made several observers worry about the fate of democratic politics in India (Bajpai 2012: 12).

Emergence of Coalition Politics

The breakdown of the minimalist national consensus among the voters with regard to giving the required bare minimum majority of seats in the Lok Sabha to any one political party since 1991 has ushered in a new era of coalition politics in India. This in turn has increased the primacy of states in the national politics. Even with respect to some large- and medium-sized state Vidhan Sabhas like those of UP, Bihar, Kerala, Punjab, Jammu & Kashmir, Karnataka and Maharashtra, meeting this minimalist condition of achieving a simple majority by a political party is becoming increasingly difficult. This has triggered a big debate as to whether this relatively new development augurs well for the health of democratic politics or not (Kumar 2011). The moot issue is whether democracy is getting further strengthened or weakened. The outcome of this debate will depend on the standpoint or theoretical perspective of democracy that one adopts. If one views it from the procedural perspective of democracy, then it is an assured yield of pessimism, frustration and disappointment; however, if viewed from the perspective of an evolving substantive democracy (Jaffrelot 2003; Jaffrelot and Kumar 2009), then there is an enormous scope for hope, optimism and celebration.

The processes of economic reforms in the wake of an increasingly globalized external environment have opened up new avenues for the states to devise innovative economic initiatives without depending on the Union (Bhambhri 2003). Perhaps the only potential danger in this development is whether the states are advancing economically at the cost of constitutionally enshrined inclusive democratic values or not. A few evidences show that an appreciable use of economic liberalism by some states is either reinforcing or breeding political ill-liberalism (Saez 2002). This is a potentially dangerous trend as it will threaten the economic and political equilibrium arduously forged and maintained by the Union (Bajpai 2012: 12).

Here the contemporary Gujarat state politics offers us a valuable scope to validate some of these apprehensions regarding the directions the state politics in Indian federal system may take. This is how the Gujarat story can be synoptically narrated. In order to electorally unseat the Congress Party from power, the mass mobilization that was launched through the polarizing politics of Hindutva communalized the state polity and society. The centre remained a mute spectator to this transformation. It behaved in the same fashion as it had in December 1992 when Babri Masjid was demolished by Sangh Parivar mobilization in Ayodhya, UP. Then in February–March 2002, the incident of burning the train compartment at Godhra, in which 57 Hindu pilgrims who were returning from Ayodhya died, came up. The anti-Muslim violence that followed this incident engulfed most parts of the state. The scales of the state governance touched new lows. The state government failed to abate it because of its alleged complicity with the rioters. This incident (like several others in the Union of states) has gone down as a blot on constitutionally committed federal democracy. It is not easy to straightaway establish the interconnection of complicity between the state and the national units of the same ruling political party at the centre and the state. At the time of post-Godhra riots in Gujarat, the BJP under the leadership of Modi ruled the state. Whereas the Union authority was in the hands of BJP-led NDA under Atal Bihari Bajpai. Even if the two levels are ruled by different political parties, the content and intensity of such disasters could be the same as evidenced during the demolition of Babri Masjid. These events considerably polarized the electorates in the subsequent Lok Sabha and Vidhan Sabha polls in both the states of UP and Gujarat. Mercifully the tide of communally surcharged electoral mobilizations ran out of their political steam and ebbed into oblivion but continues to seethe and occasionally simmer underground in a latent manner. In case of Gujarat, after the end of NDA rule at the centre in 2004, the agenda of mobilization along communal lines was softened and replaced by a 'unifier' and 'inclusive' development agenda. The central government under the Congress-led UPA was singularly targeted as a villain out to obstruct the development process of the state under the BJP regime. In the recent elections of Gujarat State Assembly in December 2012, the anticentral government campaign was launched by the BJP in such a hostile and intolerant manner that the next 'logical' step looked like making a demand for or declaration of unilateral secession from the Union. The only point of a wider concern is to know and reflect on as to how the voters would respond to such anticentre mobilizations by the rival political party in the state. The impressionistic minds of the electorates are not *uniformly* critical, receptive, politically rational and capable of seeing through the latent motives or ideological undercurrents of mobilizers and polarizers. In such cases, the spirit of federal practices, faith and partnership in governance suffer an enormous damage. Although this is generally viewed as a poll time practice, it may be sowing the seeds of anticentre and hence antifederal politics in the minds of politico-constitutionally semi-literate or illiterate and less informed electorates.

Conclusions

Despite the emergence of some serious challenges to the federal order in India, it is felt necessary to signify the gains of a mutually beneficial and evolving coexistence between the Union and states.

Both have periodically struggled in terms of striking an interdomain balance of interests between the two. Whenever the two levels of government at the centre and in the states have risen above the narrow, partisan grooves of 'political self-interest' and drawn limits with respect to party politics, there are ample evidences of a resultant bilateral, common or collective good. Realization by the most dissenting and anti centre–states that adherence to the constitutionally ordained federal institutional design is an imperative in the larger national and regional interests is a major positive development. The creation of new states out of the existing ones during last two to three decades is a good example of this collaborative and cooperative federalism in India.

References

Austin, G. 1999. *The Indian Constitution*, 1966 and 1999, Columbia, Missouri: South Asia Books, p. 186

——. 1999. *The Indian Constitution: Cornerstone of a Nation*, New Delhi: Oxford University Press.

Bajpai, K. 2012. 'Rise of Fascism in Indian Politics', *The Times of India* (Ahmedabad Edition), 8 December, p. 12.

Baruah, S. 1999. *India against Itself: Assam and Politics of Nationality*, Delhi: Oxford University Press.

Baxi, U. 2002. 'The (Im) Possibility of Constitutional Justice: Seismographic Notes on Indian Constitutionalism', in Zoya Hasan et al. (eds.), *India's Living Constitution: Ideas, Practices, Controversies*, New Delhi: Permanent Black, pp. 31–63.

Bhambhri, C.P. 2003. 'Central Government in the Age of Globalization: New Directions of Indian Federalism', in B.D. Dua, (ed.), *Indian Federalism in the New Millennium*, New Delhi: Manohar Publishers.

Birch, A.H. 1955. *Federalism, Finance and Social Legislation in Canada, Australia and the United States*, London: Oxford University Press.

Chaube, S.K. 1998. 'Unionism vs Federalism: India at the Cross Roads', in D.D. Khanna et al. (eds.), *Democracy, Diversity, Stability: 50 Years of Indian Independence*, New Delhi: Macmillan.

Jaffrelot, C. 2003. *India's Silent Revolution: The Rise of the Lower Castes in North India*, New Delhi: Permanent Black.

Jaffrelot, C. and Sanjay Kumar (eds.). 2009. *Rise of the Plebeians? The Changing Face of Indian Legislative Assemblies*, New Delhi: Routledge.

Kashyap, S.C. 2004. *Our Constitution: An Introduction to India's Constitution and Constitutional Law*, New Delhi: National Book Trust.

Kumar, A. (ed.). 2011. *Rethinking State Politics in India: Regions within Regions*, New Delhi: Routledge.

Mehta, U.S. 2010. 'Constitutionalism', in Niraja Gopal Jayal and Pratap Bhanu Mehta (eds.), *The Oxford Companion to Politics in India,* New Delhi: Oxford University Press.

Mitra, S.K. and Pehl, Malte. 2010. 'Federalism', in Niraja Gopal Jayal and Pratap Bhanu Mehta (eds.), *The Oxford Companion to Politics in India*, New Delhi: Oxford University Press.

Nigam, A. 2008. 'A Text without Author: Locating the Constituent Assembly as Event', in Rajeev Bhargava (ed.), *Politics and Ethics of Indian Constitution,* New Delhi: Oxford University Press.

Saez, L. 2002. *Federalism without a Centre: Impact of Political and Economic Reform on India's Federal System*, New Delhi: Vistaar Publications.

Wheare, K.C. 1956. *Federal Government,* London: Oxford University Press.

4

Autonomy and States' Rights in the Indian Federal Union

Original Intent, Contemporary Content

Balveer Arora

Indian federalism has been viewed through changing constitutional and judicial lenses, as the polity has evolved over the last six decades since the First Lok Sabha was convened. The polity has moved from being a federal structure initially dominated by a single party to a vibrant multi-party federal democracy marked by the federalization of the party system and the emergence in greater strength and numbers of single-state and multi-state parties.[1] The initial reticence of the judiciary to consider the Indian Constitution (1950) as genuinely federal has consequently been modified, and even transformed, through a new reading of its federal character. It has in fact moved to a robust acceptance of its federal essence. There is no longer anything 'quasi' about India's centralized federalism and the ways in which it has adapted the federal principle, its innovations and experimentations are now readily accepted by the judiciary as legitimate areas for judicial review.

Referring to India's 'undeclared federalism', Perry Anderson observes that the drafters of the Constitution of the Indian Union 'studiously avoided the word 'federal'. (...) But though less than federal in intention, in outcome the union became something like a creatively flexible federation, in which state governments came to enjoy a considerable degree of autonomy, so long as they did not offer opportunities for intervention by internal disputes or cross too boldly the political will of the centre' (Anderson 2012: 21ff).

In this chapter, our basic argument unfolds in five parts. First, we argue that the muted espousal of federalism at the outset led to a concealed identity being transformed into a mistaken identity. The earliest constitutional commentaries, barring a few notable exceptions, stressed the absence of certain commonly incorporated federal features rather than the presence of basic federal principles.[2] In the second part, we examine the gradually evolving approach of the judiciary, from a quasi-denial of the federal nature of the Constitution to a growing recognition of the significance of federal principles in the basic structure of Indian democracy. Third, we focus upon the political processes that have helped the Constitution develop its federal content. In the fourth, we look at the new ways in which Indian federalism has moved today, movements that have been propelled by competing federal coalitions. Finally, we conclude with a plea for a far-reaching reconsideration of prevailing judicial assumptions about the limited federal nature of the Constitution. Such a revisit would attach due weight to the socio-political basis of India's federal democracy and recognize that federalism is essential for its survival.

Concealed or Mistaken Identity: Clarifying Original Intent

The packaging of federal principles in the Indian Constitution and their presentation to the Constituent Assembly was a veritable *tour de force*, a masterstroke piloted by Babasaheb Bhimrao Ambedkar. He realized that the prevalent mood in the Constituent Assembly had swung against federalism, which was intended to provide the basic architecture for the nascent Union. He skilfully assuaged the fears of many notable members who saw in federalism a sure recipe for further fragmentation and eventual disintegration of India, a deeper descent into chaos and anarchy.

It was not as if Ambedkar had always been a votary of federalism; in fact, his earliest utterances on the subject were quite the contrary (Bhattacharya 1992). But when confronted with the dominant mood, eloquently articulated by K.M. Panikkar, he decided to put his weight behind a system that salvaged the essence of the federal principles he deemed necessary for the national project to survive.[3] Displaying remarkable foresight and statesmanship, he was convinced that the survival of democracy in India depended on the firm embedding of its federal character in the Constitution.

Ambedkar's espousal of federal principles was perhaps more motivated by his concern for the protection of the rights of minorities than for a commitment to the rights of subnational territorial units. His concern for an overarching judicial architecture protecting individual and group rights bears testimony to this commitment.

In a recent juridical study on the Constitution, unusual for its devotion of nearly a fourth of the book to the description of its federalism, Madhav Khosla (2012: 45–6) rightly observes, 'By the time the Indian Constitution came into being, it was decidedly federal. But because the Constitution tilts heavily in favour of the Union, many portray India as an imperfectly federal or quasi-federal nation. Such reasoning is fallacious. The Indian Constitution may give the Union more powers than it gives the states, but it does not establish the supremacy of the Union'

The objectives that Ambedkar set out to attain were well served by what are sometimes described as the 'un-federal features' of the Constitution (Alladi 2001). He portrayed the federal principles incorporated therein as being polyvalent in their application, capable of being transformed into a unitary functioning mode in times of Emergency and exceptional need. He reassured the Assembly that the Constitution that they were being called upon to approve 'can be both unitary as well as federal according to the requirements of the time and circumstances'.[4] He further assured them that 'it has sought to forge means and methods whereby India will have Federation and at the same time will have uniformity in all basic matters which are essential to maintain the unity of the country'.[5] The flexibility in reordering the internal boundaries of the Union as well as the asymmetries built into intergovernmental relations proved to be invaluable assets in providing the necessary flexibility and adaptability that the evolving union needed to assume its federal destiny.

The initial reticence of the judiciary to fully recognize this fundamental feature of the Constitution was partly influenced by the same fear of federalism that had been so forcefully articulated in the Constituent Assembly. In interpreting the original intention of the framers of the Constitution, it perforce gave due weightage to these debates. Given the historical context of partition, the apprehensions about further fragmentation and disintegration were understandable, but the directions in which the future strength of the Indian Union lay were discerned only by a few farsighted statesmen, who allowed themselves to be persuaded by the Drafting Committee chaired by Ambedkar to shun the unitary temptation.

The charismatic presence of Jawaharlal Nehru at the helm of affairs of state, in the formative years, also no doubt persuaded the Supreme Court to attach a higher level of trust in the bona fide intentions of the central government than is normally warranted in a faithful interpretation of states' rights in a federal constitution. This was especially in the context of postcolonial national reconstruction, in which the judiciary was anxious to be seen as playing its due role. The ease with which it upheld legislation declared avowedly to be for socio-economic reform is symptomatic of this phase, where obstacles and impediments were resolutely set aside, in what was perceived to be the larger national interest as defined by Parliament. One of the striking and persistent features of judicial pronouncements in matters dealing with the competing claims of national and regional aspirations is this legacy of the invocation of 'national interest', as a justification for throwing its judicial weight behind the curtailment of states' rights.

The first cases of abuse of central executive power largely went unchallenged and unchecked. Thus, the judiciary in this phase could legitimately be charged with a bias in favour of the central government, including the definition and extension of its powers. The intentions of the founding fathers to endow the states with tangible rights and resources are amply borne out by the distribution detailed given in Table 4.1, in which the states were assigned in the three key resources necessary for development: land, water and power. In fact, there were even a few lone voices in the Constituent Assembly, notably K. Santhanam, who pleaded for restraint in expanding the ambit of the powers included in the Concurrent list, as this would undermine and curtail the domain of the states.

The trend towards encroaching upon the rights of states and whittling down the domains allotted to them has been noticeable for some time. The initial method was to use omnibus articles in the Concurrent list in order to occupy the field and enact pre-emptive legislation. This was noticeably the case with item 20 of the Concurrent list, economic and social planning. The other channels frequently used were that of residuary powers (Article 248 read with item 97 of the Union List) and treaty-making powers (Article 253 read with items 11–14 of the Union List). The transfer of some items from the state to the Concurrent list was resorted by the 42nd Amendment, notably with regard to education, forests and wild animals. The control over water resources was and is already heavily vested in the Union because most major rivers are interstate. Recently, the Parliamentary Consultative Committee of the Ministry of Water Resources decided unanimously to recommend that water be shifted from the state list to the Concurrent list.[6]

Table 4.1

Distribution of Legislative Powers and Executive Responsibilities between the Union Parliament and State Legislative Assemblies in Key Areas

Domain	*List I: Union's Powers*	*List II: States' Powers*	*List III: Concurrent*
1. Defence	Defence of India (1) Armed Forces (2) Paramilitary Forces (2a)		
2. Foreign Affairs	War and Peace (15) Diplomacy (11) UN (12) International Conferences (13) Treaties (14) Citizenship (17)		
3. Money	Public Debt (35) Currency & Foreign Exchange (36) Reserve Bank (38) Foreign Loans (37)	Money lending and money lenders (30)	Bankruptcy and Insolvency (9)
4. Judiciary	Supreme Court (77) High Courts (78)	High Court Personnel (3) Prisons (4)	Criminal Law (1) & Code (2) Justice Administration (11A) Civil Code (13)
5. Internal Security	Paramilitary Forces (2a) Central Bureau of Investigation (8) Preventive Detention for Defence, Foreign Affairs (9)	Public Order (1) Police (2)	Preventive Detention for state security, public order (3)

Cont'd...

Cont'd...

6. Land	Cantonments (3)	Land rights, tenures, rents, transfer (18)	Forests (17A), Acquisition/requisition ing of land & property (42)
7. Water	Interstate rivers and river valleys notified by law in public interest (56)	Water supplies, storage, power, irrigation and canals (17)	
8. Electricity, Power & Energy	Atomic energy and related mineral resources (6)	Natural and Biogas (25)	Electricity (38)
9. Agriculture & Fisheries	Fishing/Fisheries beyond territorial waters (57)	Agriculture (14); Livestock (15), Fisheries within territorial waters (21)	Wild Animals (17B)
10. Industry	Industries notified by law for national defence (7) or to be in public interest (52)	Industries other than those in the List I (24)	Factories (36)
11. Oil, Mines, Minerals,	Mineral oil/Petroleum (53), Mines and minerals notified to be in the public interest (54)	Mines and minerals other than those in the List I(23)	
12. Trade & Commerce	Foreign trade and commerce, import/export, customs frontiers (41) Interstate trade & commerce (42)	Trade & commerce within the state (26) Production, supply and distribution of goods (27) Markets & Fairs (28)	Trade, commerce, production & distribution of foodstuffs, edible oils, cotton & jute (33)
13. Infra-structure, Transport & Communi-cations	Railways (22), national highways (23), national waterways (24), maritime shipping (25) major ports (27) airways (29) rail/sea/air transportation (30)	Roads and means of communication other than those in the List I(13)	Minor ports (31), shipping & navigation on inland waterways (32)

Cont'd...

Cont'd...

14. Education and Human Resources	Universities & Institutions of national importance for scientific/technical education and research (63–66)	Incorporation and regulation of Universities, literary and scientific societies, associations, cooperatives (32)	Technical, medical, and university education including vocational and technical training (25)
15. Informa- tion & Broad- casting	Posts/telegraph/teleph one/wireless/broadcas ting and communication (31) Cinema censorship (60)	Theatre, Cinema, Sports (33)	
16. Public Health, Social Welfare, Labour and Employ- ment	Labour in mines and oilfields (55) Port quarantine (28)	Public health and sanitation/hospitals & dispensaries (6) Relief of disabled/ unemployable (9)	Infectious and contagious diseases (29) Economic & social planning (20) Population control (20A) social security/insurance & employment/unemploy ment (23) Labour welfare (24)
17. Local govern- ment, public works & cooperatives		Municipal corporations & local self-government (5) Public works (35) Cooperative societies (32)	
18. Taxation Powers and Financial Resources	Taxes on Personal Income (82), Corporate Income (85), Capital (86), Estates (87), Rail/Sea/Air Transportation (89), Services (92).	Land Revenue (45), Agricultural Income Tax (46), Lands and Buildings Tax (49), Alcohol (51). Electricity (53), Sales of Goods (54), Vehicles (57), Cinema (62).	

Source: Compiled from *Constitution of India*, Seventh Schedule. Numbers in brackets refer to item numbers in the concerned list. Residuary powers are vested in the Union, vide Article 248 and item 97 of the Union List.

The Judiciary: From Denial to Doubt to Recognition

The trajectory of the gradual change in judicial perspectives on states' rights has run parallel to the process of adaptation of the strong centre framework to the increasing competitiveness of the political process. Heightened power struggles and new experiments in power-sharing through federal coalitions have given the states the capacity to influence the exercise of central executive power. Faced with a deteriorating power equation with the centre and its unmatched resources, the states have searched for new levers to influence central policies and exercise their rights. This change has taken place without any fundamental alterations in the constitutional distribution of powers, which has incrementally added to the reach and oversight powers of the centre rather than moving competencies in favour of the states.

The framers of the Constitution were acutely aware of the dangers of the judiciary getting sucked into intractable and intrinsically political disputes between the centre and the states. Thus, they insulated the judiciary from interstate river water disputes, for which separate tribunals were provided. They also provided for an Inter-State Council (Article 263), which was however activated only when the polity was well into its multi-party phase.

The judiciary was also acutely aware of the dangers and pitfalls of getting involved in what were essentially power struggles and even voiced its reluctance to intervene in 'the political thicket'. It finally took the plunge in the cathartic context of post-Emergency exercise of central power. It agreed to hear challenges to central intervention and extended the ambit of judicial review to cover the executive exercise of power in a key and contentious area of the federal polity, namely the imposition of direct central rule in the states (Article 356) by superseding the state legislature and executive (*Rajasthan*, 1977).

Judicial review was an integral part of the original design, but its domain was considerably strengthened and expanded after the attempts by the executive to curb judicial power failed in the mid-1970s. After the defeat of the Indira Gandhi government in 1977, the independence of the judiciary was constitutionally strengthened by the 44th Amendment. The doctrine of 'Basic Structure', initially enunciated in *Kesavananda Bharati* (1973), was further developed and progressively extended in subsequent judgements to even cover federalism, albeit to a limited extent. Thus, the judiciary moved from conditional acceptance of the federal nature of the Constitution to considering it an 'essential feature' (*Bommai*, 1994), and simultaneously increased the scope of judicial review.

In its interpretation of the powers vested in the Union government, the judiciary was initially inclined to rule in favour of the central executive, a decision made easier by a textual reading of the Constitution. The constitutional design was undoubtedly weighted in favour of the Union government and became progressively more so as the process of planned economic development further tilted the balance in its favour. Troubling evidence of the increasing and extensive misuse of central emergency powers began to emerge in the 1970s.

The Sarkaria Commission on Centre–State Relations examined this evidence and came to the conclusion that there was a compelling case for executive restraint in the use of emergency powers, intended to be used in exceptional circumstances of failure of constitutional functioning in the states. This call for restraint was further reinforced through judicial intervention when the Supreme Court read into jurisprudence the most salient recommendations of the Sarkaria Commission, in the *Bommai* (1994) case. Some of the unresolved issues were further elaborated by Justice Sarkaria in the recommendations of his panel on centre–state relations to the National Commission to Review the Working of the Constitution (2001).

The Political Process and Contemporary Federal Content

The 1980s were transitional in many ways. They were misleading on the surface if one views them as marked by central stability. The political turbulence in the states gave rise to new parties that successfully challenged the party in power at the centre. A growing number of state governments demanded space and voice: they turned to the judiciary for curbing abusive central intervention and, at the political level, demanded federal reform which would give them more participation in national policy processes.

The court was no doubt influenced in its interpretations by the impact of democratic processes on the transformation of federal practices. The strong centre was redefined and reinvented. While the Constitution remained largely unchanged, changing federal practices facilitated a process through which the states reclaimed and retrieved powers through political processes.

This period also saw the emergence of 'green federalism', marked by judicial enthusiasm and intervention. The 1990s could well be characterized as a defining decade for India's federal polity. Economic reform through liberalization and the redefinition of the relationship between the state and the markets, in turn, impacted the roles and responsibilities of the different levels of government.

Judicial interpretation of these transformative changes has been marked by careful oversight of the exercise of the regulatory functions of the central state and also a sympathetic ear for the concerns of environmental defence groups through the public interest litigation route. Similarly, it has been sensitive to the pleas of groups engaged in electoral reform with a view to cleanse the polity of undesirable elements and corrupt practices. While it is the Election Commission that is primarily responsible for the electoral process itself, the judiciary is called upon to decide petitions alleging electoral malpractices. It also hears appeals in cases that attract the antidefection law.

The judiciary has also stepped into areas that were previously considered purely matters of executive policy, invoking its own understanding of what constitutes 'national interest'. For example, the Supreme Court has thrown its weight behind the interlinking of rivers project and called upon the concerned states to cooperate, even though the Union government has yet to take a final decision on how to proceed in a matter on which experts continue to be divided.

In interpreting the shifting balance of power in India's federal polity, the judiciary has been cautious and prudent, particularly in view of the volatile nature of the political process as reflected in its federalized party system (See Table 4.2).

While the strong centre constitutional framework remains basically intact, states are emerging as strong centres of power (See Table 4.3). Confronted with the gap between constitutional texts and new political realities, the Supreme Court has steadfastly maintained its commitment to core constitutional values. However, its expanding reach raises certain apprehensions. As Pran Chopra (2006) points out, this represents a real and present danger for Indian federalism.

Table 4.2

Vote Share in Per cent of All-India, Single-State and Multi-State Parties (1989–2009)

All-India Parties	*9 LS: 1989*	*10 LS: 1991*	*11 LS: 1996*	*12 LS: 1998*	*13 LS: 1999*	*14 LS: 2004*	*15 LS: 2009*
Congress	39.53	36.26	28.8	25.82	28.3	26.53	28.52
BJP	11.36	20.11	20.29	25.59	23.75	22.16	18.84
Subtotal INC + BJP	50.89	56.37	49.09	51.41	52.05	48.59	47.36
State Parties*							
Multi-state parties	28.45	24.28	22.72	19.36	20.11	16.61	16.24
Single-state parties and independent	20.66	19.35	28.19	29.23	27.84	34.8	36.4
Subtotal state parties	49.11	43.63	50.91	48.59	47.95	51.41	52.64
Grand total	100	100	100	100	100	100	100

Source: Election Commission of India various reports available at http://eci.nic.in.

All-India parties are parties that have won seats in all four zones detailed in Table 4.4, even though they may be unevenly implanted and even absent from some states. They are also described as polity-wide parties.

*Multi-state parties are the smaller parties recognized as 'national' by the Election Commission in successive elections.

Single-state parties have won seats from a single state. Seats won by independent candidates have been clubbed with single-state parties.

Table 4.3

Division of Seats in the Lok Sabha between All-India and State Parties 1996–2009

Parties	*11 LS: 1996*	*12 LS: 1998*	*13 LS: 1999*	*14 LS: 2004*	*15 LS: 2009*
All-India Parties	*% Seats*	*% Seats*	*% Seats*	*% Seats*	*% Seats*
Congress	25.8	26.0	21.0	26.7	37.9
BJP	29.6	33.5	33.5	25.4	21.4
Sub Total INC + BJP	55.4	59.5	54.5	52.1	59.3
State Parties					
Multi-state parties*	18.8	11.8	13.3	14.9.	9.9
Single-state parties and independents.	25.8	28.7	32.2	33.0	30.8
Sub Total state parties	44.6	40.5	45.5	47.9	40.7
Grand total	100	100	100	100	100

Source: Same as given for Table 4.2 State parties as defined in Table 4.2.

Federalization Today: Competing Federal Coalitions

The new face of India's robust federalism has emerged via the mediation of federal coalitions and sharpening interparty competition. The federalization of the party system and the emergence of a fluid binodal configuration are the defining characteristics of this phase. Taking advantage of their increased political weight in the centre–state equation, assertive states are reclaiming, through the political process, their share of powers initially assigned to them. Some have taken the political power-sharing route, using to advantage the possibilities offered by federal coalitions to shape policy.

The earlier states rights discourse, which sought judicial protection for state autonomy against unwarranted and intrusive central intervention, has been supplemented in recent years by a new emphasis on more meaningful sharing of existing powers, which has superimposed itself on the long-standing demand for constitutional reform in the direction of transfer of more powers to the states. Instead, the focus has shifted to blocking attempts to further erode existing states' powers and attributions. Even the constitutionally permissible exercise of the Union's vast legislative powers has become politically fraught with danger and uncertainty. Faced with such situations, the Union is pushed into protracted consultations with the states in order to arrive at a negotiated settlement.

Table 4.4 shows that the two polity-wide parties have an uneven territorial implantation across regions. Their glaring absence in some of the most populous states illustrates the difficulties involved in negotiating agreements compromising states' rights. The label of All-India parties has been reserved here for two parties alone – the INC and the BJP – because they have obtained seats in all four zones. This does not, however, mask the fact that their regional spread is uneven and that they have pockets of strength in certain regions while having only a symbolic presence in others. This is particularly marked in the case of the BJP, which is heavily dependent on its NDA partners to establish a polity-wide presence. It has therefore emerged as a strong proponent for states' rights and federal principles.

Conclusion: Towards a New Federal Jurisprudence

Indian federalism has come a long way since it was conceived in the aftermath of partition. It is a tribute to the foresight of leaders such as B.R. Ambedkar and the acceptance of the logic of deep-rooted

Table 4.4

Zonal Distribution of Seats between Parties in the Lok Sabha elections from 1989 to 2009

Zones	*States*	*Parties*	*9 LS: 1989*	*10 LS: 1991*	*11 LS: 1996*	*12 LS: 1998*	*13 LS: 1999*	*14 LS: 2004*	*15 LS: 2009*
Zone I North and Northwest	Uttar Pradesh, Bihar, Madhya Pradesh, Rajasthan, Punjab + Chandigarh, Delhi NCT, Haryana, Jammu and Kashmir and Himachal Pradesh	INC	38	60	41	39	43	44	87
		BJP	63	87	120	128	115	70	46
		OTHERS	144	76	84	78	87	106	87
		Zone total	245	223	245	245	245	220	220
Zone 2 East and Northeast	Orissa, Assam, Sikkim + Arunachal Pradesh + Manipur + Mizoram + Meghalaya + Nagaland + Manipur + Tripura	INC	17	34	35	19	19	26	27
		BJP	0	2	1	9	13	22	23
		OTHERS	57	52	52	60	56	65	63
		Zone total	74	88	88	88	88	113	113
Zone 3 West	Goa, Maharashtra, Gujarat + Dadra and Nagar Haveli + Daman and Diu	INC	32	46	27	42	17	27	29
		BJP	22	26	34	25	35	28	27
		OTHERS	24	6	17	11	26	23	22
		Zone total	78	78	78	78	78	78	78
Zone 4 South	Andhra Pradesh + Karnataka + Tamil Nadu + Puducherry, Kerala, Lakshadweep + Andaman and Nicobar Islands	INC	110	92	37	41	35	48	62
		BJP	0	5	6	20	19	18	20
		OTHERS	22	35	89	71	78	66	50
		Zone total	132	132	132	132	132	132	132

Source: Same as given for Table 4.1. North Zone includes Uttarakhand, and East Zone includes Jharkhand and Chhattisgarh in the results for 2004 and 2009. These states were carved out in 2000 from Uttar Pradesh, Bihar and Madhya Pradesh.

realities by Jawaharlal Nehru that the foundations were laid for the emergence of a robust federal system. Just as it was difficult to initially visualize that the Constitution could provide the basis for such a system, today it is equally difficult to conceive of a nonfederal future for Indian democracy. This course taken by the polity has been irrigated by the emergence and consolidation of state parties.

The vibrancy of Indian federalism is therefore more the outcome of a political process than of a judicial revisit of the original intent. The judiciary has accepted the increasingly federal character of the polity by endorsing two of its key features: flexible boundaries and asymmetric federalism. It however clings to the notion that there is a concept of 'basic national interest' embodied in the Constitution, an extension of the idea of a 'basic structure' that is judicially defined. To the extent that these interpretations are grounded in and derived from the original intent, they are valuable judicial constructs. We have argued here that federalism was very much a part of the original intent and that the judiciary has yet to revisit its initial pronouncements to the contrary. This is all the more urgent because these pronouncements were arrived at during a phase when the voices of vital forces of India's federal society were muted and largely unheard.

Notes

1. Earlier versions of this paper were presented at the International Conference on 'Federalism, the Rule of Law and the Role of the Judiciary' organized by the Leuven Centre for Global Governance Studies, KU Leuven, Belgium (2009) and at the International Conference on 'Law and Democracy in India' Indian Institute of Advanced Study, Shimla (2012). I am indebted to the participants at both these conferences for their insightful comments.
2. The most notable mislabelling that has had a tenacious presence in textbooks was by K.C. Wheare. His 'quasi-federal' epithet clouded perceptions of successive generations of scholars. In all fairness, it is doubtful if he would use the same term today to describe India's undoubtedly federal functioning.
3. Panikkar warned that 'federation is a fair weather constitution and in the circumstances of India it is likely to be a dangerous experiment'. He further stated, 'Federation with limited powers for the Centre was an unavoidable evil in India so long as the Muslim majority provinces need to

be provided for in an all-India centre. Now (...) the necessity for a federal constitution has ceased'. Ibid.

4. 'In normal times, it is framed to work as a federal system. But in times of war, it is so designed as to make it work as though it was a unitary system'.
5. Among the means adopted for this purpose, he accorded primacy of place to a single judiciary and uniformity in fundamental laws, civil and criminal. This responsibility placed on the judiciary to uphold the unity of the country no doubt influenced its earlier interpretations of original intent.
6. Arguing that water is a national resource, it stressed the need for its coordinated use. *Indian Express* 13 July 2012.

References

Alexandrowicz, C.H. 1957. *Constitutional Developments in India,* New Delhi: Oxford University Press.

Alladi, Aruna. 2001. *Unfederal Features of the Constitution,* Chennai: Mathivanan Publications.

Anand, A.S. 1998. *The Constitution of Jammu and Kashmir* (3rd ed.), New Delhi: Universal Law Publishers.

Anderson, Perry. 2012. 'After Nehru', *London Review of Books*, Vol. 34(15), 2 August 2012, pp. 21–36.

Andhyaraujina, T.R. 2011. *The Kesavanand Bharati Case,* New Delhi: Universal Law Publishers.

Arora, B. and Nirmal Mukarji. 1992. *Federalism in India: Origins and Development*, New Delhi: Centre for Policy Research/Vikas Publishing House Pvt.Ltd.

Arora, B. and Douglas Verney. 1995. *Multiple Identities in a Single State: Indian Federalism in Comparative Perspective*, New Delhi: Centre for Policy Research/Konark.

Arora, B. 1997. 'Multilevel Federalism', in V.A. Pai Panandiker (ed.), *Survey of Research in Public Administration 1980–1990,* New Delhi: ICSSR/Konark.

——. 2000. 'Negotiating Differences: Federal Coalitions and National Cohesion', Francine R. Frankel et.al. (eds.), in *Transforming India: Socio-Political Dynamics of Democracy*, New Delhi: Oxford University Press.

——. 2002. 'Political Parties and the Party System: The Emergence of New Coalitions', in Zoya Hasan (ed.), *Parties and Party Politics in India*, New Delhi: Oxford University Press.

——. 2003. 'Federalisation of India's Party System', in Ajay K. Mehra, D.D. Khanna and Gert W. Kueck (eds.), *Political Parties and Party Systems*, New Delhi: Sage Publications.

——. 2006. 'From Reluctant to Robust Federalism: The Development of India's Political Institutions', in Mary E. John, Praveen Kumar Jha and Surinder S. Jodhka (eds.), *Contested Transformations: Changing Economies and Identities in Contemporary India*, New Delhi: Tulika.

——. 2010. 'The Indian Republic', in Luis Moreno and Cesar Colino (eds.), *Diversity and Unity in Federal Countries*, Montreal: McGill-Queens University Press.

Arora, B. and K.K. Kailash. 2012. 'The New Party System: Federalised and Binodal', in Ajay Mehra (ed.), *Party Systems in India and their Emerging Trajectories*, New Delhi: Sage Publications.

Arora, B. et al. 2013. 'Indian Federalism', in K.C. Suri (ed.) *ICSSR Research Surveys and Explorations, Political Science Volume – 2, Indian Democracy*, USA: Oxford University Press.

Austin, G. 1999. *Working a Democratic Constitution: The Indian Experience,* USA: Oxford University Press.

Baxi, U. 2008. 'Outline of a "Theory of Practice" of Indian Constitutionalism', in Rajeev Bhargava (ed.), *Politics and Ethics of the Indian Constitution,* USA: Oxford University Press.

Bhattacharyya, H. 2010. *Federalism in Asia: India, Pakistan, and Malaysia*, London: Routledge.

Bhattacharya, Mohit. 1992. 'The Mind of the Founding Fathers', in Nirmal Mukarji and Balveer Arora (eds.), *Federalism in India: Origins and Development*, Noida: Vikas Publishing.

Chaudhury, R., S.B., Samir K. Das and Ranabir Samaddar (eds.). 2005. *Indian Autonomies: Keywords & Key Texts,* Bangalore: Sampark.

Chopra, P. (ed.). 2006. *The Supreme Court versus the Constitution: A Challenge to Federalism*, New Delhi: Sage Publications.

DeSouza, P. R, Sridharan, E. (eds.). 2006. *India's Political Parties*, New Delhi: Sage Publications.

Dhavan, R. and Rekha Saxena. 2006. 'The Republic of India', in Katy Le Roy and Cheryl Saunders (eds.), *Legislative, Executive and Judicial Governance in Federal Countries*, Montreal: McGill-Queen's University Press.

Kailash K.K. 2011. 'Federal Calculations in State Level Coalition Governments', *India Review*, 10(3), pp. 246–282.

Kashyap, S.C. 2000. 'Institutions of Governance: Parliament, Government, Judiciary', in V.A. Pai Panandiker (ed.), *Problems of Governance in South Asia*, New Delhi: Konark Publishers Pvt. Ltd.

Kashyap, S.C., D.D. Khanna and Gert W. Kueck (eds.). 2000. *Reviewing the Constitution*, New Delhi: Shipra Publications.

Khosla, M. 2012. *The Indian Constitution*, New Delhi: Oxford University Press.

Noorani, A.G. 2011. *Article 370: A Constitutional History of Jammu & Kashmir*, New Delhi: Oxford University Press.

Sadanandan, A. 2012. 'Bridling Central Tyranny in India: How Regional Parties Restrain the Central Government', *Asian Survey*, 52(2), pp. 247–269.

Shastri, S., K.C. Suri and Yogendra Yadav (eds.). 2009. *Electoral Politics in Indian States*, USA: Oxford University Press.

Singh, M.P. 2011. *Indian Federalism: An Introduction*, New Delhi: National Book Trust.

Verney, D.V. 1995. 'Are All Federations Federal? The U.S., Canada and India', in Balveer Arora and Douglas Verney (eds.), *Multiple Identities in a Single State: Indian Federalism in Comparative Perspective*, Hyderabad: Sangam Books.

5

Interface of Local and Higher Governments

Nation Building and Inclusive Development in India

S.N. Sangita

In India, local governments substate (rural and urban) as a third tier of governance at the district and subdistrict levels (after higher level central and state governments) came into existence in the late 1990s, though operating, ever since, without adequate statutory powers and resources. Many provisions have been included in the Constitution (following 73rd and 74th Amendments) to make these institutions independent of higher level governments with a view to promoting national integration and inclusive growth. Powers, functions and resources have been devolved to these institutions so as to involve local people belonging to various ethnic groups (religious, linguistic and caste based) in the governance of the country (at the grassroots level, numerical strength facilitates Christian, Muslim and other ethnic minorities to provide leadership in some local governments which is difficult at higher level governments). The reservation of seats and positions in local governments enables the disadvantaged (SC/ST/OBCs/women) groups to share power with the dominant communities in terms of influencing policies and delivering goods and services beneficial to them.

Independent state election commissions (for conducting free, fair and regular elections) and state finance commissions (for allocation of financial resources) have been put in place for minimizing the influence of higher level governments. Distinct planning committees are constituted to enable local governments to formulate and implement plans based on local needs and resources. Even plan grants and resources are made available to local governments (LGs) under flagship programmes of the central government such as Mahatma Gandhi National Rural Employment Guarantee Act (MGNREGA), National Rural Health Mission (NRHM), universalization of education (Sarva Shiksha Abhiyan), Bharat Nirman, Public Distribution System (PDS) and Jawaharlal National Urban Renewal Mission (JNNURM) for building the necessary infrastructure and expanding access to health care and education. Many governance institutions such as Grama Sabha (GS) (village assembly), ward committee, social audit, ombudsman, RTI and so on have been introduced to make LGs accountable and to minimize the role of higher level governments in terms of monitoring development programmes.

Notwithstanding laudable innovations in governance design, the interference of higher level governments in the functioning of local governments is a major constraint in promoting national integration and inclusive development. The non-constitution of district planning committees, district in-charge ministers, the parallel organizations (stakeholder committees for education, health care, water, forest and so on, MP and MLA funds) undermine the autonomous status of local governments. Against this background, the chapter analyses the interface between local (rural) and higher level governments (mainly state) in promoting national integration and inclusive development. An analytical framework has been developed to examine these issues. The study is mainly based on secondary sources.

The second section outlines the analytical framework for examining the role of LGs in promoting national integration and inclusive development. The third section deals with India's federalism, empowerment and representation of the disadvantaged groups (SC/ST/women/minorities) in LGs with respect to sharing power with the dominant sections in the governance of the country. The fourth section dwells on the aspects such as participation, representation, responsiveness and accountability of LGs with regard to the provision of services through local governments in an efficient and equitable manner so as to promote inclusive development and to enjoy the trust and confidence of the minorities and disadvantaged groups. The fifth section discusses the constraints involved (in the presence of higher level governments) in the efficient and effective functioning of local governments (with autonomy and accountability) for achieving the desired goals/outcomes. The last section concludes with certain policy implications.

Local Governments (Political Decentralization) and National Integration: An Analytical Framework

Local Governments, Diversity and Nation Building

Political decentralization (devolution and transfer of power, limited self-governance and federalization) in a diverse society like ours promotes national integration, although an opposite view also prevails. The advocates of this view observe that LGs provide for opportunities to share power with other tiers of governance (central and state governments) besides promoting their own governance. LGs (decentralization), being culturally a distinctive subgroup, are regarded by many as a *sine qua non* for the survival of heterogeneous societies like ours in that they accommodate ethnic (linguistic, religious) minority groups and thereby help achieve national integration (Smith 1987: 49). LGs facilitate the participation and representation of minorities and disadvantaged groups while deepening on the democratic process (Horst et al. 2008: 4). Decentralization is, in fact, a strategy to cope up with political instability which remains threatened, simultaneously, by secessionist movements and demands for regional autonomy. LGs, by addressing regional grievances, consequently reduce the support for ethnic movements (Miodownik and Cartrite 2010: 734. Further, they act as vehicles for redressing grievances and articulating the interests of the local communities and thereby prevent the growing clamour for ethnic mobilizations against the system. Political decentralization is likely to reduce antiregime mobilizations and intercommunity conflicts. It is important to note here that the minorities express themselves in favour of remaining within the union but with a fair degree of autonomy in the form of a separate state or autonomous council. This demand is to preserve their culture, language and ethnic identity.

LG helps strengthen multi-party democracy by tempering the domination of majority communities in the area of governance. Wherever political parties also function locally, it often results in the emergence of different political parties governing at different levels of government. Multi-party democracy is thus not just restricted to elections, but also entrenches the politics of multi-party accommodation (Nico 2008: 21). Pluralist politics must be learned, and local governments make a good school (Nico 2008: 21).

However, some scholars view that decentralization threatens the unity of the general will and that it reinforces narrow sectional interests and also that it is anti-egalitarian through its support. Some studies show that moderate levels of decentralization encourage ethnopolitical mobilizations (movements seeking and hoping to gain public support for their goals by appealing and nurturing group identification based on language, region, religion, race, caste, etc.) and erect and politicize boundaries between a group residing within a demarcated political space and the rest of the state (Miodownik and Cartrite 2010: 732. It encourages the mobilization of masses on the lines of ethnic loyalties and secessionist movements; it provides opportunities for the local elite to pressurize the central government to give more powers that may lead to separation from the mainstream. Decentralization also encourages the emergence of ethnopolitical parties, thereby encouraging ethnic conflicts and secessionism.

Local Governments, Good Governance and National Integration

Local Governments, Participation and Representation

LGs enjoy legitimacy and political stability by promoting good governance in four ways: The first two relate to participation and representation, while the latter two relate to responsiveness and accountability. First, LGs enjoy legitimacy and trust, since they are elected by local people (participation), while governments nominated or imposed by higher level governments do not enjoy the same confidence. Locally elected governments allow the community to identify more with political institutions and foster a sense of ownership and belongingness to their governance and resources. Empowerment emanates from participation. Democratic decentralization, by making participation easier, makes empowerment more feasible at the local level than at the national level, especially for minorities and vulnerable groups (Blair 2000).

Second, the local people own the government, since its elected leaders represent the population in terms of ethnicity, caste, region, language and so on. The representative character of LGs has been further strengthened with the reservation of seats for the socially disadvantaged. It thus promotes participation and representation that are critical to legitimacy and trust.

Local Government and Responsiveness

LGs also enjoy respect from people, since they reflect the needs and aspirations of the people. By their very nature, local governments bring governance closer to the people, making the translation of community preferences into responsive policy and programmes more likely. They generate incentives for people to own the local government, with newly assigned responsibilities and resources relevant to them. Locally based decisions are often more practical and sustainable in that they acknowledge and accommodate local diversities and historic complexities that may exist within a particular locality. Only with the full cooperation of the local community, can development projects succeed (Nico 2008: 20) as it tends to strongly enhance speed, quantity and quality of responses from government institutions. LGs have both authority and resources to respond quickly to problems and pressures from below without waiting for approval from higher levels. LGs have more and better information regarding their constituents and are better able to enforce and coordinate policies and programmes (Bardhan 1996). LGs also harness creative energy of the local people and can promote innovations that help mobilize both human and financial resources as well. One of the underlying rationales of decentralization is the possibility of innovation and experimentation that it offers to subnational units (Nico 2008: 21). Thus, LGs promote an expected improvement in allocative efficiency, welfare and equity through increased participation, transparency, empowerment and responsiveness.

Local Government and Accountability

Political decentralization is said to strengthen accountability and contain corruption. The proximity of citizens to their elected representatives also makes it easier to make the latter accountable (Nico 2008: 21). Thus, citizens find it easier to hold LGs accountable through voter information, participation and monitoring.

However, some studies differ from these arguments. LGs, according to them, are frequently not inclusive in terms of political representation or decision making, often resulting in policies and actions not addressing the needs of disadvantaged groups, including women. It is well documented that, in general, women and weaker sections are underrepresented in LGs.

Under many LGs, the gap between the rich and poor is substantially wide. The poor, often living on employment and wages without assets and skills, do not always have access to the basic services. Their voices are not heard with respect to their basic needs such as housing, safe drinking water, fuel, transport and security. Poverty continues to be the main constraint with women bearing the major brunt of poverty. Women, as compared to men, are more concerned with basic services such as water, fuel, sanitation, primary health care, waste disposal and transport. Illiteracy or poor education exacerbates the difficulties of access to basic services (Nico 2008: 25).

The exclusion of disadvantaged groups from policy attention is a further manifestation of some LGs becoming inwardly focused – benefits for self-serving elites – rather than being community centred and development directed. The ultimate form of a self-serving institution is corruption in its various forms. Corruption and elitism, even if they exist only as perceptions, are a real threat to an effective LG as participation in elections and other processes decreases where the image of politicians and institutions is poor. Becoming inwardly focused is often the product of poor leadership; democratic institutions are not seen or used as vehicles for advancing the community interests and aspirations (Nico 2008: 25).

In this chapter, the expected outcomes of a democratic decentralization are national integration and inclusive development. Decentralization enables the minorities and disadvantaged groups to share power with the dominant communities on the basis of numerical strength and affirmative actions. Their representation in LGs helps maintain trust and local governance. They are unlikely to support secessionist and separate movements. They prefer to stay with the mainstream population while sharing political power with the dominant communities. People also tend to trust LGs, as they are presumed to promote good governance (responsiveness and accountability) and inclusive development. LGs facilitate participation of people in policy formulation in terms of articulating their needs and aspirations. Further, their participation in policy implementation and monitoring also ensures the accountability of LGs to the disadvantaged groups and thereby redressing their grievances to some extent.

However, the effective functioning of LGs depends upon the autonomy and accountability from higher level governments, that is, whether LGs are allowed to enjoy a fair degree of autonomy in relation to higher level governments (in terms of functions, functionaries and finances) in terms of promoting national integration and inclusive development?

Diversity and Political Decentralization in India

Does Indian Federalism Address Diversity and National Integration?

India has adopted federalism for governing the vast country characterized by a high degree of diversity (language, religion, ethnicity, nationality, culture and race rather than gender, class, status and occupation) on the principle of 'Shared Rule' and 'Self-Rule'. The 'shared rule' under federalism is aimed at building dynamic, efficient and modern nation–states for economic progress, national security and influence in the world arena; while self-rule is aimed at expressing and articulating distinctive identities (historical, social, linguistic or cultural) through smaller, directly democratically elected self-governing political units. By combining elements of shared rule under larger units and self-rule under smaller regional

Table 5.1

Category-wise Composition of Population across Districts (in %)

	Particulars	*SC*	*ST*	*OBC*	*Muslims*	*Christians*	*Sikhs*	*Others*
1	Above 75%	0	40		9	—	—	—
2	Above 50%	1	35		11	—	—	—
3	Above 25%	*50	**31		38	—	—	—
4	Less than 25%	542	518			—	—	—
	Total	593	593		593	—	—	—

Notes: * Above 26 per cent, ** Above 30 per cent

Source: (1) GoI, Planning Commission, Compiled from 'Report of the Task Group on Development of SCs and STs: On Selected Agenda Items of the National Common Minimum Programme', 2005.
(2) Sachar Committee Report.

Table 5.2
Statewise Composition of Linguistic Population in India, 2001

S. No.	*India/State/ Union Territory*	*Area (in sq. km)*	*Population 2001*	*1st language*	*2nd language*	*3rd language*	*4th language*	*5th language*	*Others*
	India*		**993,245,089**						
1	Andhra Pradesh (1953, 1956, 1959)	276,754	75,425,779	84.73 Telugu	8.72 Urdu	3.27 Hindi	1.02 Tamil	0.81 Marathi	1.46
2	Arunachal Pradesh (1971)	83,473	363,002	26.76 Bengali	26.15 Nepali	22.37 Hindi	14.20 Assamese	2.16 Oriya	8.36
3	Assam (1951, 1962, 1971)	78,438	24,512,931	53.08 Assamese	29.96 Bengali	6.4 Hindi	5.29 Bodo	2.30 Nepali	2.97
4	Bihar (1950, 1956, 1968, 2000)	94 163	82,821,007	73.21 Hindi	14.28 Maithili	11.42 Urdu	0.54 Bengali	0.47 Santali	0.08
5	Chhattisgarh (2000)	155 191	18,862,901	91.24 Hindi	4.34 Oriya	1.11 Bengali	0.79 Telugu	0.75 Marathi	1.78
6	Goa (1987)	3,702	1,336,151	57.62 Konkani	22.77 Marathi	5.75 Hindi	5.58 Kannada	4.05 Urdu	4.23
7	Gujarat (1960)	196,024	48,054,060	89.00 Gujarati	4.97 Hindi	2.00 Sindhi	1.59 Marathi	1.15 Urdu	1.3
8	Haryana (1966, 1979)	44,212	21,100,316	87.49 Hindi	10.59 Punjabi	1.24 Urdu	0.19 Bengali	0.1 Nepali	0.4

Cont'd...

...*Cont'd*

9	Himachal Pradesh (1966)	55,673	5,938,162	91.1 Hindi	6.13 Punjabi	1.18 Nepali	0.85 Kashmiri	0.32 Dogri	0.42
10	Jammu & Kashmir (1950)	222,236	9,795,767	55.39 Kashmiri	22.52 Dogri	19.09 Hindi	1.95 Punjabi	0.15 Marathi	0.91
11	Jharkhand (2000)	79,714	24,130,955	64.28 Hindi	11.93 Santali	10.81 Bengali	9.63 Urdu	1.94 Oriya	1.41
12	Karnataka (1950, 1956, 1968)	191,791	50,865,780	68.49 Kannada	10.89 Urdu	7.27 Telugu	3.72 Marathi	3.69 Tamil	5.94
13	Kerala (1956)	38,863	31,694,681	97.19 Malayalam	1.88 Tamil	0.36 Kannada	0.19 Konkani	0.15 Telugu	0.32
14	Madhya Pradesh (1950, 1956, 2000)	308,000	55,971,837	94.08 Hindi	2.26 Marathi	2.12 Urdu	0.46 Sindhi	0.35 Gujarati	0.72
15	Maharashtra (1950, 1960)	307,713	92,285,750	72.21 Marathi	11.57 Hindi	7.47 Urdu	2.51 Gujarati	1.52 Telugu	4.71
16	Manipur (1971)	22,327	1,374,844	92.09 Manipuri	3.35 Nepali	1.97 Bengali	1.80 Hindi	0.17 Tamil	0.63
17	Meghalaya (1971)	22,429	384,236	48.33 Bengali	13.57 Nepali	13.03 Hindi	10.06 Marathi	9.52 Assamese	5.5
18	Mizoram (1971)	21,087	111,181	72.30 Bengali	9.47 Hindi	8.05 Nepali	4.21 Santali	1.64 Manipuri	4.33
19	Nagaland (1962)	16,579	195,543	30.12 Bengali	29.14 Hindi	17.50 Nepali	8.60 Assamese	3.54 Manipuri	11.1

Cont'd...

...Cont'd

20	Orissa (1950,1960)	155,707	34,206,100	89.35 Oriya	3.05 Hindi	2.08 Telugu	2.04 Santali	1.79 Urdu	1.68
21	Punjab (1950, 1956, 1960, 1966)	50,362	24,345,424	91.74 Punjabi	7.6 Hindi	0.11 Urdu	0.08 Bengali	0.08 Nepali	0.38
22	Rajasthan (1950, 1956, 1959)	342,239	53,821,529	95.51 Hindi	2.12 Punjabi	1.23 Urdu	0.71 Sindhi	0.11 Gujarati	0.32
23	Sikkim (1975)	7,096	390,170	86.78 Nepali	9.25 Hindi	1.62 Bengali	0.75 Urdu	0.35 Punjabi	1.25
24	Tamil Nadu (1950, 1953, 1959)	130,058	62,363,004	89.47 Tamil	5.66 Telugu	1.68 Kannada	1.51 Urdu	0.89 Malayalam	0.79
25	Tripura (1950)	1,049,169	2,266,280	94.78 Bengali	2.37 Hindi	1.05 Oriya	0.91 Manipuri	0.17 Telugu	0.71
26	Uttar Pradesh (1950, 1968, 1979, 2000)	236,286	166,156,553	88.26 Hindi	5.88 Urdu	2.92 Punjabi	1.08 Nepali	1.46 Bengali	0.41
27	Uttaranchal (2000)	53,483	8,459,227	88.26 Hindi	5.88 Urdu	2.92 Punjabi	1.46 Bengali	1.08 Nepali	0.41
28	West Bengal (1950, 1954, 1956)	88,752	79,683,746	85.80 Bengali	7.21 Hindi	2.82 Santali	2.08 Urdu	1.28 Nepali	0.81
	National Capital/Territory								

Cont'd...

...Cont'd

29	Delhi State (1950, 1956)	1,483	13,818,220	81.13 Hindi	7.16 Punjabi	6.33 Urdu	1.51 Bengali	0.67 Tamil	3.27
30	Andaman and Nicobar Islands (1950, 1956)	8,249	301,381	30.39 Bengali	21.55 Hindi	20.89 Tamil	15.14 Telugu	9.58 Malayalam	2.46
31	Chandigarh (1966)	114	898,516	67.69 Hindi	27.96 Punjabi	0.81 Urdu	0.64 Tamil	0.61 Bengali	2.29
32	Dadra & Nagar Haveli (1961)	491	130,137	40.01 Gujarati	25.54 Hindi	17.52 Konkani	8.91 Marathi	1.41 Malayalam	6.6
33	Daman & Diu (1987)	112	154,180	69.46 Gujarati	19.95 Hindi	4.39 Marathi	1.34 Oriya	1.17 Bengali	3.69
34	Lakshadweep (1956)	32	52,664	97.89 Malayalam	0.73 Tamil	0.59 Konkani	0.21 Hindi	0.20 Gujarati	0.38
35	Pondicherry (1962)	492	973,075	88.53 Tamil	5.23 Telugu	4.40 Malayalam	0.73 Urdu	0.45 Hindi	0.66

Source: Compiled from Census Data 2001.

units, federal political systems provide the closest institutional approximation to the complex multicultural and multidimensional economic, social and political reality of the contemporary world (Ronald and John 2008: xii).

On the basis of the federal principle, 13 states (Andhra Pradesh, Assam, Bihar, Bombay, Jammu & Kashmir, Kerala, Madras, Mysore (Karnataka), Orissa, Punjab, Rajasthan, Uttar Pradesh and West Bengal came into existence on 1 November 1956 as per the State Reorganisation Committee report. Subsequently, many new states were formed in Northeast in the 1960s and 1970s apart from the old states. These include Tripura (1972) Nagaland (1962), Arunachal Pradesh (1971), Manipur (1972), Meghalaya (1972), Mizoram (1971) and Sikkim (1975). Three more states – Chhattisgarh, Jharkhand and Uttarakhand (bifurcated from Madhya Pradesh, Bihar and Uttar Pradesh, respectively) – came into existence in 2000 (Singh 2008). The dominant linguistic groups constitute the majority in most of the states as shown in Table 5.2. For instance, dominant language groups with above 80 per cent accounted for 20 out of 35 states in 2001.

Table 5.3

Elected Membership in PRIs (in%)

Categories	*Elected Members of PRIs in India (%)*									*Total Elected Representatives %*		
	Gram Panchayat			*Panchayat Samiti*			*Zilla Parishad*					
	2000	2008	2010	2000	2008	2010	2000	2008	2010	2000	2008	2010
SC	12.55	18.76	18.5	12.81	20.72	21.09	12.47	17.3	18.13	12.56	18.86	18.66
ST	8.74	11.91	12.13	5.69	7.28	7.43	8.07	10.84	10.27	8.58	11.65	11.83
Women	31.37	36.36	38.4	20.71	36.37	37.19	31.8	36.64	35.8	31.14	36.36	39.11
Others	47.34	32.97	30.97	60.79	35.63	34.29	47.66	35.22	35.8	47.72	33.13	30.4
Total	100	100	100	100	100	100	100	100	100	100	100	100

Note: Meghalaya, Mizoram and Nagaland – Have Traditional councils.

Source: Ministry of Panchayat Raj, Government of India (12,606).

However, this approach followed the formation of states on the principle of Self-Rule along with Shared Rule has failed to fulfil the aspirations of all groups. This is evident from the numerical strength of other linguistic groups and a demand for the creation of new

Table 5.4

States and Union Territories in India during 2001

S. No.	*Description*	*No. of States*	*1st Language*
1	Above 90%	9	Lakshadweep, Kerala, Rajasthan, Tripura, Madhya Pradesh, Manipur, Punjab, Chhattisgarh and Himachal Pradesh
2	Above 80%	11	Tamil Nadu, Orissa, Gujarat, Pondicherry, Uttaranchal, Uttar Pradesh, Haryana, Sikkim, West Bengal, Andhra Pradesh and Delhi
3	Above 70%	3	Bihar, Mizoram and Maharashtra
4	Above 60%	4	Daman and Diu, Karnataka, Chandigarh and Jharkhand
5	Above 50%	3	Goa, Jammu & Kashmir and Assam
6	Above 40%	2	Meghalaya and Dadra & Nagar Haveli
7	Below 39%	3	Andaman and Nicobar Islands, Nagaland and Arunachal Pradesh (26.76%)
	Total	35	
			2nd Language
8	Above 20%	8	Assam, Nagaland, Chandigarh, Arunachal Pradesh, Dadra and Nagar Haveli, Goa, Jammu & Kashmir and Andaman and Nicobar Islands
9	Above 10%	7	Daman and Diu, Bihar, Meghalaya, Jharkhand, Maharashtra, Karnataka and Haryana
10	Above 5%	11	Mizoram, Sikkim, Andhra Pradesh, Punjab, West Bengal, Delhi, Himachal Pradesh, Uttaranchal, Uttar Pradesh, Tamil Nadu and Pondicherry
11	Above 2%	7	Gujarat, Chhattisgarh, Manipur, Orissa, Tripura, Madhya Pradesh and Rajasthan
12	Below 1.99%	2	Kerala and Lakshadweep
	Total	35	

Source: Compiled from Census Data 2001.

states. For instance, the other language groups other than the dominant ones in some states are significant in terms of accounting for above 20 per cent in 8 out of 35 states, while it is above 10 per cent in 7 states. Similar is the case with other religious groups such as Muslims, Christians and so on. For instance, Hindus constitute more than 60 per cent of the total population in 20 out of 22 states (as shown in Table 5.5, while Muslims account for above 10 per cent in 10 out of 22 states as against Christians in 4 states.

Table 5.5

Statewise Decennial Population by Religion in 2001

S. No.		*Hindu*	*Ranking*	*Muslims*	*Ranking*	*Christians*	*Ranking*	*Others*	*Ranking*	*Total Population*
1	Andaman and Nicobar Islands	69.40	22	8.24	17	21.72	6	0.64	25	355,301
2	Andhra Pradesh	89.12	8	9.18	13	1.55	20	0.14	32	76,115,073
3	Arunachal Pradesh	34.90	30	1.90	31	18.88	8	44.32	2	1,088,666
4	Assam	64.92	25	30.93	3	3.70	13	0.45	27	26,644,159
5	Bihar	83.26	16	16.54	7	0.06	35	0.13	33	82,960,692
6	Chandigarh	78.62	20	3.95	26	0.85	24	16.59	4	900,509
7	Chhattisgarh	94.73	2	1.97	29	1.93	18	1.37	20	20,826,498
8	Dadar and Nagar Haveli	93.59	4	2.96	27	2.75	15	0.70	24	220,319
9	Daman & Diu	89.71	6	7.76	19	2.13	17	0.41	28	158,186
10	Delhi	82.02	17	11.72	11	0.94	23	5.32	11	13,848,491
11	Goa	66.11	24	6.88	20	26.81	5	0.21	30	1,341,121
12	Gujarat	89.15	7	9.07	14	0.56	27	1.22	21	50,637,439
13	Haryana	88.24	10	5.78	23	0.13	32	5.85	10	21,142,250
14	Himachal Pradesh	95.44	1	1.97	30	0.13	34	2.47	16	6,077,468

Cont'd...

Cont'd...

15	Jammu & Kashmir	29.63	31	66.98	2	0.20	30	3.19	12	10,142,444
16	Jharkhand	68.63	23	13.86	8	4.06	12	13.45	5	26,920,442
17	Karnataka	84.05	15	12.26	9	1.91	19	1.78	18	52,730,315
18	Kerala	56.21	27	24.72	5	19.04	7	0.04	34	31,816,291
19	Lakshadweep	3.66	34	95.49	1	0.84	25	0.01	35	60,640
20	Madhya Pradesh	91.17	5	6.37	21	0.28	29	2.18	17	60,331,330
21	Maharashtra	80.45	19	10.61	12	1.09	22	7.85	9	96,780,914
22	Manipur	46.03	28	8.82	15	34.06	4	11.10	7	2,165,731
23	Meghalaya	13.32	32	4.29	25	70.46	3	11.93	6	2,311,807
24	Mizoram	3.55	35	1.14	35	87.04	2	8.27	8	887,912
25	Nagaland	7.70	33	1.76	32	90.00	1	0.54	26	1,989,225
26	Orissa	94.40	3	2.07	28	2.44	16	1.08	22	36,784,465
27	Puducherry	86.68	12	6.09	22	6.94	9	0.29	29	973,786
28	Punjab	36.95	29	1.57	33	1.20	21	60.28	1	24,354,531
29	Rajasthan	88.77	9	8.48	16	0.13	31	2.63	15	56,496,840
30	Sikkim	61.06	26	1.43	34	6.69	10	30.82	3	539,683
31	Tamil Nadu	88.19	11	5.57	24	6.07	11	0.17	31	62,346,335

Cont'd...

...*Cont'd*

32	Tripura	85.65	13	7.96	18	3.20	14	3.18	13	3,198,099
33	Uttar Pradesh	80.65	18	18.50	6	0.13	33	0.72	23	166,128,481
34	Uttarakhand	84.99	14	11.93	10	0.32	28	2.76	14	8,485,995
35	West Bengal	72.52	21	25.26	4	0.64	26	1.57	19	80,121,302
36	All India	80.51		13.44		2.34		3.70		1,027,882,740

Source: Compiled from Census Data 2001.

This implies that the other dominant groups are very significant in terms of their numerical strength in a given geographical area. This may be one of the principal reasons for the demand for a further division of states by various groups on the basis of economic backwardness, apart from cultural and regional identity. The demand for separate states include Telangana in Andhra Pradesh (AP), Gorkhaland in West Bengal, Bodoland in Assam, Saurashtra and Kutch in Gujarat, Mithilanchal and Bhojpur in Bihar and Uttar Pradesh (UP), Harit Pradesh, Vindhya Pradesh in Madhya Pradesh, Maru Pradesh in Rajasthan, Koshal in Odisha, Bundelkhand and Pooravanchal in UP, Ladakh in Jammu & Kashmir (J&K), Vidarbha and Marthawada in Maharashtra and Kodagu in Karnataka. However, some people oppose the creation of small states on the basis of financial and administrative viability and security reasons.

It is evident from the above discussion that there is a need for the third tier of government at the district and municipal levels to enable minor ethnic and other disadvantaged groups to participate in the governance of the country.

Is Third Tier of Government at the District Level a Solution?

The foundation for the third tier of local self-government known as panchayat raj (PR) at the district, taluk and village levels came into existence in the late 1950s on the basis of Balwant Rai Mehta Committee recommendations. However, this attempt did not get institutionalized due to the lack of political and administrative will. Both the central and state governments undermine the significance of these institutions in promoting national integration. Most of these institutions are viewed as agents of state governments for implementing various development programmes. Besides, state governments are not enthusiastic in devolving powers and resources and holding elections regularly. However, with the constitutional amendments (73rd and 74th in 1993), the third tier of government (along with the central and state governments) for rural and urban areas with independent powers and resources got stabilized in 2000s.

After the constitutional amendments, panchayat raj institutions (PRIs) are emerging as units of local self-governance for promoting national integration and inclusive development. PRIs enjoy political, administrative and financial autonomy in many respects. First, all major responsibilities along with resources (central and state plan schemes, programmes and resources) have been transferred to PRIs for preparation and implementation of plans in addition to many centrally sponsored programmes in many states. All 29 functions (as mentioned in the schedule) and resources have been transferred to PRIs (assigning 30 specific subjects to village panchayats [VPs], 28 to taluka panchayats [TPs] and 28 zilla panchayats [ZPs] in Karnataka). PRIs have been empowered to prepare plans with respect to subjects such as agriculture, animal husbandry, primary and secondary education, public health, rural roads and housing, women and children, social welfare, public distribution, public libraries and so on. GPs undertake regulatory functions such as issuing of licenses; approval of building plans and maintenance of common properties, assets and buildings in addition to providing basic services such as drinking water and sanitation and maintaining village roads, buildings and streetlights. The elected heads of PRIs are vested with the executive powers and control over officials and women. Seats and official positions are reserved for SCs, STs (in proportion to their population) and women (not less the one-third) under PRIs so as to be able to represent and influence policies that are intended to benefit them. The State Election Commission is entrusted with the responsibility of holding free and fair elections while the State Finance Commissions are constituted to devolve financial resources to PRIs.

Panchayat Raj Institutions and National Integration in India

This section mainly analyses the contribution of PRIs in promoting good governance and national integration. These issues are analysed in terms of participation, representation, responsiveness and accountability.

Participation and National Integration

People's participation in governance of the country in terms of electing leaders and designing of policies without any discrimination (i.e. caste, class, religion, sex and literacy) is critical for ensuring the trust of the government. Similarly, freedom of expression, association and contest (highest positions of the land including President and Prime Minister) further enhance people's trust in the government and loyalty to the nation. India is one of the most developing countries in the world and its achievements in various areas can be attributed to its vibrant democracy. It has survived not only as the largest democratic nation in the world but also holds regular elections that often result in a change in governments, despite the presence of various hurdles (fatalism, terrorism, fundamentalism, low percentage of voting, poverty, human rights violations, violence, conflicts and so on).

In this regard, the participation of people in local governance in terms of voting, campaigning, contesting, attending GS meetings and other development, welfare and cultural activities are quite significant. First, establishing of PRI structures/units in the places where the population is 6,000 and 400 for GP and ward, respectively, and conducting of regular elections motivate people to participate not only in the election of responsive leaders but also selection of relevant policies (responsiveness). A high turnout in PR elections reflects this trend.

Second, people's participation during local elections in various forms (campaigning, mobilization, contributions, and membership, contesting, voting and so on) reflects their interest and trust in the local governments. Even participation by women in elections is quite significant. For instance, nearly 50 lakh women candidates file nominations for 10 lakh positions in PRIs (i.e. 3 women candidates for each position) (Baviskar and Mathew 2009: 11). An extensive participation in PR elections helps select right leaders and policies. This is evident from people's assertion in defeating nonperformers (sitting members and incumbent regimes) in PR elections.

Besides, gram sabha (village assembly) enables people to take correct decisions with respect to selecting the potential beneficiaries and localities. They can even raise their voice in case of their needs not being fulfilled or against wrongs committed by PRIs, for example, people's planning and campaigns in Kerala. Not only large numbers of residents have been mobilized in this process, but also there have been extensive debates leading to the writing of local histories and preparation of village plans (Vyasulu 2008: 69).

Local Government and Representation

Representation in the political and administrative system helps people respect and identify themselves with the government. However, people, on some occasions, want to see leaders from their own race and caste irrespective of their competence and commitment to public service. There are occasions when caste groups come to the rescue of known criminals and also corrupt and prevent the government from prosecuting and punishing the guilty. In other words representation is considered good governance rather than efficiency and commitment. People prefer to be governed by their own caste/community people rather than outsiders.

Local governments rather than higher-tier governments are more ideal for ensuring representation in two ways. First, small ethnic groups located in a particular territory are likely to have a better representation in LGs. For instance, Muslims, Sikhs and Christians who constitute a minority in India are a majority in some states. This type of representation happens more at the district-level governments. For instance, Muslims constitute a majority in 20 out of 593 districts in India (as shown in Table 5.5). In 9 districts, they constitute more than 75 per cent as against 38 districts with above 25 per cent population. Similarly, Christians constitute a majority in some districts for which information is not available. STs constitute a majority in 75 districts. However, SC population is not concentrated geographically. There is only one district with a majority population as against 50 districts with a population above 25 per cent. The districts with a minority population may go further, if other ethnic groups such as Bodos, Gorkhas and so on are taken into consideration.

It is evident from the above analysis that the third tier of government is most suited to accommodating minorities in governance structures. The existence of autonomous Hill District Councils (HDC) in the North-Eastern states is a testimony to protecting the social, cultural, political and economic rights of tribals.

Empowerment and Ownership in Local Government

Local Governments facilitate representation to the disadvantaged in that reservation helps elect the disadvantaged to various positions in LGs (as shown in Table 5.6). For instance around 36–38 per cent of women, 17–20 per cent of SCs and 7–11 per cent of STs got elected to various positions in VPs, TPs and ZPs accounting for a total of 27,31,199 positions. In fact, the participation of SCs, STs and women has increased over the years (as shown in Table 5.6). The SC membership in VPs increased to 18.15 per cent in 2010 from 12.5 per cent in 2000. The corresponding increase of SC members in panchayat samitis are 21.09 and 12.81 respectively. While the corresponding

Table 5.6

Political Empowerment and Participation of the Disadvantaged Groups in the Country's Governance

S. No.	*Details*	*No. of Units*	*Total Elected Members*	*SC*	*ST*	*OBC*	*Women Members*	*Women Ministers /Presidents*
1	Nation		*793	—	—	—	—	—
2	State	28 + 7	4,508	—	—	—	—	—
3	Municipal Corporation	112		—	—	—	—	34 (30.36)
4	Municipalities	3,551	68,554	—	—	—	—	
5	Town Municipalities <3 lakh population	1,430	—	—	—	—	—	476 (33.29)
6	Nagar Panchayats	2,009	—	—	—	—	—	670
7	District Panchayats	537	15,694	—	—	—	5,779 (36.82)	198 (1.26)
8	Intermediate Panchayats	6,094	156,609	—	—	—	58,094 (37.09)	1,970 (1.26)
9	Village panchayats	232,913	2,656,476	—	—	—	975,116 (36.71)	77,210 (2.91)
8	All panchayats	239,544	2,828,779	853,931 (30.19)	1,038,989 (36.73)	79,378 (2.81)	—	—

Note: *543 Lok Sabha and 250 Rajya Sabha Members.

Source: Compiled from George Mathew and Rakesh Hooja, 'Republic of India' in Nico Steytler (eds.), *A Global Dialogue on Federalism*, Vol. 6, McGill-Queen's University Press, London, 2007, p. 178.

figure for ZPs is 18.13 and 12.47 respectively. Similarly, the representation of STs in VPs increased to 12.13 in 2010 from 8.74 in 2000. The corresponding figures for PSs are 7.43, 5.69 and ZPs 10.27 and 7.43 respectively. The female membership in VPs increased to 38.4 in 2010 from 31.37 in 2000. The corresponding figures for PSs are 37.19, 20.71, and ZPs 35.80 and 31.80 respectively.

Women's association with PRIs has brought about a significant transformation in their attitude, empowerment, self-confidence and political awareness. Some studies highlight that women who reluctantly entered into politics have shown a great maturity in outlook, enthusiasm, increasing political consciousness and perception of their roles and responsibilities. Most of the women who got elected for the first time without political experience have started asserting control over resources and officials and challenging male authority and supremacy. Initially, many of the women members who are first timers and illiterate depend upon their men folk (husbands and other male representatives) for conducting the panchayat activities and also for shielding them from the PR officials. Gradually, they become independent and exercise control over officials. This has also resulted in a change in power relations between husbands and wives. More importantly, women belonging to the labour and lower caste groups take more interest in the activities of PRIs than the higher caste women. Now women have begun to come forward to fight for elections, to come out of homes to attend panchayat meetings and to sit with men from different caste and age groups, which is a great transformation with regard to women empowerment (Baviskar and Mathew 2009: 16)

Studies find the participation of weaker sections (SCs/STs and women) in panchayat meetings and decision making quite satisfactory (Litvack et al. 1998; Klitgaard 1991). They also find that about 80–90 per cent of women, particularly from lower income groups, attend PRIs meetings regularly. They are also found responsible for the changing work culture in PRIs and improvement of female literacy. Chattopadhyay and Duflo (2001) find that women leaders of village councils focus more on infrastructure development that is relevant to the needs of rural women (drinking water, fuel and roads). Women members in PRIs are very efficient in their developmental role (Palanithurai 2001). Similar observations are offered regarding other disadvantaged groups such as SCs/STs/OBCs.

Studies also point out that reservation has helped improve the perception levels of women besides creating an urge in them to participate at various levels of governance. Twenty-five per cent of women members perceive a visible change in their status within 'family' after they have been elected. About 60 per cent of women express that they are encouraging women to contest elections. A similar per cent of women are contemplating to contest elections (PRIA 2000).

Their representation has helped the disadvantaged groups articulate their views more effectively and improve their livelihoods. The weaker sections' hold over resources has increased due to their presence in PRIs. In states such as West Bengal, Maharashtra, Gujarat and UP, the SCs have started asserting their rights and demanding an egalitarian treatment even as they are critical of any discrimination. They are also becoming more vocal in terms of freely expressing their views while taking the full advantage of various welfare schemes meant for them. The members belonging to the dominant communities have started respecting the SC presidents, which was not the case earlier (they used to be ill treated by forcing them to sit separately, or on the floor, and having separate cups for taking tea) (Baviskar and Mathew 2009: 10). The same is the case with the STs. The ST presidents are protecting the interests of their community, though it appears symbolic in some places. It has been found that many SC, ST and women beneficiaries under different schemes who crossed the poverty line are experiencing an upward occupational mobility while at the same time many of them have started repaying their loans (Aziz 2002).

Local Government, Responsiveness and Service Delivery (Allocative Efficiency)

Democratic decentralization not only strengthens the allocative and productive efficiency but also accelerates a better service delivery. It improves efficiency, since there is a perfect match between preferences and provision of services. It reduces cost, improves output and utilizes resources more efficiently (Smith 1985: 4).

Allocative efficiency is high in the decentralized governance system rather than at the higher level governments. It facilitates a perfect match between resources and needs. Local specific information and needs can be ascertained by the local governments more accurately and thereby identify projects/schemes that have the maximum utility or welfare implication. The selection/location of projects/members is very effective, whenever they are selected by the people. The involvement of GS has brought down the selection of wrong places and persons. This is more so where needs are more diversified. For instance, some villages need water facility rather than roads. In such a situation, the utilization of the former is more than the latter provided by the central government. Many centrally sponsored rural development programmes in the past have failed due to wrong priorities, design and location. Roads, school buildings, tanks and field channels built were not effectively used as they were not strategically located to the needs of people. Similarly, many hand pumps were out of order, since people never had the feeling of owning them. Ultimately, the maintenance and sustenance of such projects and schemes under decentralized governance appears to be very high (Sangita 2007).

Local Government, Accountability and Service Delivery (Productive Efficiency)

Productive efficiency is also high under decentralized governance due to the participation of people in the implementation and monitoring of development programmes. First, people's involvement in the formulation and implementation of projects results in a reduction in transactional costs (such as administrative costs, salaries, complex procedures, waste, leakages and corruption). Late Rajiv Gandhi, the former Prime Minister, used to say that only 15 paisa out of one rupee spent would reach the poor through various antipoverty programmes. People's monitoring contributes to minimizing wastage and leakages. Their close observation prevents the procurement of substandard inputs such as goods and materials. Similarly, a close monitoring by PRIs helps improve the attendance of teachers and doctors in schools and hospitals, respectively.

Decentralization also contributes towards a better compliance and enforcement with low costs, since decisions regarding the selection of schemes and design of projects are taken in consultation with various stakeholders. This is particularly so in the management of community property resources such as forests and water tanks for which law enforcement and punitive regulations are minimal. Democratic institutions monitoring mechanisms also help improve administrative efficiency. A regular monitoring by elected representatives (monthly reviews and surveys) helps assure that the policies and programmes serve the intended sections. Further, the increased transparency and accountability resulting from the civil society enhance efficiency by reducing the potential for diversion of resources due to patronage or corruption (Brinkerhoff 2000: 604).

The productive efficiency also increases due to transparency and accountability in the delivery of services (Aziz 2002). The conducting of PR elections on a regular basis has become a powerful mechanism for ensuring accountability. This is because if the elected leaders do not work devotedly for the upliftment of rural society, they will not be able to win the election next time. The defeat of a large number of sitting members in PR elections reflects this trend. Some studies observe that the accountability of officials to the elected representatives has increased over time. Responsible officials (such as Primary Health Centre, medical officers, agricultural and veterinary officers) can be asked for their presence in the PRI meetings. In the meetings, an officer may be asked/questioned regarding his/her performance. Productive efficiency can also be improved through social auditing and monitoring. Social auditing (Jamabandi) through GS and ward sabha (population = 400) in Karnataka has enabled citizens in monitoring the progress of works as well as ensuring that the administrators are accountable to the entrusted tasks and responsibilities (Sivanna 2004).

Productive efficiency can also be achieved by ensuring a reduction in corruption under PRIs. The present study finds that decentralized governance enhances a greater transparency and reduces the incidence of grand corruption. Another study finds that corruption among PRI functionaries is minimal where media and civil society are alert. The rent seeking is more visible in areas where institutions such as GS, media and civil society organizations are nonfunctional.

Productive efficiency can also be improved under decentralized governance in that it helps mobilize additional resources (voluntary contributions such as land, capital and labour) for promoting rural development. Such contributions accounted for 20–40 per cent of the expenditure of the community development blocks in the 1950s with many villagers donating lands for the construction of schools and hospitals. There also exist instances where repair of field canals and tanks, and construction of buildings and roads were evident. Also, involvement of the people has helped manage common property resources of the village more effectively. People's involvement has also resulted in an improvement in the collection of levies, betterment and user charges.

Local Government and Service Delivery

Decentralization has improved the provision of public services. Sectors such as education and health care have improved substantially under the PRI regime. It is observed that there has been a significant improvement in the area of medical and public health facilities and the supply of drugs in Karnataka. The attendance of doctors and paramedical staff has improved considerably under the constant monitoring of local leaders in many PHCs and hospitals. VP leaders are playing a positive role by exerting a moral pressure on the staff not to avoid their regular duties. The availability of doctors and paramedicals in medical centres works out to 74 per cent and 93 per cent, respectively. Households (31 and 26%) are found satisfied with the behaviour of doctors and teachers, respectively.

The utilization of resources transferred to the PRIs is much better than it used to be under the line departments. Developmental works are being executed more speedily with field staffs better controlled under PRIs (Sundaram 1994). In Madhya Pradesh, gram panchayats and Janpad panchayats played a very important role in improving literacy in the 1990s (Vyasulu 2008: 69).

Local Government and Service Delivery (Equity)

Decentralized governance ensures an effective delivery of services such as education, health care and poverty elimination programmes. Decentralized governance is more sensitive to poverty and unemployment according to the World Bank (2002) and Harriss (2000). According to these studies, PRIs in India have done remarkably well with regards to devolution of powers, implementation of the centrally sponsored employment generating and antipoverty programmes National Rural Employment Programme (NREP), Public Distribution System (PDS), and IRDP Integrated Rural Development Programme (IRDP), especially in Karnataka, West Bengal, Andhra Pradesh, Madhya Pradesh, Rajasthan and Kerala.

Westergaard's (1986) study suggests that NREP had achieved a considerable success in providing employment to the rural poor. Some studies on 'food for work' programme attribute or fair degree of success to the accorded programme. Dreze (1990) also finds IRDP overwhelmingly benefiting the landless labourers. Swaminathan (1990) also notices a similar success while comparing the state performance with respect to implementing IRDP in West Bengal and Tamil Nadu, while Webster (1992) finds the benefits under the employment generation programme and IRDP going to the poor besides improving their living conditions.

Leakages and wastages have come down in the implementation of poverty alleviation programmes under PRIs. Bardhan and Mookherjee (2004) in their study on IRDP and agricultural mini-kits for the period 1978–1998 with respect to West Bengal find the proportion of GP seats secured by landless doubled (10% to 20%). The distribution of IRDP leakage rate to the medium and large landowners works out to a very low per cent (less than 4%) as against 87 per cent of benefits for small and marginal farmers.

In West Bengal, in the late 1970s and early 1980s, the gram panchayats played an important role in the implementation of Operation Barga – identifying those who tilled land and registering their rights with agricultural output showing a dramatic increase in agricultural production in the state since then. Subsequently, in the late 1990s, in Midnapore, the panchayats played an important role in disseminating an innovative sanitation package that has now become a model for the country (Vyasulu 2008: 69).

Constraints Involved in the Effective Functioning of Local Governments

Local governments in both urban and rural India, although constitutionally mandated, have a very weak existence in their own right. They are controlled by state governments, which have retained numerous powers. Among them is the power to make rules, to make changes in the content of schedules, to appoint officials, to dismiss the sarpanch, to cancel resolutions or decisions of panchayats, to dissolve panchayats and to inspect records and works. Local governments are thus subservient to state governments. The local governments have no power to legislate, nor have capacity to approach courts to rule upon disputes over the respective constitutional powers of the second and third orders of government. In fact, there is no case law on local governments in India like in the United States (Horst et al. 2008: 9).

The constitution of in-charge ministers for districts further undermines the autonomy of rural local governments. The in-charge ministers are responsible for all the activities including developmental, welfare and social security. They head committee to monitor and review the implementation of development and welfare programmes, particularly the centre and state sponsored schemes. The ZP president is one of the members of the committee. Similarly in Karnataka, MLAs chair the committees at the taluk level for identifying beneficiaries for schemes such as allotment of houses, sites, as well as the selection of water supply schemes (Chandrasekhar 2011).

The non-constitution and ineffective functioning of district planning committee are also a major constraint involved in the autonomous functioning of local governments. The participative district planning has received prominence with the eleventh five-year plan with an emphasis on inclusive growth. District planning is an important instrument towards achieving the optimum outcomes in terms of a balanced development with the convergence of resources and enforcement of intersectoral priorities. Unfortunately, many state governments have failed to support the district planning committees with the required capacity, expertise and resources to prepare long- and short-term plans matching the resources and needs and aspirations of people (Kumar and Sangita 2011.

Most of the centrally sponsored schemes (CSSs) dealing with employment, education, health, nutrition, child and women care, infrastructure and so on fall outside the purview of PRIs. The implementation of flagship programmes of the central government include MGNREGA, NRHM, universalization of education (Sarva Shiksha Abhiyan), Bharat Nirman programme, Indira Awas Yozana, Mid-day Meal, PDS and JNNURM. These schemes are very significant in terms of their number, administrative network and resources. However, these schemes numbering around 213 in 2003–2004 have come down to 147 in 2011–2012 (likely to be reduced further to 49). Second, the resources spent on the flagship programmes in the districts, taluks and villages levels constitute around 70–80 per cent of the development expenditure. Third, parallel level bodies (para state bodies or registered societies) consisting of administrators, experts and NGOs are constituted outside the PRIs. Such bodies number 10–40 at each of the levels (state, district, taluk and village). Examples for such bodies include special agencies such as District Rural/Tribal/Watershed Development Agency for implementing CSSs. For instance, 571 District Rural Development Agencies (DRDAs) cells were engaged in the implementation of IRDP in the country in 2004 (Chandrasekhar 2011: 50. The same is the case at the taluk and village levels. Most of these bodies are headed by the minister, Deputy commissioner/collector concerned at the district level, while administrator, MLA or Taluk president at the taluk level (Chandrasekhar 2011: 50).

The parallel bodies of the Constitution for implementing programmes/schemes (state and central governments and international organizations) appropriate the functions of VPs. In every village, 5–10 committees with separate office bearers and budgets for activities such as development, health, water, sanitation, education, forest and so on appropriate the functions of VPs. Most of these committees are constituted with the representatives of stakeholders, NGOs, PRIs and administration. Sometimes the budgets of these committees are many times higher than those VPs. There are even instances where keen contests have taken place for positions in these organizations.

Some of these committees are above the VP (vertical), while others are horizontal. The former are known as village development committees with nominated members to supervise and monitor the development activities including the village panchayat. Some of the committees are the village development committee in West Bengal, gram vikas samiti in Haryana, gram swaraj system in MP and vigilance committee in Himachal Pradesh (Chandrasekhar 2011: 62), while the latter include the village committees for water, forest, health and education. The committees are responsible for the formulation and implementation of plans as well as their operation and maintenance.

The initiation of many development programmes by the chief ministers of the state also undermines the functioning of PRIs. For instance, Andhra Pradesh Chief Minister, Chandrababu Naidu, started a massive programme known as Janmabhoomi, which claimed to be a government at the door steps (Prajalu Vadakku Palana) for addressing the problems of the villagers. This was the biggest event of the state government held twice in a year for 2–4 weeks. The cluster meetings used to be held in the villages in which ministers, MPs MLAs/MLCs, elected representatives of local bodies and officials with big budgets and support of the entire district administration outside the purview of PRIs participated. The structure of Janmabhoomi Programme was dominated by bureaucrats, NGOs and political leaders and there was practically no role for the elected PR leaders except in a customary way. Janmabhoomi covered the activities reserved for PRIs including the major development programmes such as enrolment, immunization, organization of free medical camps, desiltation of tanks, laying down of roads, construction and whitewashing of school buildings, chlorination of water and so on (Chandrasekhar 2011: 83). Even the identification of beneficiaries for pensions, houses and sites available under various programmes of the central and state governments were carried out in these meetings. The succeeding CMs have followed similar programmes with different names. For instance, one programme is called as Rachabanda by Dr Rajasekhara Reddy who succeeded Chandrababu Naidu and Palle Bata by the next CM, Kiran Kumar Reddy. These two programmes resemble Janmabhoomi in many respects.

The allotment of local area development funds/grants to federal and state legislators (MLA/MLC/MP grants) also undermines the effective functioning of these institutions. Members of Parliament Local Area Development (MPLAD) was introduced in 1993 with each MP getting Rs. one crore (raised to 2 crore subsequently) for each year to undertake development works for the creation of durable assets in his/her constituency with the support of DC concerned. Although this scheme is not implemented outside the purview PRIs, it has resulted in the duplication and wastage of resources as it remains isolated without getting integrated with the local planning and also without accounting and accountability. Similar schemes are also introduced by the state governments. For instance, Karnataka Legislators Local Development Scheme (KLLADS) was introduced in 2003 (Chandrasekhar 2011: 58).

Local governments are yet to achieve real financial autonomy. They still depend upon higher level governments for about 70–80 per cent of their expenditure. Even this has been declining over the years. The total expenditure of local governments as a proportion of the combined expenditure of the Union, states and local governments amounts to 6.4 per cent for 1998–1999 and 5.1 per cent for 2002–2003. The decline in the expenditure of panchayats (covering nearly 73% of the population) from 3.9 per cent in 1998–1999 to 3.3

per cent in 2002–2003 is quite disappointing as against 20–35 per cent for some countries and 45 per cent for Denmark (Oomen, 2006: 897). Even the revenues raised by panchayats from the sources assigned to them are very low. For instance, the revenues of panchayats constitute around 0.07 per cent of GDP and 0.35 of total public revenues (central, state and local revenues taken together) for 2002–2003 (Rao and Rao, 2008: 56). The own revenue resources of local governments amounts to only 0.39 per cent of GDP for 2002–2003 (of which more than 82% is from urban local bodies) (Oomen 2006: 897).

Local governments in many states are yet to develop their own cadre of administrators with most of the senior-level staff being drawn from higher level governments, over which the local governments have no control.

Although local governments enjoy a constitutional status, which are not amendable by the state governments, they are unable to function as units of self-government. They are dependent on state governments, which have conceded only political decentralization, not the fiscal or administrative decentralization of powers and functions to localities (Horst et al. 2008: 9).

Enabling Environment for Success of PRIs

The effective functioning of local governments depends upon the commitment of the central and state governments and the support of civil society organizations and movements as well. Political regimes (parties and leaders) with a strong commitment towards decentralization and development are responsible for devolving adequate powers and resources to local governments. For instance, PRIs have come into existence following the initiative taken by the Congress Party under the leadership of Nehru and S.K. Dey in the late 1950s. A further attention was provided by Rajiv Gandhi in the 1990s, which ultimately led to the conferring of a constitutional status to PRIs. Similarly, Ramkrishna Hegde, the then chief minister of Karnataka, along with a dedicated team of bureaucrats was responsible for devolving major powers and resources to PRIs in the 1980s in Karnataka. However, democratic decentralization has not received sufficient attention in some states with powers given to them having been withdrawn and no elections held regularly.

Leftist governments in Kerala and West Bengal have provided supporting legislations along with resources to strengthen PRIs for reducing poverty and promoting social development. At the same time, civil society organizations and movements are instrumental in mobilizing people for devolving powers and resources to PRIs. Reform-minded political parties in Kerala and West Bengal have created opportunities for collective action from below by mobilizing the small and marginal farmers and landless so as to take advantage of the benefits associated with PRIs and antipoverty programmes (Mark, 2007). Even civil society organizations and movements have mobilized people for devolution of powers and resources to PRIs by empowering PRIs through protests, advocacy, capacity building and so on. In the recent years, NGOs in Karnataka have fought for the rights of PRIs, when the state government was trying to dilute the powers given to PRIs. Similarly, Kerala Sasthra Sahitya Parishath played a significant role in terms of shaping and implementing the people's campaign for decentralized planning in the late 1990s (Mark 2007; Crocker 2008).

Conclusions

It is evident from the above review that political decentralization (local governance, federalism) promotes national integration and inclusive development by enabling the minorities and disadvantaged groups to share power with others in the governance of the country. People's participation promotes trust in the local governments, since they get an opportunity to select their own governments and policies. The representation also enables people to trust their government. Third, local governments help formulate policies reflecting the needs and aspirations of the people. Fourth, LGs promote accountability and thereby reduces wastages and corruption. In spite of these advantages, the local governments are not able to function as autonomous institutions due to political, administrative and financial interference from the higher level governments.

References

Aziz, A. 2002. *Decentralised and Planning: A Comparative Study in Three South Indian States*. New Delhi: Macmillan.

Bardhan, P. 1996. 'The Nature of Institutional Impediments to Economic Development', Working Paper No. 1041, UC Berkeley: Institute for Business and Economic Research.

Bardhan, P. and Mookherjee, D. 2000. 'Capture and Governance at Local and National Levels", *American Economic Review*, Vol. 90, No. 2, pp. 135–139.

Baviskar, B.S. and George Mathew (eds.) 2009. Inclusion and Exclusion in Local Governance: Field Studies from Rural India, Delhi: Sage Publications Pvt. Ltd.

Brinkerhoff, D.W. 2000. 'Democratic Governance and Sectoral Policy Reform: Tracing Linkages and Exploring Synergies', *World Development*, Vol. 28, No. 4, pp. 601–615.

Chandrashekar, Lalita. 2011. *Undermining Local Democracy: Parallel Governance in Contemporary South India*, New Delhi: Routledge.

Chattopadhyay, R. and E. Duflo. 2001. 'Women as Policy Makers: Evidence from a India Wide Randomized Policy Experiment', Unpublished, Cambridge, Mass.

Crocker, D.A. 2008. *Ethics of Global Development: Agency, Capability and Deliberative Democracy*, New York: Cambridge.

Dan, Miodownik and Britt Cartrite. 2010. 'Does Political Decentralisation Exacerbateor Ameliorate Ethno-Political Mobilisation? A Test of Contesting Propositions', Vol. 63 (4), December, pp. 731–746.

Dreze, J. 1990. 'Poverty in India and the IRDP Delusion', *Economic and Political Weekly,* Vol. 25, No. 39, pp. 95–104.

Harriss, J. 1993. 'What is Happening in Rural West Bengal? Agrarian Reform, Growth and Distribution', *Economic and Political Weekly*, Vol. 28, No. 24, June 12, pp. 1237–1247.

Harry Blair. 2000. Participation and Accountability at the Periphery: Democratic Local Governance in Six Countries', *World Development Report,* Vol. 28 (1), pp. 21–39.

Horst, R., Andrew, C., Singh, D., and Keswani, S. 2008. 'Local Government in Federal Systems' (sub-theme paper), in John Kincaid and Rupak Chattopadhyay (eds.), *Unity in Diversity: Learning from Each Other, Volume 4 – Local Government in Federal Systems,* New Delhi: Viva, pp. 3–18.

Jennie, L., Ahmad, J., and Bird, R. 1998. *Rethinking Decentralization in Developing Countries*, Washington DC: World Bank.

Klitgaard, Robert. 1991. *Controlling Corruption*, University of California Press, Berkeley.

Kumar, Anil and Sangita S.N. 2011. *Decentralised Governance and Planning in Karnataka, India*, Newcastle upon Tyne, UK: Cambridge Scholars Publishing.

Mark, R. 2007. 'Does Decentralisation Improve Equity and Efficiency in Public Service Delivery Provision', *IDS Bulletin,* Vol. 38, No. 1.

Oommen, M.A. 2006. Fiscal Decentralisation to the Sub-State Level Governments, (Special Article), *Economic and Political Weekly*, Vol. 41 (10), March 11–17, pp. 897–903

PRIA. 2000. *Programme for Strengthening Panchayati Raj Institutions: Narrative Report*, New Delhi: PRIA.

Rao, G.M. and Rao, U.A.V. 2008. 'Expanding the Resource Base of Panchayats: Augmenting Own Revenues', *Economic and Political Weekly*, Vol. 43, No. 4, January 26–February 1, pp. 54–61.

Ronald, W.L. and Kincaid, John. 2008. 'Introduction', in John Kincaid and Rupak Chattopadhyay (eds.), *Unity in Diversity: Learning from Each Other, Volume 4 – Local Government in Federal Systems*, New Delhi: Viva, pp. xi–xvii.

Sangita, S.N. 2007. 'Decentralisation for Good Governance and Service Delivery in India: Theory and Practice', *The Indian Journal of Political Science*, Vol. LXVIII, No. 3, July–September, pp. 447–484.

Singh, M.P. 2008. 'Reorganisation of States in India', *Economic and Political Weekly*, Vol. 43, No. 11, March 15–21, pp. 70–75.

Sivanna, N. 2004. 'Panchayat Jamabandhi in Karnataka: A Case of Transparency and Accountability in Good Governance', *ISEC*, No. 142, Bangalore.

Smith, Anthony D. 1987. *The Ethnic Origins of Nations*, UK: Blackwell.

Smith, B.C. 1985. *Decentralisation: The Territorial Dimension of the State*, Boston: George Allen & Unwin.

Steytler, N. 2008. 'Enhancement of Democracy through Empowerment of Disadvantaged Groups' (sub-theme paper), in John Kincaid and Rupak Chattopadhyay (eds.), *Unity in Diversity: Learning from Each Other, Volume 4 – Local Government in Federal Systems,* New Delhi: Viva, pp. 19–35.

Sundaram, M. 1994. *Decentralisation in Developing Countries*, New Delhi: Concept.

Swaminathan, M.S. 1990. 'Village Level Implementation of IRDP-Comparison of West Bengal and Tamil Nadu', *Economic and Political Weekly*, Vol–XXV, No. 13, March 31.

Vyasulu, V. 2008. 'The Functioning of Local Government in Federal Systems: Perspectives from India' (Sub-theme paper), in John Kincaid and Rupak Chattopadhyay (eds.), *Unity in Diversity: Learning from Each Other, Volume 4 – Local Government in Federal Systems*, New Delhi: Viva, pp. 55–70.

Webster, N. 1992. *Panchayati Raj and the Decentralisation of Development Planning in West Bengal*, Calcutta: K.P. Bagchi and Company.

Westergaard, K. 1986. *People's Participation, Local Government and Rural Development: The Case of West Bengal*, CDR Research Report.

World Bank. 2002. *Decentralizing Indonesia: A Regional Public Expenditure Review, Overview Report East Asia*, Washington DC: World Bank.

6

Whither Decentralization in India?

The Interesting Story of a Nobody's Child

Anil Kumar Vaddiraju

India is considered a unitary-federal state in that the balance in the basic constitutional structure in administrative, political and fiscal terms is more towards the centre, not the states. However, ever since independence, the *de facto* nature of this structure and its operation has been changing. There are some scholars who have recently called Indian federalism a 'cooperative federalism' (Mozoomdar 1995, 1999) and yet others as 'asymmetrical federalism' (Saxena 2007, 2012). What these recent characterizations of Indian federalism indicate is that there has been a change in the nature of Indian federalism over time and is reflected quite clearly in the changing relationships between states and the centre (Manor 2001; Mitra and Malte 2011).

However, there are other basic characteristics associated with the constitutional structure. The Constitution, drafted by the founding fathers, with a two-tier structure, has become a three-tier structure after the amendments in the Constitution in 1992 – 73rd and 74th Amendments. However, these amendments did not occur in isolation in that they were effected in 1992 at a time when the economic reforms started rolling out in 1991 in a big way with the latter making a significant difference to the nature of state-centre relations (Jenkins 1999). Ever since the economic reforms, the nature of federalism has been undergoing significant changes.

In the context of the changing Indian federalism ever since the reforms, Rudolph and Rudolph (2001: 1541ff) argue that the Indian polity, which had an inherent bias towards the centre, has changed after the reforms. Further, they have persuasively argued that reforms have transformed what is basically a command economy into a 'federal market economy'. They observe,

> The heart of our argument about India's emergent federal market economy [is that]: the decline of central public investment and growth of private investment gives the federal states, the immediate sites of private investment, a greatly expanded role in economic liberalisation and promoting investment and growth. They do so in highly variable ways that are contingent on agency – i.e. policy initiatives, leadership, good governance – as on structure, e.g. previous economic position.

While concluding that what is emerging is a federal market economy they maintain that the central government retains its role more as a regulator, while the responsibility of the states with respect to economic matters has expanded manifold. They conclude by observing that,

> The states in India's federal market system command more economic and political sovereignty than they did under a Nehruvian planned economy; their voices matter more in economic and political decisions. States are challenged to be more self-reliant; increasingly, they have to navigate as tubs on their own bottoms. But they are also faced with new restraints on their enhanced autonomy. While the centre's interventionist and tutelary role has faded, its role as a regulatory state has expanded. The states have found that the price of more freedom is more responsibility for growth and fiscal discipline. (Ibid.: 1548)

What Rudolphs argue is the evolution of Indian federalism in the post-reform period. While the economic reforms have vastly increased the economic clout of the states, they are still dependent on the centre. The debate on federalism in India has thrown up many views. Rob Jenkins (1999), for example, argues that the states of India, contrary to the argument that their sovereignty has expanded, are still dependent on the central government in their attempts to attract foreign direct investment (FDI) and also in their dealings with multilateral agencies such as International Monetary Fund (IMF) and the World Bank. Jenkins examines the Indian federalism from the viewpoint of 'constituent diplomacy paradigm'. As per this paradigm, states have a prominent role to play in the making of foreign economic policy. According to Jenkins, this 'constituent diplomacy' paradigm, when applied to India, has its limitations.

Further evidence on the increasing autonomy of states in policy making comes from Stephen Howes, Ashok K. Lahiri and Nicholas Stern. They observe that:

> A number of political factors have led to increased levels of state autonomy over the nineties. In many ways, the political authority of the central government has weakened over the nineties, providing more 'political space' for states to plough their own course. (Howes, Lahiri and Stern 2003)

Going further, they observe

> Few state governments now exist at the mercy of the central government: state governments are either important regional allies of the Central government, or are in the opposition. Reflecting this power shift from the Centre to the states. (Howes, Lahiri and Stern 2003)

While examining the increasing role of states from a class perspective, Sanjaya Baru (2000) argues that the emergence of states should be attributed to the emergence of regional capitalists and regional bourgeoisie in the Indian polity. Sanjaya Baru attempts to demonstrate this trend through specific cases of Gujarat, Maharashtra Tamil Nadu and Andhra Pradesh. He also includes Karnataka in the same list.

Rudolphs, Jenkins (2004), Howes, Lahiri and Stern, and Sanjaya Baru all agree broadly on the increasing role of federal states in the post-reform period. The economic liberalization has expanded the space of states under the federal economy.

The discussion of federalism is important in the context of economic reforms and political decentralization for two reasons: (a) the nature of federalism has changed since the reforms and (b) the changed nature of 'federal market economy' has ramifications for the process of decentralization further down the political system. An increase in the overall strength of the states under the 'federal market economy', as Rudolphs describe, needs not necessarily lead to a further decentralization of the political system. The latter depends on 'agency', that is, political leadership, and other crucial factors such as political culture and political history of the states.

The question whether the economic and fiscal bias is still tilted more towards the centre in the centre–state relations is worth raising.

It is said that the situation would be tantamount to a 'huge paradox' if the centre does not provide economic and political powers to the states but expects them to devolve such powers further down. The position of this author is that while the macro economy is still largely under the control of the centre and Planning Commission, as, for example, Ajit Mozoomdar (1999) states, the situation appears to be in a transition. It is not a paradoxical situation but a transitional situation with more leverage for states: both economically and theoretically. Writing in 1995, Mozoomdar takes a view of the future as follows:

> In India the political system is moving towards greater federalism, that is, towards enlarging the area of the states' functional autonomy. The need for a less centralised system of economic decision-making and development planning is accepted, if reluctantly. (1995: 230–231)

Therefore, we would like to contend here that the situation now is not paradoxical but transitional: the centre has pressures upon it for devolving more powers to the states even as the states find themselves under a greater obligation to devolve more powers to the local governments. There is no 'huge paradox' involved here but a gradual transition towards more and sustainable federal relations is evolving. Therefore, the situation conforms to the arguments put forth by Rudolphs that we are moving towards a more federal polity where economic relations are apt to put more pressures on the centre to devolve enhanced fiscal powers to the states.

Another trend that has significantly strengthened the states is the emergence of coalition politics – particularly at the national level. Coalition politics – the regional and state-based parties lending their support to national parties in forming coalitions with an eye on sharing power – has played a crucial role in terms of vastly increasing the bargaining power of the regional and other smaller parties with the centre, a fact well reflected under the previous NDA government as well as the previous/present UPA government. Regional and quasi-regional parties have used this enhanced bargaining power, almost to the extent of holding the central government to ransom, to clinch economic deals and also loans from multi-lateral donors. While discussing the changing nature of federalism, we need to keep this crucial aspect in view.

If economic reforms are crucial from a macro perspective, what is the nature of governance and decentralization reforms then? The reforms as they are talked of today are both economic and governance reforms. These include economic measures and changes as well as what is called 'institutional reforms' or 'governance reforms'. The policy makers constantly claim this in their reform-rhetorics. According to this categorization, political decentralization falls within the orbit of 'governance' or 'institutional reforms'. Interestingly, both do not necessarily go hand in hand, that is, if one is implemented, the other may be ignored by the state-level regimes.

States are becoming increasingly stronger and relatively more assertive. The emergence of coalition politics (since 1989) has also contributed to this trend. It well appears now that in the *longue duree* of Indian history, the days of 'imperial Delhi' are over. States are becoming more powerful strengthening because of economic reforms, private investments and coalition politics. Increasingly either regional parties at the state level assert themselves or regional satraps of national parties are more important than ever. In the post-economic reform period, the trend has been towards a steady nationalization of regional parties and regionalization of national parties (Mooij 2005). Even across the Hindi belt, quasi-regional parties are gaining more importance. The Rashtriya Janata Dal and Samata Party in Bihar and Samajwadi Party and Bahujan Samaj Party in UP are nothing but quasi-regional parties with hardly any political or electoral base outside the states of Bihar and UP. And these massive states and their regional leaders exercise a tremendous power in determining not only the outcomes, but also the very stability and continuity of the government in Delhi. Coalition politics has made these and many other state-level regional parties/leaders more powerful in terms of determining the political outcomes at the national level. Therefore, the states have emerged as crucial players in the national political arena. The regional leaders of national parties are too stronger today, calling shots in an assertive manner within their national parties than was the case during the charismatic political regimes of Jawaharlal Nehru, Indira Gandhi and Rajiv Gandhi. It is an open secret that, as the recent elections in many states have shown, the dynasty is not doing well anymore despite its desperate efforts – 2014 is likely to witness further changes.

The question, however, is what implications the strengthening of states under the Indian federalism will have for further deepening and broadening of Indian democracy? This is the central question we are addressing in this chapter. Do the states have relatively more room for manoeuvre and freedom for economic growth and prosperity? And do decentralized powers further down the constitutional hierarchy of governance? Our major contention is that states have become stronger over time, but they need not decentralize further down in three-tier federalism (Vaddiraju 2008). States continue to ignore decentralization (Singh and Sharma 2007). Contemporarily, it is private investments, managing capital, coalition politics and enjoying both fruits and spoils of economic growth that matter to the states. However, such a trend tends to concentrate powers at the state capitals. Interestingly, often in the earlier times, it was the rural upper castes that were the vanguard at the state level and they used to be the loyal followers of their superior bosses at the centre. Sociologically this is not true any longer. It is a well-recognized phenomenon all over India that the rural upper castes have declined sociologically over time, leading to the emergence of backward and lower castes in most states, while these emerging backward castes need and assert power at the state capitals. The net consequence of this configuration of circumstances is that while federalism is likely to thrive somewhat in Indian polity, decentralization is set to suffer. As said above, decentralization is a state subject after all. Unless state regimes *promote* decentralization, decentralization does not happen. Decentralization is a function of four prerequisites as James Manor (2011) note (a) devolution of powers; (b) devolution of finances; (c) accountability of bureaucrats to representatives and (d) accountability of representatives to local, ordinary people and the effective promotion of decentralization by state level regimes (Manor 2011) Interestingly, all or most of these four requisite characteristics are not to be seen in most Indian states. In such a context, the states in a relatively stronger position may or may never decentralize. However, except civil society organizations, no other state is brought to bear upon the pressure to decentralize further. In order to illustrate these points, we take the examples of three states: (i) Karnataka, (ii) Andhra Pradesh and (iii) Tamil Nadu. These three states in the recent past have been under the rule of Bharatiya Janata Party, Congress Party and one or the other regional party, respectively. It would be interesting to explore their experiences vis-à-vis decentralization (Similar such exercise for earlier period was done by Aziz, Abdul et al. (eds.). 2002). Their varied developmental trajectories are provided elsewhere by different scholars (Balasubramanyam and Balasubramanyam 2008).

Karnataka

Decentralization, particularly rural decentralization, has always been high on the agenda of policy makers in Karnataka despite ups and downs throughout. The 1983 Act pertaining to rural local bodies was more progressive than the 1993 Act. In fact it is often held that the 1983 Act had inspired the national legislation of 1992 itself (Satishchandran 1995). When it comes to inspiring the national amendment many states make that claim, but of all, Karnataka was the first state to have implemented 25 per cent of reservation for women in the local bodies even before the national act was passed to that effect (Aziz 2007). Karnataka is also the first and perhaps the only state that has provided state secretary rank bureaucrat as a secretary to the district panchayat that is zilla parishad apart from Deputy Commissioner or Collector (Natraj and Ananthpur 2004). Traditionally, ever since the days of Ramakrishna Hegde's Janata Party government, Karnataka firmly stood for decentralization.

Post-liberalization, economic reforms have also been carried out vigorously in Karnataka (Manor 2004, 2006a). In Karnataka, the growth rate in the post-reform period has been around 8 per cent. The fiscal reforms are also high. Even though there are sectoral imbalances as well as regional imbalances, Karnataka appears to be a state with significant economic reforms and also a relatively high level of decentralization. In this context, Karnataka is an exceptional state. In fact, Kadekodi et al. note this as:

> This emphasis on technology-led growth coupled with local governance reform is, at least in theory, a singularly innovative strategy to address the challenge of generating growth with equity and can be described as 'Karnataka Model' of Development. (2008: 17–18)

They further observe that:

> The Karnataka model should more accurately be called the 'Mysore Model' because the strategy was not arrived at serendipitously. It has century-old roots in policy decisions taken by the princely state of Mysore. (Kadekodi et al.: 18–19)

Although Karnataka traditionally had a considerable focus directed towards decentralization, only 17 subjects out of a total of

29 have been devolved to panchayats (Rajasekhar and Satapathy 2007; Vaddiraju 2009a). Not all subjects of the Constitution have been devolved. Besides, considerable finances are devolved; as of now, each panchayat gets about Rs. 40 lakh per year. However, functionaries have not been devolved and are a major problem (Vaddiraju and Sangita 2011). As elsewhere, the functionaries of the government have a marked reluctance to come under the decentralized bodies. The District Planning Committees are in the same situation and as in many other states, often they are not functioning very satisfactorily. The weakest point of 'Karnataka model' is urban decentralization. In the entire state, urban decentralization is just nominal. Under urban bodies, it is the district collector and the bureaucrats who call all the shots. As elsewhere, the zilla panchayats do not take up the work of urban decentralization. They focus on rural decentralization. Zilla panchayats remain basically zilla rural panchayats without a fair urban component. As Lalita Chandrashekhar (2011) argues in her book *Undermining Local Democracy*, recently the governance culture of parallel bodies to panchayats has rubbed off on the rural and urban local bodies in Karnataka too, while the trend in the future (considering the current situation) is unlikely to be any different. Parallel bodies to panchayats are the order of the day (Manor 2005). Over the past seven years, the situation of the local governance institutions – both rural and urban – has worsened considerably with no focus directed towards them any longer. Given the routine political crisis at the state level, the agenda of decentralized governance has taken a backseat since long. The BJP government in the years recent has done nothing for the promotion of decentralization. Not only this, the discussion on decentralized governance in the public interest among the media, academia, intellectuals and the public sphere in general has dissipated in Karnataka totally of late. Karnataka too is going the way of many other states.

Andhra Pradesh

Interestingly, in India, Andhra Pradesh and Rajasthan were the first states to have started panchayati raj and decentralization (Haragopal and Sudarshanam 1995). However, the local bodies continue to receive a very low priority. The local bodies are highly politicised, discriminated against and at best ignored when it comes to the governance of the state (Narayana). This has been the story particularly since the advent of economic reforms. Regarding the experience of Andhra Pradesh, one cannot help observing that in the post-reform period the economic reforms were given the top priority while at the same time, the political decentralization was given a low priority (Rao and Dev 2003). The same international donors that encouraged economic reforms also discouraged the decentralization process through panchayats. In fact, the 'parallel bodies' to panchayats were donor driven (Reddy 2007). In this situation, economic reforms, pushed by donors, ran counter to decentralization, again at the instance of donor-driven policies.

There is a direct linkage, in the case of Andhra Pradesh, between economic reforms and political decentralization. Had economic reforms focused on the rural sector, carried out land reforms (in the older sense of the term) and implemented decentralized governance, the democratic processes and politics would have got strengthened. Instead, the successive governments in Andhra Pradesh have focused more on Hyderabad-centric high technology led development, neglecting rural development and democratic governance in rural areas in the process (Mooij 2007). The emphasis on IT, BT, pharmaceuticals and such sectors is in itself not incorrect, given the recent developments on various fronts. But the problem is that such economic and governance reforms and associated focus on donor-driven policies have happened at the expense of rural development and rural governance. The syndrome of 'parallel bodies' continues to persist.

Although the Congress Party has been in power for the last nine years, the condition of the decentralized bodies has not improved any further under its regime as compared to the regional Telugu Desam Party (TDP). The status of devolution of powers continues to be same as it was during the TDP rule. TDP itself had ignored panchayats badly, treating them as hostile bodies and the Congress policy is no different either. Parallel bodies promoted by the TDP continue; TDP Chief Minister Naidu's favourite 'Janmabhoomi' programme became Congress Chief Minister Y.S. Rajasekhara Reddy's 'Racha banda' programme later. Rural schemes and funds continue to be managed by District Rural Development Authorities and bureaucrats rather than the local bodies, while poverty alleviation programmes are promoted by GONGOS. SERP (Society for Elimination of Rural

Poverty – a World Bank funded and the state government founded NGO) of Naidu's time has acquired a new name under the Congress Party. The aspect of decentralization has not received much attention since a decade, while panchayats and urban bodies are being neglected for the last nine years or so. In many ways, it is a case of a spectacular opportunity lost; because the same Congress Party was in power all through the period at the centre. The state government could have taken advantage of it to promote decentralization. The Congress government at the centre, which initially promoted decentralization, does not seem inclined to pressurize its own states to decentralize in any meaningful manner.

Tamil Nadu

Although there is a substantial amount of progress achieved following the constitutional amendments (Aram 1995), the overall situation is not very encouraging. The bureaucracy and higher level political representatives seem to dominate the elected representatives of local self-governing institutions. The Tamil Nadu Development Report (TNDR) puts this succinctly in the following manner:

> While all the enactments were passed with the objective of creating Self Governing Local Institutions, in practice, they did not or could not function as Self Governing Institutions, but function mainly as agencies of the State and Central Governments. The 29 items indicated in the 11th Schedule of the Constitution have not been entrusted to *Panchayats*. Similar is the case in respect of Urban Local Bodies. (Planning Commission, TNDR 2005: 40–4)

The above picture indeed portrays a bleak picture of local self-governance in Tamil Nadu. Why is this so? We venture some explanation and this explanation is based on the political process of Tamil Nadu.

1. Partly because of the history of backward caste and Dravidian movements with a focus on strengthening powers at the state level.
2. Partly because of the focus on centre–state relations in which the state-level governments and regimes jealously guard their interests vis-à-vis the centre and central government.
3. Probably also, the creation of local self-governments is seen as the dilution of powers of the state-level government by giving

the centre a direct access to grassroots institutions by-passing the state government.

4. Partly because of a strong tradition of bureaucratic governance where line departments of the government are accorded a priority with respect to handing over of powers to the local self-governing institutions.

We try to elaborate on these propositions below as these are also some reasons underlying the strengthening of the state economy through economic reforms that have actually make the state regimes insensitive to the devolution of powers to local government institutions. The stronger the state regime, the weaker will be the local self-governments (Vaddiraju 2009b).

First, Tamil Nadu has a history of progressive backward class movements (Pandian 1992). The roots of these movements stretch as far back as the nineteenth century. The backward class movements have been quite active in state politics since their beginning, demanding their representation in politics, government jobs and educational institutions. These demands have persisted from the nineteenth century through to the present times. These have been essentially non-Brahmin or even anti-Brahmin movements with backward classes claiming a share not only in the economic pie but also regarding social change and self-respect (Radhakrishnan 1996). These movements have persistently viewed Brahmins as Aryan invaders waging wars against the local Dravidians, through their own language, culture and civilization. From the beginning, there has been a fusion of backward class movements and the Dravidian movement. This has led to progressive affirmative actions such as reservation in educational institutions and government jobs as well as political representation in the state government. However, all the demands of the backward classes have not been met as there exist many divisions among the backward classes themselves. But two things are clear: one, there is a larger accommodation of the middle and lower tiers of the social structure in social, economic and political power sharing; and two, backward class movements combined with the Dravidian non-Brahmin self-respect ideology have increased the regional politics at the state level. These movements have given rise to strong Dravidian political parties such as Dravida Kazhagam (DK), DMK, AIADMK and the other more recently formed political parties.

The net result of the articulation of regional and backward classes focusing on politics at the state level is the concentration of politics at the state level. The state government is seen as an important terrain for political contestation, sharing of power and political and economic accommodation. The Dravidian parties have always operated at the state level with a focus on governance. An interesting result of this concentration of political power at the grass-roots level is that the sub-state or the tiers of governance at the state level have never received their due attention. All the political parties have always mobilized their constituencies for capturing and maintaining power at the state level. This is the main feature of the regional party regimes in Tamil Nadu and Andhra Pradesh. When regional parties concentrate their power at the state level, these parties show reluctance to strengthen the lower tiers of governance. The Dravidian parties in Tamil Nadu and the regional party in Andhra Pradesh, the TDP, show a similar trend in this respect (Vaddiraju 2012). The net result of these processes is that political power has got concentrated at the state level without being devolved down the political order.

The second aspect is the centre–state (federal) relations. This refers to the general dissatisfaction among the states in general and states led by regional parties in particular that the federal relations are skewed more in favour of the centre. The general dissatisfaction with the federal relations has forced the regional parties to jealously guard their interests at the state level. This is because it is at the state level that these parties have their strong social and political bases. This has led to frequent demands made on the centre for the devolution of more powers to the states in political and economic arenas. Federalism and fiscal federalism are the most favoured and significant issues underlying the political discourse of regional parties. The political mobilization of people and voters at the state level also moves along these lines.

The Story

Karnataka, which had earlier enjoyed a fair record with respect to decentralization, has fallen in line with other states over the last seven years. BJP as a party-in-power has done nothing in terms of furthering the decentralization process in the state. The Congress Party regimes in AP have done little precious either. They have neither interest nor pressure from the above to do anything substantial in this respect. The TDP policy continues as before, though with changed names and titles. The Tamil Nadu story of decentralization has never been encouraging, especially since the promulgation of decentralization laws. In this story, we have comparatively considered three states ruled by BJP, Congress and regional parties with respect to the recent past and present. None of them has shown much interest in the decentralization process and the story, as Professor James Manor notes, is one of 'missed opportunities'. Karnataka could have done better with respect to its historical record, while AP could have fared better because of the Congress Party being in power at both the levels. However, none of them has displayed any genuine interest either in the immediate past or present. What follows is an interesting story. While states are more interested in the share of sovereign power, they are, on their own, not willing to share the same with local governments. Economic reforms have helped states attract more investments and strengthen the state capitals; their political clout has got enhanced because of coalition politics as also the status of regional leaders in national politics and parties. As mentioned earlier, there is an increasing trend towards the nationalization of regional parties and regionalization of national parties. But neither of the above guarantees nor promotes the third tier of federalism. National parties at the state level, be it BJP or Congress, are not much interested in local governments. Regional parties have never been enthusiastic to share power with local bodies. Then the question is who else can be expected to be interested in decentralization and local government in the Indian polity? Will decentralization whither from now on?

References

Aram, M. 1995. *'Tamil Nadu': Status of Panchayati Raj in the States of India*, New Delhi: Concept Publishing Company, pp. 189–197

Aziz, A. 2007. 'The Decentralization Experience in Karnataka', in Singh, Satyajit and Pradeep K Sharma (eds.), *Decentralization: Institutions and Politics in Rural India,* New Delhi: Oxford University Press, pp. 120–135.

Aziz, Abdul et al. (eds.). 2002. *Decentralised Governance and Planning: A Comparative Study of Three South Indian States,* New Delhi: Macmillan.

Balasubramanyam, V.N. and A. Balasubramanyam. 2008. 'Differing Approaches to Development: The Case of Four South Indian States', paper presented at the Seminar on 'Development Through Planning, Market, or Decentralization?' at The Department of Humanities and Social Sciences, Indian Institute of Technology, Bombay, Mumbai, 21–23 January.

Chandrashekhar, L. 2011. *Undermining Local Democracy: Parallel Governance in Contemporary South India*, New Delhi: Routledge.

Haragopal, G. and G. Sudarshanam. 1995. *'Andhra Pradesh': Status of Panchayati Raj in the States of India*, New Delhi: Concept Publishing Company.

Howes, S., Lahiri, A. and Nicholas Stern (eds.). 2003. *State Level Reforms in India: Towards More Effective Government,* Delhi: Macmillan.

Jenkins, R. 1999. *Democratic Politics and Economic Reform in India,* Cambridge: Cambridge University Press.

——. (ed.). 2004. *Regional Reflections: Comparing Politics across India's States*, Delhi: Oxford University Press.

Kadekodi, G. K, Kanbur, R. and Vijayendra Rao (eds.). 2008. *Development in Karnataka: Challenges of Governance, Equity and Empowerment,* New Delhi: Academic Foundation.

Manor, J. 2001. 'Centre-state Relations', in Atul Kohli (ed.), *The Success of India's Democracy*, Cambridge: Cambridge University Press, pp. 78–102.

——. 2004. 'Explaining Political Trajectories in Andhra Pradesh and Karnataka', in Rob Jenkins (ed.), *Regional Reflections: Comparing Politics across India's States,* New Delhi: Oxford University Press.

——. 2005. 'User Groups: A Potentially Damaging Second Wave of Decentralisation?', *European Journal of Development Research*, Vol. 16, No. 1, pp. 193–213.

——. 2006a. 'Successful Governance Reforms in Two Indian States: Karnataka and Andhra Pradesh', IDS Discussion Paper: 385, Sussex: Institute of Development Studies.

——. 2011. 'Local Governance', in Jayal Niraja Gopal and Pratap Bhanu Mehta (eds.), *The Oxford Companion to Politics in India,* New Delhi: Oxford University Press, pp. 61–79.

Mitra, S.K. and Malte Pehl. 2011. 'Federalism', in Jayal Niraja Gopal and Pratap Bhanu Mehta (eds.), *The Oxford Companion to Politics in India,* New Delhi: Oxford University Press, pp. 43–60.

Mooij, J. (ed.). 2005. *The Politics of Economic Reforms in India*, New Delhi: Sage Publications.

——. 2007. 'Hype, Skill and Class: The Politics of Reform in Andhra Pradesh, India', *The Journal of Commonwealth and Comparative Politics*, Vol. 45, No. 1, pp. 34–56.

Mozoomdar, A. 1995. 'The Political Economy of Modern Federalism', in Balveer Arora and Douglas V. Verney (eds.), *Multiple Identities in Single State: Indian Federalism in Comparative Perspective*, Delhi: Konark, pp. 197–233.

——. 1999. 'The Indian Federal State and its Future', in V.A. Pai Panandiker and Ashis Nandy (eds.), *Contemporary India*, New Delhi: Tata McGraw-Hill, pp. 261–296.

Natraj, V.K. and Kripa Ananthpur. 2004. 'Delegation to Devolution: Karnataka', Working Paper No. 184, Chennai: Madras Institute of Development Studies.

Narayana, E.A., 'Panchayati Raj in Andhra Pradesh: An Appraisal of Its Working since Seventy Third Constitutional Amendment', *The Indian Journal of Political Science*, Vol. 38, No. 4, pp. 809–814.

Pandian, M.S.S. 1992. *The Image Trap: MG Ramachandran in Film and Politics*, New Delhi, Newbury and London: Sage Publications.

Planning Commission. 2005. *Tamil Nadu Development Report*, New Delhi: Academic Foundation.

Radhakrishnan, P. 1996. 'Backward Class Movements in Tamil Nadu', *in* M.N.Srinivas (ed) *Caste Its Twentieth Century Avatar,* New Delhi: Viking, Penguin publishers, pp. 111–134.

Rajasekhar, D. and Sachidananda Satapathy. 2007. 'The Functioning of Gram Panchayats in Karnataka', in T.M. Joseph (ed.), *Local Governance in India: Ideas, Challenges and Strategies,* New Delhi: Concept Publishing Company, pp. 363–383.

Rao, Ch. H. and S. Mahendra Dev. 2003. *Andhra Pradesh Development: Economic Reforms and Challenges Ahead,* Hyderabad: Centre for Economic and Social Studies.

Reddy, G. 2007. 'Panchayati Raj Institutions and Parallel Bodies in Andhra Pradesh: A Model for Synergy', *The Indian Journal of Political Science,* Vol. 38, No. 2, pp. 247–257.

Rudolph, L.I. and Susanne Hoeber Rudolph. 2001. 'Iconisation of Chandrababu: Sharing Sovereignty in India's Federal Market Economy', *Economic and Political Weekly,* Vol. 36, No. 5, pp. 1541–1552.

Satishchandran, T.R. 1995. 'Karnataka' in Institute of Social Sciences', in *Status of Panchayati Raj In the States of India,* New Delhi: Concept Publishing Company.

Saxena, R. 2007. 'Treaty-Making Powers: A Case for 'Federalisation' and 'Parliamentarisation', *Economic and Political Weekly*, Vol. 42, No.1, January 6, pp. 24-28.

——. 2012. 'Is India a Case of Asymmetrical Federalism?', *Economic and Political Weekly*, Vol. XLVII, No. 2, January 14, pp. 70–75.

Singh, S. and Pradeep K. Sharma (eds.). 2007. *Decentralization: Institutions and Politics in Rural India*, New Delhi: Oxford University Press.

Vaddiraju, A.K. 2008. 'Decentralisation as a Policy Process in India', paper presented at the Seminar on 'Development through Planning, Market, or Decentralization?' at The Department of Humanities and Social Sciences, Indian Institute of Technology, Bombay, Mumbai, 21–23 January.

Vaddiraju, A.K. 2009a. 'Comparing Rural Decentralisation Across Indian States: Karnataka and Andhra Pradesh', *The Indian Journal of Political Science*, Vol. LXX, No. 1, January–March, pp. 21–30.

——. 2009b. 'Federalism and Decentralisation in India: Andhra Pradesh and Tamil Nadu', ISEC Working Paper: 208, Bangalore: Institute for Social and Economic Change.

——. 2012. 'Federalism Yes, What About Decentralisation? Politics and Governance in Andhra Pradesh and Tamil Nadu', *Journal of Polity and Society*, Vol. 4, No. 1, pp. 28–50.

Vaddiraju, A.K. and Satyanarayana Sangita. 2011. *Decentralised Governance and Planning in Karnataka*, New Castle upon Tyne: Cambridge Scholars Publishing.

7

Fiscal Federalism in Operation

Case of India

Tapas Sen

The idea of federalism, from an economist's viewpoint, is less demanding than that of a political scientist. It only requires more than one level of independent decision making, while the concept of democracy that is embedded into the political definition is not a *sine qua non*. It is viewed essentially as a construct to realize the advantages of both responsive decision making that better characterizes smaller units and a larger common market that is the advantage of large size. However, for a federal system to be relevant and significantly efficiency enhancing, there should be differing tastes and preferences across the federating units. Also, economies of scale in producing/supplying publicly provided services should not be large enough to outweigh the efficiency gains of a federal system in too many services. This is the basic message of 'decentralization theorem' based on a conventional idea of fiscal federalism.

India as a nation fits well into the theoretical construct, but is still sometimes characterized as a 'quasi-federal' system, not a full-fledged federation because (a) its Constitution does not allow for secession of a federating unit; (b) the federating units can be, and have been, reshaped by the centre (actually, the Parliament), thus rendering the federating units obviously as unequal partners of the centre and (c) the assignment of specific functional domains to the centre and states as also the concurrent domain, but of all residuary powers in the centre, and the prescription of overriding authority of the centre in the concurrent domain. The last two factors hold an important operational significance that will be reverted to a little later. The Indian federal structure has stood the test of time so far despite strains; politically, the federal structure has become more mature with the ruling political entities at the centre and the states being increasingly different. The issue of whether the structure of fiscal federalism, as it has been described in the Constitution and as it has evolved over the years, has kept pace with the developments in the political sphere is, therefore, a pertinent question at this juncture. This review is aimed at highlighting several such issues in the actual system of fiscal federalism in India that could be candidates for a fresh assessment and possible reform. The review is structured around four major aspects of fiscal federalism – assignment of functions (powers and responsibilities), imbalances, intergovernmental transfers and subnational borrowing and indebtedness.

Assignments: by Constitution, by Intent and by Default

The Constitution of India lays down the domain of the states, the centre and the concurrent domain in black and white. On the revenue side, the states have only sales tax (now changed to a truncated value added tax or VAT in most states covering wholesale and retail trade) as a major source of revenue – about 60 per cent of their tax revenues originate from this source alone. Other revenue generating taxes at the state level include stamp duties and registration fees, state excise (on alcoholic beverages and other products using alcohol), motor vehicle taxes, electricity duty, profession tax and a few others. The centre, in contrast, has both personal and corporate income taxes, excise duties/VAT (again a truncated version covering stages prior to sale of output), customs (import and export duties) and now services tax. The last tax mentioned was not originally included in any list of the Constitution. It is now being levied by the centre on the strength of its domain including all residual items. This is a significant issue because the pattern of economic growth over the long run has seen the share of services sector rise from a small one in the 1950s to more than half in the gross domestic product (GDP). Obviously, a rather skewed distribution of tax handles between the centre and the states has become even more skewed because of the introduction and widening of the services tax base. Table 7.1 provides some data on the share of the centre and the states (along with union territories) in tax revenue. But it should be added here that this description relates to the collection of tax revenues only; the mechanism of tax sharing changes the picture substantially as can be seen from the Table 7.1.

Table 7.1

Revenue Sharing in India (Rs. crore)

Year	*Combined Revenue Receipts*	*Revenue Receipts of States before Central Transfers*	*Central Transfers to States*		*Revenue Receipts of States after Transfers*
			Shared Taxes	*Grants*	
1980–1981	23,835	8,448 (35)	3,792	2,796	15,036 (63)
1985–1986	51,011	13,486 (26)	7,491	7,067	28,044 (55)
1990–1991	99,282	34,926 (35)	14,535	13,293	62,754 (63)
1995–1996	207,170	80,903 (39)	29,285	21,577	131,765 (64)
2000–2001	349,979	132,162 (38)	51,945	37,684	221,791 (63)
2005–2006	696,285	265,198 (38)	95,887	73,677	434,762 (62)
2006–2007	870,543	326,834 (38)	122,330	90,185	539,349 (62)
2007–2008	1,007,221	327,434 (33)	153,600	108,377	589,411 (59)
2008–2009	1,052,670	365,841 (35)	161,979	124,090	651,910 (62)
2009–2010	1,175,444	452,420 (38)	167,992	140,955	761,367 (65)
2010–2011 (RE)	1,571,611	580,624 (37)	223,203	160,318	964,145 (61)

Note: Figures in parentheses represent percentage shares in combined revenue.

Source: Indian Public Finance Statistics, Ministry of Finance, Government of India; various issues.

The biggest issue in the area of revenue assignment at present is the structure and administration of the proposed goods and services tax (GST). If both the state-level sales taxes/VAT and the central-level excise/VAT are to be operated in a way that would maximize the benefits of this reform, it is imperative to coordinate these levies (or even merge them together) and integrate the taxation of services into a single or a split GST. However, this has proven to be a difficult task so far despite some progress made initially in rationalizing a variety of tax structures and rates. Although a high powered committee is representing the states in thrashing out the details with the central Ministry of Finance, there are several roadblocks in the process of reaching an agreement in terms of protecting the interests of winners and losers, particularly with respect to the central sales tax (a tax on interstate trade legislated by the centre but collected and appropriated by the states; this is slated to be abolished eventually as it goes against the idea of an Indian common market). It is now almost certain that the single GST structure featuring revenue sharing with the states as suggested by the Kelkar Committee (Kelkar 2003) and later by the Thirteenth Finance Commission will not materialize, and that a two-part GST is likely. But there are additional problems regarding the administration of the tax, collection, jurisdiction, appropriate rates and other details that have made an agreement elusive. Repeated announcements of dates for the introduction of an integrated GST have not actually resulted into an actual implementation, but have converted this issue into a live example of centre–state (as also interstate) conflicts of interest preventing concerted actions.

Revenues other than taxes include interest incomes, dividends, user charges, fees and fines. How much revenue is raised from these sources depends essentially on the extent to which these sources are exploited by each unit, and how wisely they invest (in terms of rates of return). However, a few sources with large revenue potential need special mention.

The revenue from minerals has remained a controversial issue since long. The principles of assigning revenues from natural resources are not unequivocal; while their uneven distribution calls for national ownership, the large costs of exploitation of such resources borne by the jurisdiction in which they are located argue for localized control. Even lessons from international practices are not helpful, in view of a bewildering variety. In the case of India, the issue becomes further complicated because the states in which most of the natural resources are located happen to be typically low-income states for whom natural resources constitute a substantial source of revenue. In practice, environmental compulsions as expressed by an apex court judgement limited the exploitation of a natural resource such as forests. While the concerns are probably genuine ones, an unfortunate outcome of this restriction was the loss of public revenue from forests in states such as Assam, Orissa, Jharkhand, Chhattisgarh and Madhya Pradesh, all of which are low-income states. Since the restrictions were applied without any compensation for the states that were to maintain these 'national assets' as the forests are now called, it was somewhat inequitable. Subsequently, this inequity was better appreciated, and the Thirteenth Finance Commission was asked to work out an appropriate scheme of compensation. Though a compensation scheme was recommended and put into practice, its appropriateness is a matter of opinion.

With respect to minerals deposits located inland, the states in which they are located control the extent of exploitation, but the revenue claim of the concerned states is limited to the paltry land revenue that can be charged and the royalty on the amount of minerals extracted. In the case of mineral oils and natural gas, these are fully under the domain of the centre, though the concerned states are entitled to royalties (the centre appropriates the royalties for offshore oil wells and any cess charged).[1] Other minerals are divided into two categories: major and minor, the latter essentially comprising stones and sand only. For all major minerals, the centre fixes the royalty rates from time to time; the grouse is that royalty rates are too low even when the prices of these minerals are skyrocketing. Further, the centre is alleged to do this rather deliberately so as to provide a cost advantage to its publicly owned mining companies. In the end, the states hold that while the entire burden of costs other than the direct costs of extraction are borne by the concerned states, royalties are unacceptably low,[2] depriving them of substantial revenue. Apart from the issue of royalties, there were some central policies in the past that also prevented the mineral-rich states from leveraging this advantage to promote industrialization. For example, the previously applicable freight equalization policy made available coal across all parts of India at the same cost through a policy of subsidies.

The principles of sharing revenue sources and those for sharing of expenditure responsibilities are independent of each other. In general, for most revenue sources other than those impacting relatively immobile assets and activities, assignment to the central level is suggested. In contrast, barring a few public goods of nationwide benefit area such as national defence, railways, foreign trade and policy and macroeconomic policy, most public services are theoretically better provided at the subnational level. The Indian system of assigning expenditure responsibilities reflects this rather faithfully. Going purely by the constitutional scheme of functional assignments, the states account for a larger share of expenditure responsibilities. Almost the entire category of social services is primarily under the domain of states; additionally, they share major expenditure responsibilities in the areas of agriculture and allied activities, physical infrastructure such as irrigation, roads and inland water transport, and power. The share of actual public expenditure incurred by states in the combined expenditure of the centre and states (Table 7.2) shows a larger role for the states. Quantitatively speaking, there does not appear to be much of a centralization in expenditures. But the qualitative aspect is a different story.

Assignments in a federation are often influenced by history. A 'bottom-up' federation (coming together of federating units) usually restricts the powers and responsibilities of the federal (or central) level, while the converse is true for a 'top-down' federation like India. Additionally, in the past, the overwhelming presence of a single party at the centre and the states did promote a *de facto* centralization in terms of key policies. This has changed over the years, but political diversity has created new compulsions in the changed context resulting in centralizing tendencies, albeit differently. Essentially, the increased competition in the political arena has underlined the importance of making the most of public expenditures in terms of votes; to do this, it has become necessary to ensure that possible electoral gains from central policies and schemes are not shared with states. Perhaps with this compulsion in view, untied transfers from the centre that allow the states sufficient leeway to frame their own expenditure priorities are being increasingly converted to specific-purpose transfers. Moreover, an ever-increasing proportion of these are bypassing the state budgets, being provided to parastatals that are created specifically for channelling these transfers through, possibly to convey the central sponsorship to the voters. This is resulting in smaller state budgets than they would have been if all the transfers were provided to the state governments in the first instance as was the practice in the past. Also, the substitution of specific-purpose transfers for untied ones implies that an increasing part of the state-level public expenditures reflect not the state governments' but the centre's priorities, bringing about a qualitative change. This type of centralization has been buttressed by some amendments to the Constitution to shift some of the functions formerly under the exclusive domain of the states to the concurrent jurisdiction (e.g. agriculture).

Table 7.2

Expenditure Share of States and UTs in India (Rs. crore)

Year	*Combined Total Expenditure (Revenue + Capital)*	*Total Expenditure (Revenue + Capital) of States & UTs*	*Share of States (%)*
1980–1981	34,845	19,389	56
1985–1986	75,458	40,666	54
1990–1991	155,142	86,279	56
1995–1996	293,104	156,990	54
2000–2001	552,124	364,685	66
2005–2006	933,642	560,218	60
2006–2007	1,086,592	533,039	49
2007–2008	1,243,598	629,272	51
2008–2009	1,519,081	768,374	51
2009–2010	1,814,610	974,859	54
2010–2011 (RE)	2,194,483	1,161,624	53

Source: Same as given in Table 7.1.

Some of the blame for this type of centralization must be laid at the doors of the state governments also. Apart from not fully utilizing the tax handles within their jurisdiction (e.g. agricultural income tax), states have been guilty of not paying adequate attention to basic public services such as education, health care, water supply and sanitation owing to their infatuation with starting too many new developmental projects without being able to do justice to most of them in terms of allocation of financial resources. They also have failed to efficiently manage the power sector largely under the state domain through state electricity boards, mainly because of the poor operational policies designed to be populist in terms of garnering political gains. These failures of the states have provided a convenient reason to the centre to intervene in many areas (that were originally under the state domain) through specific-purpose schemes, and even to bypass the state government budgets. In reality, a large part of the central bureaucracy administering a plethora of such schemes would be unnecessary if the states met their constitutional obligations with a fair degree of diligence.

Fiscal Imbalances

The assignment of revenue sources and expenditure responsibilities, as mentioned above, is in principle based on different and independent sets of considerations, leading to some degree of centralization of revenues with relatively larger expenditure responsibilities at the state level. This results in a mismatch between revenue sources and expenditure responsibilities at the subnational level as a whole, known as 'vertical imbalance'. As per the logic of vertical imbalance, the centre enjoys a pre-transfers fiscal surplus, while the states as a whole would normally face a pre-transfers deficit. While this did hold true in India over the years, intergovernmental transfers were relatively low until the 1980s, but were enough to cause post-transfer deficits in the revenue account at the central level and surplus at the state level. The quantum of transfers increased substantially from the early 1980s, but oddly enough, from around 1987–1988, states also started showing gradually increasing deficits in their revenue account. This situation elicited a tongue-in-cheek comment from an observer that changing the quantum of intergovernmental transfers essentially amounted to redistributing deficits!

Also there is a substantial 'horizontal imbalance' in India that refers to differences among individual states (units at the same level) in the ability to meet their expenditure responsibilities with revenues at their disposal. Such an imbalance arises mainly because of varying levels of economic development across states; a more developed state has a higher revenue base to tap and would normally raise higher revenues per capita, while greater economic activities and higher private incomes reduce its public expenditure obligations. The opposite would normally be true with respect to less developed states. Thus, horizontal imbalances are expected to be larger with respect to less developed states.

In practice, it is only the fiscal and revenue deficits (or other budgetary concepts of deficits) that can be observed as approximations of fiscal imbalances. For each of the states, such deficits would be a combination of vertical and horizontal imbalances. Conceptually, if each of the states raised its entire revenue potential (R*) and spent according to need (X*), thus having deficits equal to ($X_i^* - R_i^*$), then the same for the most developed state (i.e. with the highest per capita income) would represent only the vertical imbalance, as horizontal imbalance should be zero by definition. Given this, the vertical imbalance for other states could be estimated by scaling it up or down, using a relative population ratio, assuming per capita vertical imbalance to be the same across all states. The horizontal imbalance could then be taken to be the remaining deficits. Unfortunately, actual deficits are also affected by the departures of actual revenue collections and expenditures from the normative (X* and R*), and these departures do not necessarily follow any pattern. The end result is that a relatively high-income state such as Punjab exhibits large and persistent deficits, while a low-income state such as Orissa shows an occasional fiscal surplus! This completely confounds any attempt to empirically distinguish between the vertical and horizontal imbalances. Since these two types of imbalances constitute the two most important reasons for intergovernmental transfers, the lack of clarity about them makes the job of designing a rational system of intergovernmental transfers rather difficult. The actual transfer mechanisms have adopted various less-than-ideal methods for distributing intergovernmental transfers among individual states as a result. The preceding discussion should serve to indicate that if the transfers are to compensate for the two imbalances discussed above, the only appropriate way would be to base them on X* and R* or what is known as a system of transfers on a normative basis.

Intergovernmental Transfers: How Effective?

Intergovernmental transfers are used in almost all federal systems, as they can be designed to serve various purposes apart from ameliorating vertical and horizontal imbalances, such as correcting subnational decision making in the presence of benefit spillovers across jurisdictions, or ensuring minimum standards of defined basic services. There are different types of transfers that can be used, and the design of the transfers should ideally be suited for the purpose. For example, tackling vertical imbalance requires unconditional transfers, and both tax sharing and block grants can be used. In contrast, if minimum standards of basic services are to be ensured, grants to meet this objective must be specific purpose (to be spent on specified services), and linked to the shortfall from the minimum defined. Transfers to address horizontal imbalances, known as equalization transfers, should be positively linked to the degree of such imbalances and should preferably be unconditional in order to avoid changing budgetary priorities of the recipient governments. But if the intention is indeed to modify the priorities, matching grants are best suited for it.

In India, intergovernmental transfers (shared taxes and grants) flow through three channels: the Finance Commission, the Planning Commission and the line ministries of the central government. Tax sharing is exclusively based on a formula that is specified in the awards of the Finance Commission, reassessed every five years. The Finance Commission also awards other grants based on assessed revenue deficit, those for passing on to the local bodies, for natural calamity relief and even ad hoc grants. The Planning Commission also provides several categories of grants, but the main one is the formula-driven grant for supplementing state resources to implement their Five-Year Plans. The line ministries administer specific-purpose grants (often matching) related to centrally sponsored schemes and central plan schemes. These are focused on relatively narrow departmental objectives. The transfers through the Finance Commission are expected to manage vertical imbalances besides meeting the objective of fiscal equalization (reducing horizontal imbalances), while the Planning Commission grants are meant to serve the causes of socio-economic development as also equalization.

In practice, the problem of vertical imbalance is reasonably well met by the system of intergovernmental transfers in that the post-transfer share of revenues of states in the combined revenues of both the centre and states is roughly in line with their share in public expenditures (Tables 7.1 and 7.2). But equalization has not been addressed by the transfers with much success, with the horizontal imbalances remaining at least as large as ever. Although this could be partly attributed to other reasons, empirical analyses indicate the failure of the intergovernmental transfer system (barring the Finance Commission transfers) to effectively address this issue (Rao et al. 2000). In this connection, sometimes objections have been raised against assigning 'too much' weight to equalization, as it might militate against efficiency in the sense that it might provide perverse incentives to recipient governments' fiscal behaviour. Implicit in this line of argument is the presumption that the observed fiscal imbalances are more because of fiscal mismanagement rather than any exogenous reasons, and aligning substantial transfers with such imbalances would amount to rewarding such mismanagement while punishing prudent fiscal management. While this presumption can easily be seen to be false with a moment's reflection (even a rudimentary understanding of the path of economic development of various regions of India is enough for it), it does contain some truth that has to be carefully gleaned and addressed. And the truth is that observed or actual fiscal imbalances with respect to various states do not indeed reflect horizontal imbalances accurately. A state can be wanting in revenue effort (West Bengal is an example) or it can be a spendthrift populist government (the case of Punjab is an example); the result could be a large deficit without a large fiscal handicap. Conversely, a less developed state could be clamping down on public expenditures too much (Bihar and Odisha) and exhibit surpluses. As mentioned above in the previous section, only a normative assessment of revenues and expenditures can reveal the true extent of horizontal imbalances on which to base equalization transfers. This would also be efficient, since it would be independent of actual fiscal behaviour of the states, thereby making strategic revenue and expenditure policies irrelevant.

Of course, there can be alternative ways of looking at efficiency; for example, efficiency in the context of intergovernmental transfers can be defined as a system that allocates transfers in such a way that national economic growth is maximized. Conceptually, it can be achieved by providing transfers to the states according to their potential for economic growth or their ability to channelize these transfers into economic growth. However, this line of reasoning is difficult to implement in practice, primarily because of the difficulty in assessing growth potential of transfers with respect to individual states with any degree of accuracy, but also because it would then make the transfers similar in nature to private investments, obliterating the special role of the government in promoting balanced economic development, which may not be permissible in view of its obligations towards equalization (Sen 2011).

The agenda in the area of intergovernmental transfers, apart from promoting equalization through normative assessments of revenue and expenditure of the states, should also seek to limit the discretionary transfers through the centrally sponsored schemes, the specific-purpose grants used to bring about a qualitative centralization as described in the previous section. While a few of them may be necessary to cover the states' failures in meeting their responsibilities, most of them do not fall under this category, and even such grants can be redesigned to impose minimum curbs on state autonomy, which is an important ingredient of a federal system.

Subnational Borrowings and Fiscal Responsibility Legislation

Debt is one of the legitimate financing options for any government looking for funds to invest in assets that yield adequate returns. Strictly speaking, a government should be taking into account the social rate of return rather than simply the financial return, but budgetary considerations may not allow a state government to prudently apply this principle. This is particularly so when there is not much of revenue surplus to finance capital expenditures. Not all countries allow their subnational governments to borrow from the market (e.g. Sri Lanka). There is an apprehension that pressures to spend too much may increase borrowings beyond a prudent level, which in turn might create a bailout dilemma for the centre. This is not an entirely baseless fear considering the history of Indian state finances in some cases. But the Indian Constitution does allow the states to borrow from any source within the country, and even indirectly (through the central government) from outside the country or from multilateral agencies. However, a key restriction is that the market borrowing of any state (through government bonds) will be controlled by the central government as long as it is indebted to the centre. Since all states in India do have outstanding debt repayable to the centre, the centre can control the market borrowings of all states, and it does actually allocate the quantum of market borrowings among states through a consultative process involving the Ministry of Finance and the Planning Commission. However, this control does not extend to several other methods of borrowing that the states employ. For example, negotiated loans are outside this control, and the states can easily evade the control by borrowing through their non-departmental public enterprises. This is mainly related to long-term loans; short-term loans, normally required to tide over liquidity problems, are available from the Reserve Bank of India (RBI) (ways and means advances and overdrafts), as also commercial banks. The state provident funds also constitute in practice a method of borrowing from their employees; another notable source is the small savings made by residents of the state in the specified schemes of the centre – the proceeds are given to the states as central loans after deducting a service charge.

If the above discussion gives an impression that the states can borrow as much as they want from so many sources, it would not be quite correct. Every lender makes some assessment of the credit-worthiness of the borrower, and this holds true even if the borrower is a sovereign state government. Typically, a lender would assess creditworthiness of borrowers by examining their income, expenditure and stock of debt already outstanding, and this remains true when a state government is the borrower. There have been cases of state bonds not being fully subscribed by the market in the past; the RBI (the manager of the bond issues of most state governments) had to bundle bonds of some states that were not much in demand with those of other states that were in demand in the past, with all bonds bearing fixed interest rates in the primary market. This practice has been discontinued by the RBI and now state bonds have to stand on their own through an auction mechanism reflecting the demand for these bonds in the interest rate payable by the concerned state. It is even possible that part of the issue is not subscribed at all. Even too high a rate of interest (reflecting poor creditworthiness) constitutes a clear discouragement to further borrowing since this additional cost is likely to further increase indebtedness, which would negatively affect creditworthiness even more. Thus, there are some built-in checks and balances in the system, though they cannot be claimed to be foolproof. There are instances to show that the market does not go by the fiscal condition of a state and that it uses other simple indicators possibly such as per capita income to assess debt sustainability.[3] However, this runs against fair play and is particularly unfair for low-income states that have to struggle hard to show 'good' fiscal outcomes. Some reforms to correct the market biases without affecting the basic structure of market discipline may be called for here (Sen 2003).

Since around 2005–2006, there has been a more serious constraint on the states' borrowings. The Twelfth Finance Commission had recommended an incentive-based system of state-level fiscal responsibility legislations that saw most of the states (barring two) passing such legislations incorporating a reduction of fiscal deficits to 3 per cent or below of the gross state domestic product (GSDP) and of revenue deficits to zero by the end of its award period. This was continued, with the other two states joining in by the Thirteenth Finance Commission. Since fiscal deficits roughly equal net borrowings from all sources for state governments, this constitutes a strong statutory ceiling on the states' borrowings from all sources. What needs emphasis here is the fact that the target deficit levels are uniform across states with important implications that are discussed below.

The Plight of Less Developed States

In this concluding section, the main failure of the Indian federal system – not achieving much of equalization despite more than 60 years of its operation – is intended to be brought into focus. Historically, the initial socio-economic conditions of low-income states were not conducive to achieving a rapid growth, and national policies regarding public sector investment as also the regional spread of its own expenditures did not compensate for these problems. The system of planning in India essentially depends on own resources, and hence, the limited resources of these states did not allow them to develop rapidly with the help of planning; even the plan transfers have not been particularly equalizing. Private investment gravitates to states with better infrastructure and/or larger markets; less developed states did not have either by definition. They had some advantage in the form of natural resources, particularly minerals, but national policies such as the freight equalization policy, the low royalties and the licensing system that was part of physical planning severely limited their ability to leverage this advantage to the fullest extent. An origin-based tax on domestic trade, the central sales tax, even allowed the more developed states to tax their 'exports' to low-income states and thus exporting their taxes; with much smaller productive capacity, this option was not really available to the less developed states. All these constraints taken together did not allow low-income states to realize their full growth potential in the past.

Some of these constraints have been removed or loosened over time, but others remain. To be sure, there is a substantial amount of central transfers flowing into these states through various centrally sponsored schemes, particularly those meant for poverty alleviation. But much of the expenditure out of these resources is predetermined to be in the nature of palliatives and does not actually go far towards unlocking the development potential of these states; further, the matching requirements of centrally sponsored schemes (uniform across states) have either distorted the spending patterns of low-income states when they tried to maximize receipts of these transfers or have not allowed them to fully utilize the available transfers because of their inability to provide the entire matching requirement. Among the transfers through different channels, only those through the Finance Commission have been somewhat equalizing. Now, the fiscal reform legislations promoted by the successive Finance Commissions in recent years have effectively barred these states from using borrowed resources to invest in even financially viable asset creation with the ceilings on fiscal deficit. In this scenario, the system practically condemns the less developed states to remaining so forever.

For the fiscal federal system to be really equalizing, further reforms are needed, as has been pointed out in the preceding sections. The central government has to rethink policies that tilt its own expenditures away from low-income states – these include an unnecessarily large farmer's subsidy in the food subsidy that benefits only two or three states that are not among the relative poor ones, and a poorly designed and hugely expensive fertilizer subsidy system. It also needs to convert the taxation of interstate trade from an origin-based system to a destination-based one. In the area of intergovernmental transfers, the primary mechanism for equalization, the thrust must be on a system based on normative assessments. The plan transfers need to be made more equalizing overall (i.e. all plan transfers taken together, and not only for the state plan schemes), while the central ministries overseeing centrally sponsored schemes should consider ways of not only making the allocations more equalizing, but also the actual utilization. In this context, even the option of varying matching ratios across states can be considered. There is also a need for an institutional mechanism that would educate the market (without affecting its basic features) about the sustainability of debt of the states that issue fresh bonds. Finally, the uniform targeting of deficits across states requires a reassessment and serious examination of the option of fixing the deficit targets by taking resource requirements of each state into consideration.

Notes

1. In some cases, new lease agreements for oil fields waive payments of cess and royalty in favour of sharing output (called profit petroleum); in such cases, as per the award of the Finance Commission to which this issue was referred, the profit petroleum is shared 50: 50 between the concerned state and the centre.
2. Earlier, the royalty rates were specific rates in nature, implying a rate applicable to physical output of the mines and thus totally nonresponsive to the price of minerals. In most cases, these have been changed to *ad valorem* rates in the previous decade, but there are still complaints regarding how the applicable price is determined. In the case of petroleum, however, this problem is minimized as the applicable price is the international price taken from a reputed source.
3. 'Markets do not differentiate between the borrowings of various States, notwithstanding their very different financial conditions' (Bose et al. 2011).

References

Bose, D., Jain, R. and Lakshmanan, L. 2011. 'Determinants of Primary Yield Spreads of States in India: An Econometric Analysis', Working Paper 10/2011, Department of Economic and Policy Research, Reserve Bank of India, Mumbai.

Kelkar, V. 2003. *Report of the Task Force on Implementation of the FRBM Act 2003*, New Delhi: Ministry of Finance, Government of India.

Rao, M.G., Sen, T.K. and Jena, P.R. 2008. 'Issues before the Thirteenth Finance Commission', *Economic and Political Weekly*, Vol. 43, No. 36, September 6, pp. 41–53.

Sen, T.K. 2003. 'Finances of Governments and their Capacity to Spend', in *India Infrastructure Report 2003: Public Expenditure Allocation and Accountability*, published for the 3i Network, New Delhi: Oxford University Press, pp. 140–150.

——. 2011. 'Horizontal Imbalance in Indian Federation', in Praveen Jha (ed.), *Progressive Fiscal Policy in India*, New Delhi: Sage Publications.

8

Fiscal Decentralization to Subnational Governments (SNGs) in Indian Federalism

Anirudha Barik

> An efficient fiscal system calls for a substantial degree of decentralization in meeting its allocation function.
>
> —Musgrave and Musgrave

Over the last two decades, a very important part of the programme for stabilization and structural reforms has centred around economic reforms. While recognizing this fact, the government has incorporated fiscal reforms as an integral part of economic reforms in India. The intent is to make governments more efficient in term of equitable service providers and to open new spaces for the democratic participation of the society. The strategy it has adopted to achieve these objectives relates to the decentralization of functions, resources and responsibilities from the central government to the subnational governments (SNGs). Hence, the primary argument is that decentralization increases the overall efficiency of governance besides bringing governance closer to the people in terms of an optimal mix of local policies. Based on these ideas, many countries all over the world have started devolving more and more resources and functions to SNGs so as to increase their efficiency and thereby economic growth. With this shift in the approach, India ushered in a landmark reform in favour of decentralization through 73rd Amendment to the Constitution in 1992 provided in Part XI (Articles 245 to 263). Before going to undertake an appraisal of the fiscal decentralization, it would be desirable to define the term 'fiscal decentralization'.

'Fiscal decentralization', as the focus of this chapter, can be defined as 'it comprises the financial aspects of devolution from the central government to the lower-tier governments'. It is the currently fashionable term. The alternative descriptions include 'central-local (or intergovernmental) financial relations' and 'fiscal federalism' and are often used by European and American writers respectively. In other words, it refers to the devolution of policy responsibilities from the central government to the regional governments with regard to spending and revenue collection decisions.

However, effective decentralization involves the calibration of administrative, political, and fiscal dimensions (Table 8.1). Without political decentralization, participatory decision making is not possible. Thus, administrative decentralization is necessary to implement political decisions, and an important precondition for fiscal decentralization. The latter assumes greater importance, because the other two cannot be implemented in the absence of fiscal decentralization. Therefore, this chapter mainly focuses on fiscal decentralization in view of its significance.

Table 8.1

Types of Decentralization and their Characteristics

Types	*Administrative*	*Fiscal*	*Political*
Characteristics	Independent decision making by SNGs on spending activities.	Independent decision making power by SNGs for raising revenues and allocation of financial resources.	Free election for selecting officials (e.g. mayor, council) of SNGs through secret ballots.

Although fiscal decentralization covers a broad policy area, it can be looked at in terms of four basic 'pillars': *first*, expenditure assignments – what are the functions and expenditure responsibilities of each level of government?; *second*, revenue assignments – which tax or nontax revenue sources are made available to SNGs in order to meet their responsibilities?; *third*, intergovernmental fiscal transfers – central governments may provide regional and local governments

(LGs) with additional resources through a system of intergovernmental fiscal transfers or grants; and *fourth,* subnational borrowings – SNGs can borrow to finance revenue shortfalls. The worldwide trend towards fiscal decentralization has also been accompanied by intense debates regarding its costs and benefits. While there exist some perceived costs in terms of the reduced ability of the central government to implement macroeconomic stabilization programmes and the possible efficiency losses due to poor local capacity, it has been strongly argued that decentralization results in better service delivery, active involvement of the local people in governance and revenue mobilization.

After having a good idea about the nature of decentralization and the principles involved, the next task is by asking how do we measure the extent of fiscal decentralization. Because measuring fiscal decentralization is very important to determine its relationship with the variables of interest. Now we take up this task in this section.

Following the public finance literature (Oates 1972), this chapter dwells on two standard measures (expenditure ratio and revenue ratio) of fiscal decentralization along with a new ratio, that is, composite ratio (CR). The *first*, expenditure ratio (ER) involves comparing the SNGs' share of expenditure to that of the total central government's (Oates 1972). On the other hand, the *second* measure, revenue ratio (RR) compares the SNGs revenue with that of the total government's (Akai and Sakata 2002). However, this chapter has used a modified ratio (known as composite ratio [CR]) for measuring the degree of fiscal decentralization from a different perspective with a greater degree of accuracy. *This measure is a ratio of the sub national government's self-financed expenditure to the central governments expenditure on its own projects.* In order to avoid double counting, grants given to the state governments have been subtracted. This is because when a higher level of government gives grants to a lower level of government it amounts to an expense. Hence, subtracting the grant amount ensures that the expenditure is recorded only once by own. Thus, the equation of CR would be as follows,

$$CR = \frac{\text{Total SNG Expenditure} - \text{Grants received by the SNG}}{\text{Central Government Expenditure} - \text{Grant given by the Central Government}}$$

However, the closer the ratio is to 1, the higher the degree of fiscal decentralization. Based on this understanding of fiscal decentralization, the trends in fiscal decentralization structure (since its introduction/inception in 1992) are presented in Figure 8.1. Based on these trends, there is likely to be a shortfall (from 2005–2006 onwards) in expenditure and revenue ratios on account of a substantial decline in indirect taxes and the likely lower than budgeted nontax revenues. The CR is relevant mainly in the context of fiscal marksmanship.

Figure 8.1

Trends in Fiscal Decentralization in India: 1992–2011

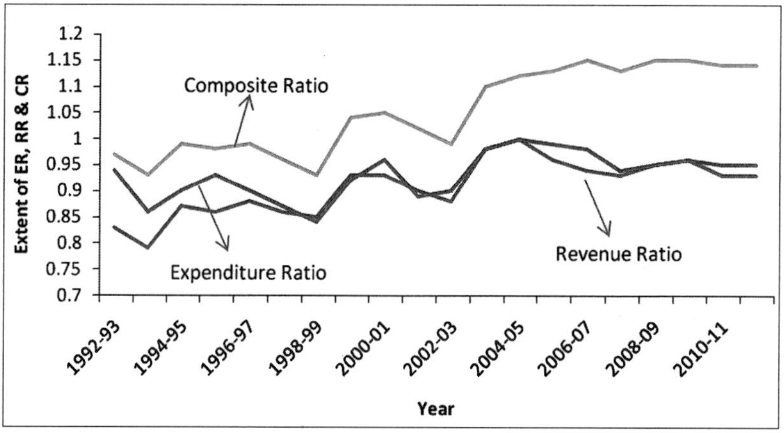

Source: Indian Public Finance Statistics 2011–2012, Ministry of Finance, Government of India, 2012.

Fiscal System and Decentralization in the Indian Context

The Historical Background

At the time of its inception, the Indian Constitution envisaged a two-tiered federal structure of governance with executive and legislative powers shared between the centre and the states, while not assigning any specific provisions for *panchayats*. The role of *panchayats* was, however, articulated.

In what can be considered as the first substantial effort, the Balwant Rai Mehta Committee (1957) made recommendations on the devolution of powers and resources to PRIs. However, its recommendations were not effectively implemented. Later, the Ashok Mehta Committee (1978) recommended a two-tier system of *panchayati raj* with 'block' as the base, and 'district' as a key administrative unit for planning, coordination and resource allocation. The committee also recommended the devolution of financial powers to PRIs. However, it was not until the Singhvi Committee (1986) that the constitutional recognition of *panchayats* became a serious issue for the government. The recommendations of this committee led to the introduction of the *Panchayati Raj* Bill in the Parliament in 1989. While the bill was passed by the Lok Sabha, it was rejected in the *Rajya Sabha*. Consequently, a Joint Parliamentary Committee was set up to prepare a revised bill. In 1992, the new bill, the 73rd Constitutional Amendment, was introduced in the Parliament. The bill was finally passed in 1993, providing an exclusive legal basis for *panchayats*. The devolution of political power to the third tier appears to make an eminent sense in the Indian context.

The Structure of Indian Federalism: Assessment and Comparative Performance (Political)

India, a federal union of 28 states and 7 centrally administered territories, is home to a population of more than 1.2 billion people with more than 400 ethnic groups, speaking a variety of languages and dialects. The centre–state fiscal relations in the Indian context evolved as a two-tier federalism until the 73rd and 74th Constitutional Amendments in 1992, through which an attempt was made to place the fiscal arrangements under a three-tier framework by statutorily specifying the roles and finances of the governmental administrative units below the state level (i.e. rural and the urban local governments).

In the current system, all these three tiers of SNGs have executive authority and are supposed to be independent of one another. However, the administrative regulation, supervision and reporting requirements, and capacity differences have resulted in a hierarchical structure (see Figure 8.2).

An overview of the diverse structure of LGs is shown in Table 8.2. Of this, about 3842 come under urban areas and the remaining under rural areas. In the rural context, local governments are called *panchayats*. Further, the rural local governments (RLGs) consist of a

Figure 8.2
Hierarchical Decentralization Structure in India

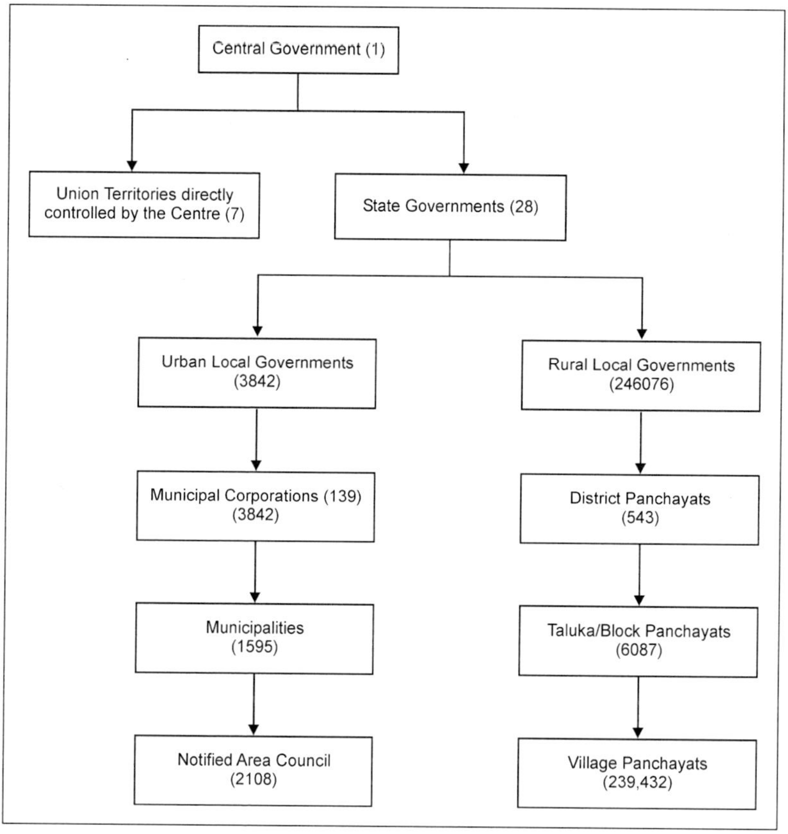

three-tier *panchayat raj* system at the district, block and village levels, while the urban local governments (ULGs) consist of notified area committees, town panchayats, municipalities and municipal corporations, depending upon their size. The LGs in both urban and rural areas carry out functions concurrently with state governments with the latter enjoying overriding powers. However, the structure of LGs differs across various states in the country and so does the degree of fiscal decentralization. In some regions, fiscal decentralization has been more successful, not in terms of delivering public services, and mobilizing physical and human resources, but in unleashing a host of incentives to exploit the developmental potential relative to others.

Table 8.2

Local Government Units under Different Tiers

State	*RLB*			*ULB*		
	District Panchayat	*Block panchayat*	*Village Panchayat*	*Municipal Corporation*	*Munici-palities*	*NAC*
Andhra Pradesh	22	1,097	21,809	15	103	6
Arunachal Pradesh	16	150	1,751	ULBs do Not Exist		
Assam	20	185	2,202	1	29	59
Bihar	38	531	8,463	11	43	84
Chhattisgarh	16	146	1,620	10	28	24
Goa	2	—	189	1	13	—
Gujarat	26	224	13,738	7	159	2
Haryana	19	119	6,187	1	24	51
Himachal Pradesh	12	75	3,243	1	20	28
J&K	0	0	4,139	2	80	—
Jharkhand	24	212	4,562	2	15	22
Karnataka	29	176	5,652	8	138	73
Kerala	14	152	999	5	53	—
Madhya Pradesh	48	313	23,040	14	88	236
Maharashtra	33	351	27,916	22	222	5
Manipur	6	4	165	—	10	18
Meghalaya	3	—		—	6	—
Mizoram	—	—	707	—	1	—
Nagaland	—	—	1,110	—	3	16
Orissa	30	314	6,234	3	36	64
Punjab	20	141	12,447	5	97	33
Rajasthan	32	237	9,184	3	11	169
Sikkim	4		163	1	2	9
Tamil Nadu	29	385	12,618	8	150	561
Tripura	4	23	513	—	1	12
Uttar Pradesh	70	820	52,000	12	194	422
Uttarakhand	13	95	7,227	1	31	31
West Bengal	18	341	3,354	6	118	3
Total	543	6,087	239,432	139	1,595	2,108

Source: FC-XIII: Data Submitted by the State Governments to the Thirteenth Finance Commission.

Fiscal Aspects of Indian Federalism: Assessment and Comparative Performance-Economical

Revenue and Expenditure Shares of Three Levels

Although it is difficult to bring out qualitative aspects of decentralization through quantitative measures, the respective share of different levels of government in raising revenues and incurring expenditures provides insights into the working of fiscal federalism – to get a comprehensive picture of fiscal decentralization in India (see Table 8.3).

Table 8.3

Revenue and Expenditure Trends across Different Tiers of Government

Tiers	*Ratio of Expenditure to GNP*			*Share of Expenditure in Total Government Expenditure*			*Ratio of OR to NSDP*		*OR to Total*	
	1991–92	*1997–98*	*2002–03*	*1991–92*	*1997–98*	*2002–03*	*1997–98*	*2002–03*	*1997–98*	*2002–03*
Centre	16.3	17	18.5	49.2	49	47.4	15.4	16.4	60.49	60.58
State	14.8	17	18.8	44.4	48	48.2	9.35	10.2	36.67	37.51
Local	2.1	1	1.71	6.4	2.9	4.39	0.72	0.51	2.83	1.9
1. Rural	0.9	0.6	1.1	2.9	1.7	2.8	0.1	0.09	0.2	0.35
2. Urban	1.2	0.4	0.6	3.5	1.1	1.6	0.7	0.42	2.64	1.55
Aggregate of all	33.2	35	38.9	100	100	100	25.5	27.1	100	100

Note: Central own revenue inclusive transfers to state governments; OR = Own Revenue.

Source: Datta (1992, for 1997–1998, Rao and Author's own calculation from the report of the Thirteenth Finance Commission, GoI.

There has been a dramatic increase in the significance of the government expenditure in the post-reform period from around 33.2 per cent at the time of reforms to 39 per cent for 2002–2003. The tier-wise composition of the government expenditure has also undergone significant changes over time. During the nineties, the consolidated expenditure of the state governments was lower than that of the central government. By 2002–2003, however, the state government expenditure overtook the expenditure of the central government. The expenditure ratio of the local self-government, on the other hand, was very low with no significant trends observed. It would appear that there was an improvement from the early nineties up to the second half of nineties, but began to decline thereafter. Although the trend is observed to have reversed from 1997–1998, the ratios remained still as compared to those for 1991–1992 period. The ratios for India are found to be one of the lowest among developing countries.

Now, let us consider the level of fiscal autonomy vested with the local governments in India. The ratio of own revenues to the total expenditure is treated as a measure of fiscal autonomy (Table 8.4). It gives a summary picture of the changes in the composition of revenue, tax and nontax sources of revenue of RLGs and ULGs for the period 1991–1992 to 2002–2003. The ULGs have always been more self-reliant than RLGs. The revenues collected by RLGs (tax and nontax) from own sources are found to have accounted for 85 per cent of the total income for 1991–1992, while the share of own revenues in the total revenues is observed to have declined to 58.43 per cent in 2002–2003. In contrast, the ULGs are found to have depended on grants to the extent of nearly 40 per cent, while the RLGs to the extent of nearly 90 per cent of the aggregate income, thereby indicating a low degree of financial autonomy.

Table 8.4

Share of Different Sources of Income of LGs in India (in%)

Sources of Income	*Rural*			*Urban*		
	1991–1992	*1997–1998*	*2002–2003*	*1991–1992*	*1997–1998*	*2002–2003*
Taxes	8.1	1.95	3.87	54.4	48.38	39.23
Nontaxes	2.7	1.55	2.98	26.9	17.47	19.2
Total own revenue	10.8	3.5	6.84	84.9	65.85	58.43
Grants and other revenues	89.2	96.5	93.16	18.7	34.15	41.57
Total own revenue	100	100	100	100	100	100

Source: Datta (1992, for 1997–1998, Rao and Author's own calculation from the report of the Thirteenth Finance Commission, GoI.

Relative Share of Centre and States in Revenue and Total Expenditure

The relative shares of the centre and states in the combined revenue receipts as well as combined expenditure show vertical imbalances with respect to the Indian federation. Table 8.5 presents the relative shares of the centre and states in the combined revenue and total expenditures. The centre's share in the combined revenue expenditure varies from 40 per cent to 46 per cent across the period covered by FC-I to FC-XII. But the period covered by FC-VIII, shows a remarkable stability in the relative shares of the centre and states in the combined revenue expenditure with the share of the centre fluctuating in the narrow range of 43 to 44 per cent. As far as the combined total expenditure is concerned, the share of the centre is found to have varied from 43.14 per cent to 50.51 per cent through the award periods of the XII Finance Commission (here after TwFC).

Table 8.5

Relative Shares of the Centre and States in Revenue and Total Expenditure

Averages for Finance Commission Periods	*Relative Shares (in %)*			
	Total Expenditure		*Revenue Expenditure*	
	Centre	**State**	**Centre**	**State**
FC-I	48.83	56.17	40.77	59.23
FC-II	49.47	50.63	41.83	58.17
FC-III	50.51	49.49	46.1	53.9
FC-IV	47.69	52.31	41.77	58.23
FC-V	43.14	56.86	40	60
FC-VI	47.35	52.65	44.19	55.81
FC-VII	44.79	55.21	41.98	58.62
FC-VIII	47.86	52.14	44.22	55.78
FC-IX	45.58	54.42	43.45	56.55
FC-X	43.35	56.65	43.18	56.82
FC-XI	43.77	56.23	44.03	55.97
FC-XII*	43.47	56.26	44.45	55.55
Overall average	45.92	54.08	43	57

Note: *Average of three years (2005–2008).

Source: Report of the Thirteenth Finance Commission, Ministry of Finance, Government of India, 2010.

On the other hand, Figure 8.3 shows the finance commission (FC) period-wise variations in the shares of states in the combined revenues and total expenditure.

Figure 8.3

Relative Shares of States in the Combined Revenues and Total Expenditure

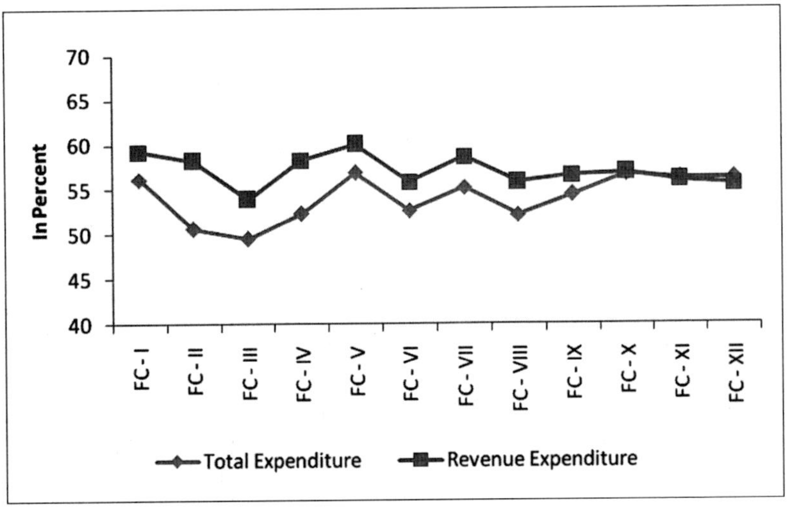

Source: Report of the Thirteenth Finance Commission, Ministry of Finance, Government of India, 2010.

Asymmetry in Indian Federalism

Another salient feature of the fiscal federalism in India is that decentralization is taking place mainly in terms of incurring expenditures, not raising revenues. The central government could exercise control over one-third of the revenues, but its share in raising revenues accounts for two-thirds. In contrast, state and LGs are found to have raised only about one-third of revenues but the revenue accrual to them amounts to about two-thirds. Hence, each of the three levels is observed to have incurred about one-third of the total expenditures. In fact, asymmetry in revenue and expenditure decentralization is particularly glaring at all levels of governance (Table 8.6).

Table 8.6
Revenue and Expenditure Decentralization in India

	Total Revenue	*Total Expenditure*	*Total Revenue*	*Total Expenditure*
	I. As Per cent of GSDP		*II. As Per cent of Total Expenditures*	
Centre	16.92	16.93	59.22	22.08
States	13.27	16.53	34.32	33.85
Local governments	0.8	12.4	3.23	22.07
ULGs	0.7	10	2.74	18.45
RLGs	0.06	1.38	0.24	1.89
SNGs	14.07	28.93	37.55	55.92
Total	31.81	58.62	100	100

Source: Datta (1992, for 1997–1998, Rao and Author's own calculation from the report of the Thirteenth Finance Commission, GoI.

It is evident from the Table 8.6 that at local level, ULGs have accounted for 18.45 per cent of the total expenditures incurred while the share of RLGs works out to less than 2 per cent (Table 8.6). Like in all federal systems, the states enjoy significant revenue raising powers and in fact, the states account for 34.32 per cent of the total revenues raised. The expenditure share of the state governments after giving grants to local governments amounts to 34 per cent. Of course, the states still have to depend on the central government transfers to finance a significant portion of their expenditures. Almost 37 per cent of states' revenues accrue from transfers. As mentioned above, the total revenue raised by LGs constitutes just about 0.8 per cent of GDP or 2 per cent of the total revenues. Thus, more than quarter million LGs in rural India incur less than 2 per cent of the total expenditures. The expenditures incurred by them also include expenditures on various centrally sponsored schemes (CSSs) such as poverty alleviation and social development programmes. However, the asymmetric arrangements need not necessarily be the outcome of constitutional arrangements for they can also result from the way in which administrative, political and fiscal systems are managed in a federation, which differs across various parts of the country. Thus, despite the constitutional recognition LGs in India, they are not in a position to raise significant revenues and have to depend on higher level governments for grants. As a result, the revenue accrual to the LGs is not adequate enough for them to effectively deliver the assignments. To sum up, the type of fiscal decentralization at local levels seen in India may be characterized as deconcentration rather than decentralization.

Fiscal Decentralization and Macro Economic Implications

Ensuring/maintaining macroeconomic stability is considered the main function of the central government (Oates 1972). Nevertheless, the method involved raising resources and spending at the subnational levels can hold macroeconomic implications. Therefore, the issue to be examined is that to what extent, the existing fiscal systems have contributed to the fiscal imbalances in India.

Fiscal Imbalances: Trends and Issues

It is also often said that 'India lives in its states'. This is obviously true, but it is becoming increasingly a means for passing on governmental responsibilities from the central to the state levels. Under the constitutional provisions, state governments have always had very significant responsibilities (e.g. for health care services and education). However, at the same time, they have not had commensurate powers either to raise revenues to fulfil their responsibilities. That is why there is a fundamental fiscal difference between the centre and states – that state governments necessarily face a hard budget constraint unlike the central government.

Figure 8.4

Fiscal Deficits of the Centre and States as Per cent of GDP

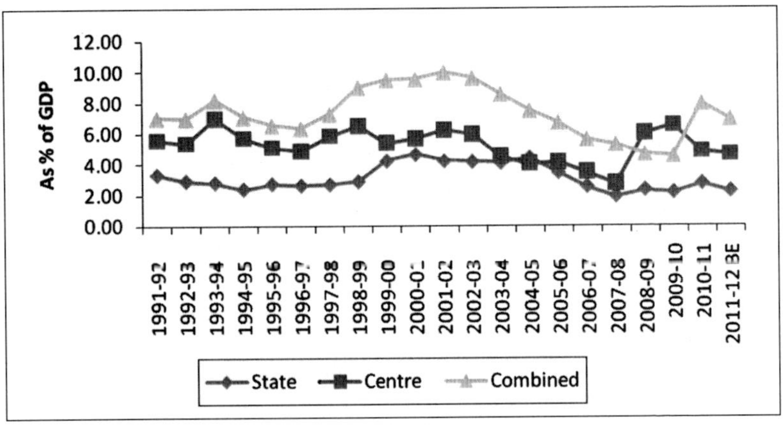

Source: Budget Documents, Government of India.

The consolidated fiscal position of the central and state governments witnessing a severe fiscal crisis in the early years of this decade is no longer as pervasive and has even showed a significant improvement in the recent years as reflected in major deficit indicators, namely, revenue deficit, gross fiscal deficit and primary deficit (Figure 8.4). An improvement in the fiscal situation in the recent years (since 2003) has been achieved by pursuing the fiscal correction and consolidation process under a rule-based fiscal framework. The efforts of the state governments towards reducing fiscal imbalances have been aided by larger devolutions, from the central government and transfers by the FC through shareable central taxes (a higher buoyancy of central taxes has aided larger devolutions) and grants. Consequent upon these developments, the state governments achieved revenue surpluses for the second successive year in 2007–2008. However, due to a moderation in the economic growth during 2008–2009, the revenue buoyancy suffered a setback, while the aggregate expenditure shot up. As a result, the key fiscal indicators were estimated to deteriorate further in 2009–2010.

Intergovernmental Transfers in India

Intergovernmental transfers have been employed to fulfil a variety of objectives and the design of such transfers depends on the purpose for which they are made. In Indian fiscal literature, federal transfers are recommended for (i) closing the fiscal gaps, (ii) equalization and (iii) spillovers and merit good reason. It is generally recognized that (i) the transfer system should be formula based rather than negotiations and (ii) the design of transfers should not allow for adverse incentives with respect to fiscal management. The general purpose transfers should be so designed as to offset horizontal inequity – shortfalls in revenue capacity and excess expenditure needs of SNGs and specific purpose transfers should be designed to ensure minimum standards of targeted services with significant spillovers at the subnational levels or for merit good reasons. In addition to the Finance Commission, with central planning gaining in importance, the Planning Commission has also become a major dispenser of funds – to the states for plan purposes. The funds are distributed according to the formula evolved and modified by the National Development Council (NDC) from time to time. Besides these two agencies, various central ministries also make some transfers, through CSSs, for specific purposes. Major programmes related to poverty alleviation, family planning and education fall under this category. The trends in the relative shares of these transfers are presented in Table 8.7.

Table 8.7

Composition of Central Transfers from the Centre to States (in%)

Years	*Finance Commission Transfers*			*Other Transfers*			*Total Transfers (4 + 7)*
	Share in central Taxes	*Grants*	*Total FC Transfers (2 + 3)*	*Plan Grants*	*Nonplan Grants*	*Total Other Transfers (5 + 6)*	
FC-VIII (1984–1989)	53.48	6.65	60.13	35.8	4.07	39.87	100 (4.83)
FC-IX (1989–1995)	52.98	8.48	61.46	35.91	2.63	38.54	100 (4.89)
FC-X (1995–2000)	62.06	6.55	68.61	29.52	1.87	31.39	100 (4.09)
FC-XI (2000–2005)	58.38	11	69.38	28.65	1.97	30.62	100 (4.16)
FC-XII (2005–2010)	56.48	11.55	68.03	28.55	3.43	31.98	100 (5.21)
2005–2006	57	14.95	71.95	25.36	2.7	28.06	100 (4.69)
2006–2007	57.93	13.47	71.4	25.54	3.05	28.59	100 (5.11)
2007–2008	58.82	10.21	69.03	27.69	3.29	30.98	100 (5.46)
2008–2009	56.04	9.69	65.73	30.92	3.34	34.26	100 (5.37)
2009–2010 (BE)	53.62	11.22	64.84	30.88	4.28	35.16	100 (5.23)

Note: Figures in parentheses are indicative (column 8) as % of GDP

Source: Report of the Thirteenth Finance Commission, Ministry of Finance, Government of India.

Transfers through FCs appear predominantly significant in terms of an increase in the share of transfers from 60.13 per cent in the award period of FC-VIII to 68.03 per cent in the period of FC-XII. Further, within the FC transfers, there has been an increase in the share of grants, particularly in the periods covered by FC-XI and FC-XII. FC-XII observe that grants could be targeted better and that distributive considerations could be addressed more effectively through grants rather than through tax devolutions per se. The commission, accordingly, increased the share of grants in the transfers in accordance with its own recommendations. The share of plan grants has been steadily increasing since 2006–2007, and in fact it has been increasing more pronounced from 2007–2008 onwards owing to a shift in the composition of plan grants as well as higher transfers through CSSs.

Table 8.8
Criteria and Relative Weights for Determining Inter Se Share of States and LGs

Criterion for Inter Se Share of States	*Weight Allotted (%)*	*Criterion for Grants to Local Governments*	*Weight Allotted (%)*	
			PRIs	*ULBs*
1. Population	25	1. Population	50	50
2. Income	47.5	2. Income	10	20
3. Area	10	3. Area	10	10
4. Index of infrastructure	–	4. Index of devolution	15	15
5. Tax effort	8.75	5. SC/STs proportion in total population	10	–
6. Fiscal discipline	8.75	6. FC LGs grants utilization index	5	5
Total	100	Total	100	100

Source: Same as given for Table 8.7.

Table 8.8 shows the criteria and the fiscal weights, adopted by the Thirteenth Finance Commission (TFC), for determining *inter se* share states and LGs

Figure 8.5
State Transfers to LGs for the Years 1998–1999 and 2007–2008

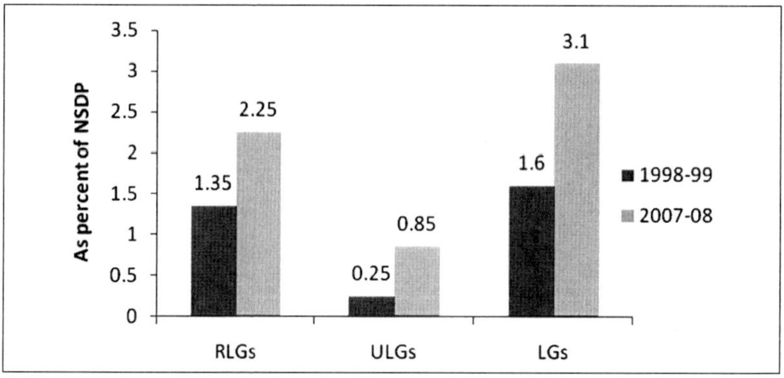

Moreover, the states are required to appoint an FC every five years for making recommendations on the transfers to be made to ULGs and RLGs. They are required to make recommendations on the assignment of tax revenues to LGs, sharing of tax revenues between the states and the LGs and their distribution and grants to be made to them (Figure 8.5).

Equalizing impact of Central Transfer Schemes

The efficiency and equity implications of the Indian fiscal transfer system have for long remained a subject of critical scrutiny. In this context, Figures 8.6 and 8.7 throw some light on the fiscal health of states and financial devolutions. The relatively low and even declining share of central taxes is confirmed by the evidence observed of the states' share (of central taxes) as a proportion of the total central tax revenues (Figure 8.6). It shows that the relative shares of states have been on the decline since the observed peak for 2001–2002, and also that the average with respect to the recent years is well below the average with respect to a similar period a decade earlier. All the state governments currently receive just around one-fourth of the central tax revenues, even though they are directly responsible for delivering most of the public services that directly affect the lives of people.

Figure 8.6

States' Share in the Central Governments Total Tax Revenues

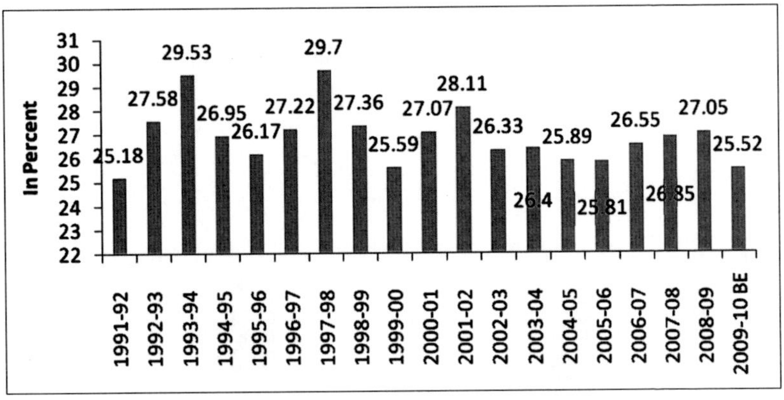

Source: Budget Documents, Government of India.

Figure 8.7

Gross Devolutions from the Centre to Sates over the Years (%)

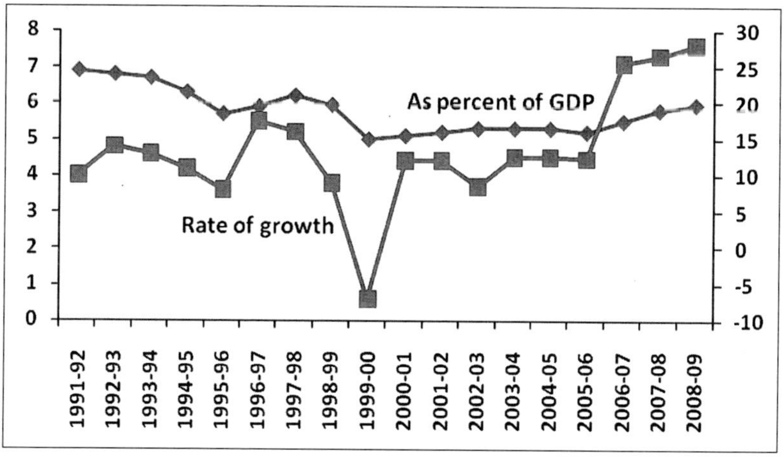

Figure 8.8

Gross Devolutions and Revenue Deficits of States over the Years

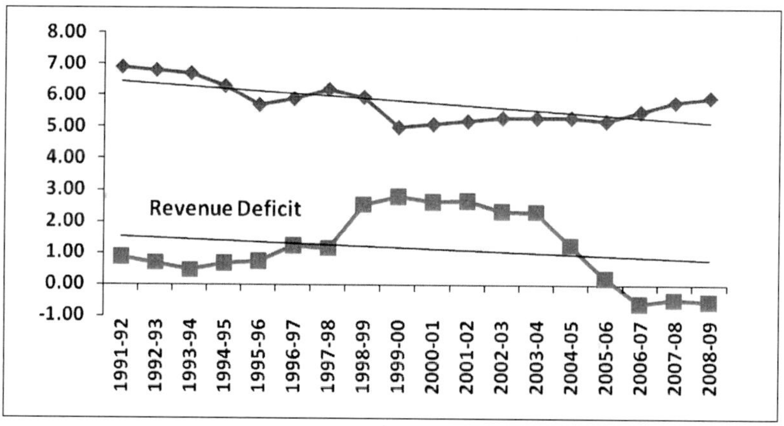

In current nominal terms that has certainly been rising, as indicated by Figure 8.7, which shows the nominal rate of growth (on the right hand scale). As per cent of GDP of states, it has been mostly stagnant in the recent period. In view of the efforts of the state governments being aided by larger devolutions, the state governments have managed to achieve improvements in the revenue account (Figure 8.8). The linear trend lines show the long-term relationship between the central government's devolutions to states and the resultant revenue deficits of the states.

Despite the design of the transfer system noted above, the overall impact of the central government's transfers to states is equalizing for all states (Table 8.9). The equalizing impact is primarily due to the FC transfers, particularly tax devolutions and current transfers. Neither the plan grants nor the nonplan grants given by the Planning Commission (during EFC and TwFC) have a significant equalizing impact.

Table 8.9

Equalizing Effect of Centrally Transferred Schemes

Centrally Transferred Schemes	*Income Elasticity#*					
	Eleventh Finance Commission			*Twelfth Finance Commission*		
	GCS	**SCS**	**All States**	**GCS**	**SCS**	**All States**
Tax devolution	–0.414*	–0.328*	–0.471*	–0.532*	–0.507*	–0.564*
Total plan grants	–0.236	–0.041	–0.282	0.041	–0.060	–0.585
Total nonplan grants	–1.027	–0.997	–1.001	–0.054	–0.070	0.302
Total FC transfers	–0.403*	–0.280	–0.514	0.508*	–0.478*	–0.558*
Total current transfers	–0.277*	–0.268	0.408	0.375*	–0.345*	–0.594*

Note: *Significant at 1 per cent level.
#Income elasticity has been estimated by regressing the transfer items on NSDPin a log-linear model.

Source: Estimated using the data taken from the Budget Documents of theGovernment.

Conclusions

This chapter analyses fiscal decentralization in terms of a three-tier federal framework in India. The analysis helps understand the relative roles of the three levels of government with respect of fiscal decentralization. It brings out the anomalies in assignments both between the centre and states and states and local governments. The findings of the chapter indicate that, the inclusion of LGs shows the aggregate fiscal deficits being much higher than they are usually measured to be.

The transfers from the centre to the states have inherent moral hazard problems in that it is more difficult to meet the objectives of transfers system if multiple agencies make transfers. Notwithstanding these weaknesses, the central transfers are generally equalizing. A major contributor to equalization is FC transfers. However, the Planning Commission transfers and the assistance given by CSS are not equalizing. Preferably, the entire transfers should be the responsibility of the Finance Commission, while the Planning Commission should focus on the physical infrastructure. However, transfers to LGs do not follow a clear pattern. Constitutional sanction has enabled the institution of LGs, but they do not play a significant role in providing public services, much less in terms of raising resources. It is, therefore, necessary to redesign the transfer system by factoring in the formula, accountability, incentives and equity. And the fiscal devolutions to LGs should be considered an integral component of the restructuring of centre–state fiscal relations.

Before concluding, it is worth to note here that reforms on these lines would call for a radical change in the strategy of decentralization with respect to Indian federalism. Thus, this present chapter is a modest attempt at exploring the possible directions in which reforms should proceed in order to overcome asymmetries existing with regard to fiscal decentralization in the context of economic liberalization.

References

Akai, Nobuo and Sakata, Masayo. 2002. 'Fiscal Decentralization Contributes to Economic Growth: Evidence From-State-Level Cross-Section Data for the United States', *Journal of Urban Economics,* Vol. 52, pp. 93–108.

Bardhan, P. 2002. 'Decentralization of Governance and Development', *Journal of Economic Perspectives*, Vol. 16, pp. 185–205.

Bardhan, P. and Dilip Mookherjee. 2000. 'Capture and Governance at Local and National Levels', *American Economic Review*, Vol. 90, No. 2, pp. 135–139.

Buchanan, J.M. 1950. 'Federalism and Fiscal Equity', *American Economic Review,* Vol. 40, No. 4, pp. 421–432.

Dutta, Bhaskar. 2000. 'Fragmented Legislatures and Electoral Systems: The Indian Experience', in Anthony Lanyi (ed.), *Institutions, Incentives, and Economic Reforms in India*, New Delhi: Sage Publications.

Mundle, S. 2001. *The State of Government Finances, Fiscal Reforms and the Role of ADB,* Government of India: Planning Commission.

Musgrave, R.A. 1959. *Theory of Public Finance,* New York: McGraw Hill.

Oates, W.E. 1972. *Fiscal Federalism,* New York: Harcourt Brace Jovanovich.

Oates, W.E. 1999. 'An Essay on Fiscal Federalism', *Journal of Economic Literature,* Vol. 37, No. 3, pp. 1120–1149.

Rao, G.M. and Raja J. Chelliah. 1995. *A Survey of Research in Fiscal Federalism in India,* New Delhi: Indian Council of Social Science Research.

Rao, G.M. and Tapas K. Sen. 1996. *Fiscal Federalism in India: Theory and Practice,* New Delhi: Macmillan India.

Rao, M.G. 2004. 'Linking Central Transfers to Fiscal Performance of States', *Economic and Political Weekly,* Vol. 39, No. 18, pp. 1820–1825.

Rao, M.G. 2001a. 'Taxing Services: Issues and Strategy', *Economic and Political Weekly,* Vol. 36, No. 42, pp. 3999–4006.

Rao, M.G. and Nirvikar Singh. 2001a. 'The Political Economy of Center-State Fiscal Transfers in India', Working Paper No. 107, Center for Research on Economic Development and Policy Reform, Stanford University.

——. 2004. 'Asymmetric Federalism in India', Working Paper 04'08, Santa Cruz Center for International Economics, University of California, Santa Cruz.

Shah, A. 2004. *Fiscal Decentralization in Developing and Transition Economics: Progress, Problems and the Promise,* World Bank Working Paper.

9

An Analysis of Fiscal Relation and Adjustment with the Centre

A Case of Gujarat

Sangita Agrawal and Dinkar Nayak

In India, fiscal adjustments have always been viewed in the context of economic planning. Recognizing the fact that the financial resources of the states may prove inadequate for undertaking welfare, maintenance and development activities, the Indian Constitution has provided an arrangement for transferring funds from the centre to the states through the mechanism of finance and planning commissions. The intergovernmental resource transfers from the national to sub-national governments (SNGs). SNGs are expected to play a crucial role to smoothen the fiscal imbalances experienced by different states in the country.

Gujarat is one of India's most developed states. It is also one of the highly urbanized states of the Indian Union with 39 per cent of its population living in urban areas. Further, in terms of economic growth, Gujarat happens to be one of the most prosperous and fastest growing states in India. Its position relative to all other states shows that the state's annual average growth rate at current prices is always ahead of the national average. However, as compared to the eighties, the difference is found narrowed for the nineties and 2000s. Thus, in the post-economic reform period, the average growth rate of Gujarat shows a decline in comparison to the average growth rates of all the other states.

However, Ahluwalia, M (2000) points out that during the post-reform period, the economic growth of Gujarat grew at rates normally associated with 'miracle growth'. Gujarat's superior performance was not the result of any conscious policy of limiting benefits of liberalization, but was due to the fact that the state was able to provide an environment most conducive to take advantage of the new policies.

However, in order to achieve sustained growth rates in future, Gujarat needs a corrective action with respect to its fiscal performance. Over the last two decades, the fiscal deficit of Gujarat has increased by 5 per cent of state domestic product (SDP). The factors responsible for the increase in deficit include (i) growing interest burden; (ii) increasing wages and salaries; (iii) pension liabilities; (iv) losses incurred by the state public sector undertakings; (v) charges/cost recoveries and (vi) deceleration in the central transfers.[1] It is also pointed out that interest payments of some of the states (West Bengal, Orissa, Punjab, Rajasthan, Gujarat and Uttar Pradesh) absorb 30–50 per cent of revenue receipts. However, it is pointed that the factors influencing the budget outcomes of states are mainly structural and cyclical in nature. Structural deficit is defined as an expansionary fiscal stance of the government. Long run structural weaknesses of the states are identified as expenditure growth tending to outpace the growth of revenues. Thus, states are vulnerable to fiscal imbalances that affect their ability to undertake and perform the developmental functions.

It is also felt that the state needs to direct its efforts towards promoting its social sectors, especially health and education. The state education programmes reveal that it is not enough to allocate resources to education, it is also necessary to ensure that education is imparted in proper school buildings, and through trained teachers. Thus, a substantial investment is needed on all fronts such as schools and health care facilities, power system, irrigation and water management system, land development, etc. It is, therefore, essential that the state strengthen its existing financial position in order to identify the potential and to promote growth and development.

Although the Gujarat fiscal health has shown some improvement following the enactment of the Fiscal Responsibility Management Act 2005, still, the existing system lacks a link that could hold its fiscal position for a long period. It is in this light that this chapter attempts to enumerate the issues related to the devolution of resources from the centre to the states. The main focus here is to analyse the role of the centre in determining the fiscal performance of Gujarat state.

There are well-researched papers and studies on the state finances in India pertaining to centre–state fiscal relations.

Rao (2002: 3267) examines the trends in fiscal imbalances at the state level. He points out various reasons for the slow growth of revenues, expansion in expenditure and the central government transfers to states going further, he observes that most of the schemes proposed by the Ministry of Finance have serious design problems. The author quotes, 'The problem with the scheme is that the amount of funds available for payments may not be enough to transfer the incentives. The schemes are designed to incentives only the incremental changes in revenue deficit irrespective of the size of the deficit'. Both political will and administrative competence are needed for achieving consolidation and generation of quality infrastructure and a competitive environment for fiscal balance at the state level.

Dholakia (2005) examines various parameters of Fiscal Performance Index to measure the fiscal performance of states. He argues that the fiscal crisis that started around 1985–1986 aggravated further during the post-reform period. In view of the severity of fiscal problems experienced by the states, it is argued that the fiscal self-reliance and improvement index (FSRII) adopted by Tenth and Eleventh Finance Commission was based on a single fiscal performance indicator which in itself was narrowly based, unstable and biased against the better fiscal performer state.

The writer highlighted that the successive Finance Commission of India has not been in a position to provide adequate incentives to the states to become fiscally efficient. The criterion of fiscal discipline was explicitly added in the devolution formula of the Eleventh Finance Commission and later suggested in the Tenth Finance Commission formula for measuring fiscal discipline is totally unjustified against the better performing states. FSRII recommended by both the commissions suffers from serious limitations and can affect the allocation and distribution of resources and thereby, growth, development and welfare of the state economies.

Rao et al. (2008) view that in general the state finances has shown a marked improvement recently (with both fiscal and revenue deficits declining during 2007–2008 as compared to 2003 from 8.4% to 5.5% and 5.9% to 1.3%, respectively), but the situation in some of the states still remains grim. According to this study, the improvement in deficit has been brought about by cutting down on developmental expenditure. Thus, fiscal adjustment has been achieved at the cost of economic growth and macroeconomic stabilization.

A concern has also been expressed on the wordings used in the TORs (Terms of References) of the Commission, which raise two important issues, that is, macroeconomic stability and sustainability while recommending transfers. Authors argue that the Commission has to take a holistic view of the requirements with respect to social services without making a distinction between plan and nonplan or revenue and capital sides. Second, it will avoid the perverse incentives from the gap-filling approach. Third, it is possible to design grants to ensure that the states do not substitute their own expenditure for these services. Fourth, this will facilitate human development of poorer states by improving the standard of public services besides contributing to the increase in the productivity.

Bagchi (1997) throws light on cooperative federalism. He points out the evolution of federalism in the United States from dualism (national and subnational units) to 'cooperative federalism'. He argues that when the centre takes on too many functions at their disposal, checks and balances get weakened. For a federal constitution to be stable, the checks and balances must be strengthened in every possible way and a spirit of cooperative federalism must be accommodated in the constitution.

There are other substantive studies on state finances such as the papers by Kochhar, (2004) and Kishore (2007), who argue that federal fiscal relations constitute a vital component in the fiscal arrangements between the centre and states. They favour a leadership role for the centre regarding fiscal consolidation.

The studies cited above either look at the state finances as a whole or are interstate comparative studies. However, the studies pertaining to Gujarat in the post-reform period are lacking. It is this gap that the present study attempts to fill. The rest of the chapter is divided into three sections: Section I presents an introduction; Section II outlines the methodology and Section III highlights the results followed by concluding remarks in the final section.

Methodology

The study uses the annual data provided by the various RBI bulletins on the state finances and Gujarat State Domestic Product, GOG publications. The time period considered for the study spreads over 1980–1981 to 2009–2010. This is further divided into three decades. A comparative analysis of Gujarat with other nonspecial category states has been carried out using ratios and a simple linear regression analysis.

The Findings

Performance of Nonspecial Category States (Aggregate Receipts & Expenditure)

The total receipts and expenditure of the government are the aggregation of the consolidated fund of the state and the balance from the Public Account. Basically, it is divided into revenue and capital account. An analysis of the total receipts and expenditure of nonspecial category states is depicted in Table 9.1 for the period 1980–2010.

Total receipts/SDP ratio accounts for 17–19 per cent in the case of Gujarat, while for all states, it ranges between 18 and 19 per cent. For the year 2010, both receipts and expenditure of Gujarat are found to have declined to 10 and 11 per cent respectively of SDP. In comparison to non-special category states, Gujarat seems to be in a disadvantageous position. Gujarat had occupied ninth position in the eighties and the nineties, while for the year 2000, its rank improved to third position. However, for the year 2010, its rank decreased to 14th position. Over the period 1980–2010, Gujarat receipts growth rate was around 12.73, lower than the all states growth rate of 14.23 per cent.

The state with the highest receipts/SDP ratio was Orissa followed by Bihar. The states that had improved during the period included West Bengal, Madhya Pradesh and Uttar Pradesh.

The aggregate expenditure/SDP ratio of Gujarat ranged between 19 and 24 per cent during the eighties and the nineties (Table 9.1). However, it fell drastically to 15.80 per cent in the year 2005, amounting to a positive sign. Among the nonspecial category states, the position of Gujarat at 9th and 12th rank seemed to be lower as compared to the other states. Bihar accounted for the highest position (ranked 1) with respect to expenditure/SDP ratio

(24%) during the period 1980–2010. The other states that showed high expenditure/SDP ratios were Orissa, Karnataka and Madhya Pradesh.

Table 9.1

Statewise Share of Total Receipts and Expenditure as Per cent of the Gross SDP – NSCS of India

States	*1980 (R)*	*EXP*	*1990-R*	*EXP*	*2000-R*	*EXP*	*2010 (R)*	*EXP*
AP	19.41 (6)	19.65 (8)	19.82 (8)	19.74 (8)	19.15 (9)	19.38 (7)	15.4 (5)	14.7 (7)
Bihar	22.99 (2)	24.35 (1)	22.84 (4)	23.52 (3)	30.55 (1)	29.59 (1)	21.8 (2)	15.3 (6)
Gujarat	18.44 (9)	19.42 (9)	19.68 (9)	19.54 (11)	24.22 (3)	24.45 (3)	10.2 (14)	11.3 (13)
Haryana	17.01 (8)	17.94 (10)	17.99 (12)	17.58 (12)	15.69 (14)	15.77 (4)	11.1 (11)	12.9 (12)
Karnataka	20.32 (5)	20.97 (4)	22.50 (5)	21.37 (6)	19.23 (8)	19.10 (8)	14.5 (7)	14.1 (9)
Kerala	18.21 (10)	19.96 (7)	23.78 (2)	23.95 (9)	17.64 (11)	18.23 (11)	12.1 (10)	13.5 (11)
MP	19.11 (8)	20.41 (6)	19.13 (10)	19.36 (13)	21.84 (4)	21.37 (4)	21.9 (1)	19.9 (1)
Maharashtra	15.38 (12)	15.71 (13)	17.07 (13)	16.72 (14)	16.95 (13)	16.84 (12)	10.4 (13)	11.0 (14)
Orissa	23.47 (1)	23.64 (3)	29.16 (1)	27.98 (1)	24.38 (2)	25.40 (2)	17.5 (4)	17.6 (3)
Punjab	15.20 (13)	16.26 (12)	18.21 (11)	18.00 (9)	19.24 (7)	18.89 (9)	13.8 (8)	15.4 (5)
Rajasthan	21.55 (3)	24.15 (2)	22.42 (6)	22.83 (4)	21.68 (5)	21.22 (5)	15.2 (6)	15.5 (4)
Tamil Nadu	21.03 (4)	20.87 (5)	20.91 (7)	21.13 (7)	16.85 (12)	16.64 (13)	13.2 (9)	13.8 (10)
UP	16.73 (11)	17.15 (11)	23.65 (3)	22.05 (5)	21.38 (6)	20.21 (6)	19.2 (3)	19.0 (2)
WB	14.09 (14)	15.00 (14)	17.06 (14)	17.32 (10)	18.64 (10)	18.63 (10)	10.9 (12)	14.6 (8)
All states	17.78	18.51	19.08	19.06	19.08	23.22	12.6	12.9

Note: Figures in brackets indicate ranks.

Source: *Handbook of Statistics on State Government Finance*, 2004, *State Finance: A Study of Budget*. RBI, CSO. New Delhi.

In terms of the growth rate of expenditure, Gujarat accounted for around 12.73, much lower than the all states growth rates of 14.23 per cent. The states with the highest expenditure growth rate were Maharashtra (14.02), West Bengal (14.01) and Andhra Pradesh (14.00). With respect to nonspecial category states, Gujarat ranked 9th and 13th during the period 1980–2010 except the year in 2000 when it ranked 3rd (Table 9.2).

Table 9.2

Gross Fiscal Deficit of Non Special Category States as Per cent of Gross SDP

	1980	*1990*	*2000*	*2010*
AP	2.71	2.90	5.04	2.4
Bihar	4.57	6.03	8.53	4.1
Gujarat	3.32	6.42	7.19	3.1
Haryana	3.31	2.83	3.90	3.5
Karnataka	3.64	2.40	4.10	2.9
Kerala	4.20	5.66	5.38	2.9
MP	4.33	3.35	3.42	3.5
Maharashtra	2.79	2.50	3.58	2.4
Orissa	3.62	5.65	7.65	2.6
Punjab	3.18	6.58	5.23	3.2
Rajasthan	4.46	2.63	5.23	2.5
Tamil Nadu	2.60	3.59	3.46	3.2
Uttar Pradesh	3.55	5.53	5.61	3.9
West Bengal	2.80	4.69	7.61	4.6
All States	3.03	3.93	4.65	2.7

Source: Handbook of Statistics on State Government Finance, 2004, *State Finance: A Study of Budget*. RBI, CSO. New Delhi.

A look at the final rankings of the states based on the table reveals a pattern that can be clearly categorized as in Box 1:

Bihar and Orissa are found to have registered the highest aggregate receipts/SDP ratio mainly backed by the largest central transfer ratio of 20–35 per cent over the period 1980–2010. The states such as Uttar Pradesh, Madhya Pradesh and Kerala also recorded relatively higher receipts/SDP ratios for the years 2000 and 2005. With regard to all these states, the central transfers accounted for more than half of the revenue receipts.

Box 1

Highest receipts/SDP ratio: Bihar, Orissa, Punjab, Rajasthan, Uttar Pradesh, Karnataka, Andhra Pradesh.

Average receipts/SDP ratio: Gujarat, Kerala, Haryana, Maharashtra, Tamil Nadu.

Poor-receipts/SDP ratio: MP, West Bengal.

Highest expenditure/SDP ratio: Bihar, Orissa, Rajasthan, Uttar Pradesh, Karnataka, MP, Tamil Nadu.

Average expenditure/SDP ratio: Gujarat, Kerala, Haryana, Maharashtra, Andhra Pradesh.

Poor-expenditure/SDP ratio: Punjab, West Bengal

The states such as Karnataka, Kerala, Tamil Nadu and Andhra Pradesh with receipts from their tax sources accounted for nearly 9–12 per cent of SDP over the period 1980–2010. In the case of Gujarat, it is observed that its receipts included own tax revenue followed by central taxes.

The aggregate expenditure as a ratio of gross SDP shows an increase for all the nonspecial category states barring Gujarat, Maharashtra, Haryana and West Bengal. It is also noticed that the increase in expenditure on the part of most of the states was mainly due to an increase in the capital outlay with nondevelopment expenditure playing a significant role.

Some states such as Bihar, Orissa and Haryana also recorded the highest development expenditure, that is, 8–13 per cent of the SDP for the period 1980–2005.

Also revenue expenditure is found greater than revenue receipts, while capital expenditure greater than capital receipts for most of the years over the period 1980–2010. This led to a negative trend in the state finances as an increase in revenue expenditure results in revenue deficit and thereby leading to fiscal deficit. Most of the nonspecial category states are found to have experienced a high deficit/SDP ratio (Table 9.2).

A deficit trend is found on a higher side with respect to Gujarat as compared to other nonspecial category states. Besides an increase in the revenue expenditure, the centre has also failed to provide proper incentives as evidenced by the transfers from the successive

Finance Commissions with Gujarat always ranked 9th and 13th among the nonspecial category states.

Table 9.3

Resource Transfers from the Centre to the States on the Recommendations of Finance Commission – Per cent of Total Assistance Given to All States

States	*VII FC*	*VIII FC*	*IX FC*	*X FC*	*XI FC*	*XII FC*
AP	7.30 (5)	7.34 (5)	7.45 (3)	8.2 (3)	6.90 (4)	6.54 (4)
Bihar	10.67 (2)	10.70 (2)	11.46 (2)	10.6 (2)	10.47 (2)	9.42 (2)
Gujarat	4.62 (9)	3.77 (9)	3.15 (12)	3.76 (11)	3.17 (11)	3.22 (10)
Haryana	1.48 (12)	1.11 (12)	1.1 (14)	1.17 (14)	0.8 (14)	1.02 (13)
Karnataka	4.82 (7)	4.38 (8)	4.20 (10)	4.80 (9)	4.66 (8)	3.96 (9)
Kerala	3.70 (11)	2.27 (10)	3.17 (11)	3.22 (12)	2.86 (12)	2.84 (11)
MP	7.66 (4)	7.50 (4)	6.90 (4)	7.26 (4)	6.27 (5)	5.75 (5)
Maharashtra	8.23 (3)	6.68 (5)	6.49 (6)	5.70 (7)	4.20 (10)	4.56 (8)
Orissa	4.72 (8)	4.84 (7)	4.82 (9)	4.16 (10)	4.52 (9)	4.56 (8)
Punjab	2.01 (12)	1.64 (11)	1.80 (13)	1.63 (13)	1.07 (13)	1.19 (12)
Rajasthan	4.33 (10)	4.25 (9)	5.59 (8)	5.20 (8)	5.62 (6)	5.59 (6)
Tamil Nadu	7.21 (6)	6.05 (6)	6.38 (7)	5.99 (9)	4.81 (7)	4.94 (7)
Uttar Pradesh	15.91 (1)	15.47 (1)	15.09 (1)	16.64 (1)	16.95 (1)	18.56 (1)
West Bengal	7.66 (4)	8.74 (3)	6.82 (5)	6.92 (5)	8.38 (3)	7.57 (3)

Note: Figures in brackets indicate ranks.

Source: Various Finance Commission Reports and Reserve Bank Bulletins.

The total devolution of resources from the centre to Gujarat increased from Rs. 471.9 Cr. in 1980–81 to Rs. 10,594 Cr. in 2008–09, that is, by 22 times (Table 9.3). However, with the increased transfers of resources, the relative importance of components has also changed over time. In 1980–81, tax sharing contributed 40 per cent of the total devolution, while the grants and loans contributed 34 and 25 per cent, respectively. But by 2008–09, tax sharing increased to 57 per cent and grants to 36 per cent while the loans declined to 4 per cent (i.e. the share of loans drastically declined from 25% to 4%). However, it is important to note that during the mid-eighties, when the fiscal crisis had just begun in Gujarat, the share of loans increased to 63 per cent of the total devolution, while the share of tax and grants declined to 13 and 23 per cent, respectively. Thus, Gujarat resorted to borrowing whenever there was a fiscal crisis to supplement its needs. The trend shows that for the entire period, tax sharing became relatively more important as compared to grants and loans. A similar trend is observed across all the states, with the share of tax being higher as compared to grants and loans.

Table 9.3 shows the percentage share of the total resource transfers from the centre to the states in the light of the recommendations of different Finance Commissions. The major aim of the federal financial transfers to the states is to reduce and minimize the inter-state regional and economic disparities and to assess the impact of financial transfers made to the states on the basis of the recommendations. Although each Finance Commission has given its own devolution formula on the basis of its recommendations, still we find that there is not a substantial variation in the total assistance given to states from VII FC to XII FC. Bihar and Uttar Pradesh are found to have been provided with the maximum assistance, while the share of other nonspecial category states varies by 1 or 2 per cent.

Trends in resource transfer show that the total transfers to Gujarat (which comprise tax sharing, loans and grants) have steadily declined over time with the state always remaining at 9th to 12th position among the nonspecial category states. Table 9.3 shows that Bihar and Uttar Pradesh account for 28 per cent of the total share given to all states. However, the states that are found to have improved their ranks include Maharashtra and Andhra Pradesh.

Gujarat is always at a disadvantageous position as compared to other states. Each Finance Commission evolves its own principles for determining the relative share of states. The Finance Commissions have failed to do justice to one of the main objectives of resource transfers in terms of always disfavouring the industrially prosperous states, and their schemes of tax sharing have not been able to fetch the required revenues to the poorer states.[2]

The Gujarat Government has always urged the respective Finance Commissions for a fair share of revenues in order to have more resources at its disposal. The Gujarat Government has stressed the need for sharing the revenues on the basis of other criteria (industrialization, urbanization, etc.) besides population, realizing that this would favour a few states as against all others.

The Tenth Finance Commission recommended uniformity in the allocation of tax proceeds. A major criticism levelled against them is the gap-filling approach[3] underlying them. This gap-filling approach has fortunately led to rewarding those states that have been either lax in their tax collection or incurred large revenue expenditures beyond their potential revenue receipts, while states that follow prudent fiscal policies are being penalized by denying them of their due share in the central transfers.

A major criticism levelled against the Finance Commissions is that in the process of assessing the states, they create an 'artificial equilibrium' in that revenues are overestimated and expenditures are underestimated to reach an artificial equilibrium. This approach of nonmaterialization is disadvantageous to deficit states prior to devolution and not much advantageous to advanced state post-devolution. As a consequence, revenue deficit states have found it difficult to maintain the available base of development services as well as infrastructure, inadequate as it has been all through.

Major Issues in Fiscal Adjustment of Gujarat[4]

Gujarat State and Devolution Formula

Gujarat experienced a low per capita real income of 1.38 per cent per annum before 1980. But after 1980, its per capita income growth rate has hovered around 3.69 per cent per annum. Gujarat's high growth rate can be attributed specially to the massive capital investments in industries, assisted by the oil discoveries and the abundant use of natural gas, which has freed the region from dependence on coal, while the completion of Narmada project has made the state more prosperous as compared to other states in India. Also considered a better performer on the fiscal front, especially in the beginning of the eighties, it enjoys some specific revenue generating resource potential that can play a crucial role in the fiscal disciplining of the state. However, all these positive developments have gone against Gujarat state as devolution is largely made on the basis of a set of criteria, such as population, as well as the so-called socio-economic backwardness and/or economic distance. It is argued that 'the degree of freedom available with the state economies both with respect to revenue collection as well as expenditure is quite less as compared to centre. More importantly, under the name of regional equity the efficiency factor is totally sacrificed'.[5]

Tax Efforts

Second, in the devolution formula, contribution made by a given state to the national basket is not regarded as an important factor. The NFC, TFC and EFC propose to give 10 per cent weight to tax efforts by a state instead of the contribution factor. But the amount is indeed a very meagre incentive as tax efforts are measured by the ratio of per capita own tax revenue of a state to its per capita income as it can be seen from Table 9.4.

Table 9.4

Total Tax Shared by Gujarat as a Proportion of SDP, Growth Rate, Per Capita Tax

Year Gujarat	*Per cent of SDP*	*Growth Rate*	*Per Capita Tax Shared*
1980–1990	1.86	16.51	74.69
1991–2000	1.65	24.84	256.58
2001–2008	1.45	20.04	592.81
1980–2008	1.68	20.49	287.68
All States			
1980–1990	3.00	14.28	108.16
1991–2000	3.06	13.75	343.97
2001–2008	2.92	16.82	888.75
1980–2008	2.97	14.82	415.40

Source: *Handbook of Statistics on State Government Finances*, RBI, 2004, Various State Finance Reports of RBI.

As a proportion of the gross SDP, the ratio of per capita own tax revenue accounts for 1–2 per cent for the period 1980–2010, which is quite less than the Gujarat own tax revenue which ranges between 5 and 7 per cent of the gross SDP. However, the growth rate seems to hover between 16 and 24 per cent. This means it could be an elastic source of revenue, depending on the will and desirability of the central government. The per capita tax shared works out to Rs. 287, much less than the national average of Rs. 415.

As mentioned earlier, there are three types of major taxes shared between the centre and the states with the most important among them being income tax.

Inequitable Basis of Distribution

The Finance Commission supports a positive discrimination (i.e. to reduce the regional disparities among the states) on the basis of responsibilities towards the poor states. Therefore, the main justification for giving a larger share of tax on the basis of collection seems to be an inequitable basis of distribution. In this regard, Vittal (1988) pointed out that both the Planning Commission and Finance Commission have similar approach of penalizing the efficient and rewarding the inefficient states, as both of them have somewhat subjective approach for devolving the resources among the states. Gujarat is one among them.

The corporate tax and customs duty, which are known to be more income elastic in nature, are not shared at all with the states in accordance with the constitutional arrangements. The TFC has suggested in its alternative scheme that all central taxes be pooled together and that 29 per cent of the total tax revenues be allocated to the states. Somehow, the FC has dropped the idea as experts feel that this would not in any way result in any substantial difference in the revenue allocation unless a drastic change is effected in the formula.

State Right

The state can't exercise its right to impose sales tax on sugar, tobacco and the textiles as the centre levies additional excise in lieu of sales tax. Not only that the proceeds from this duty are distributed among all the states and that according to the progressive formula as well. The progressive formula indicates relatively higher shares to relatively poor states except the state of Gujarat.

In this regard, Dholakia (2000: 3219) observes, 'The changes in the distribution formulae shows that the Eleventh Finance Commission has been particularly against the interest of industrially prosperous, trade intensive and marginally better-off states, like Gujarat. This is because the growth of industries and trade in Gujarat which is in the range of 10 to 12 per cent in real terms during the late eighties and nineties would have certainly led to larger and larger contribution to the central exchequer during all these years'. Moreover, over the last few years, income from agriculture in Gujarat has declined significantly relative to other sectors despite the fact that agricultural incomes are not taxed like the nonagricultural incomes. Gujarat's contribution even in terms of income tax will be growing substantially over the years.

State Indebtedness

Gujarat, a revenue surplus state before 1985, has changed into a revenue deficit state. This means that what was earlier a nondebt creating source of financing has become a source of rising internal indebtedness. Earlier, the revenue receipts were used to cover part of the capital expenditure, but now an increasing part of the capital receipts are used to finance revenue expenditure. The consequent build up of public debt and the interest burden (now the largest and fastest growing item of expenditure) has further increased the growth of revenue expenditure, leading in the process to a spiral of growing deficit, rising debt and interest costs and further expansion of deficit.

Second, sectors such as irrigation, power, and road transport that constitute a major part of the state government investment do not seem to yield enough returns.

Grants

The central government extends grants on average and percentage basis and does not take into consideration the actual needs and performance. Besides the provision of grants are covered by many conditions and constraints. The various memorandums submitted by Gujarat urge the Commission that the grants be considered as needs-oriented assistance.

Table 9.5

Grants as Per Cent of Gross SDP and Their Growth Rates

Year	*Per cent of gross SDP*	*Growth rate*	*Per capita grant shared*
Gujarat			
1980–1990	1.44	17.50	61.50
1991–2000	1.09	24.50	168.54
2001–2008	1.32	16.98	504.75
1980–2008	1.28	19.85	226.37
All States			
1980–1990	2.25	10.05	102.97
1991–2000	2.26	12.08	229.79
2001–2008	2.46	19.24	166.89
1980–2008	1.08	16.26	166.53

Source: Handbook of Statistics on State Government Finances, RBI, 2004, Various State Finance Reports of RBI.

The share of Gujarat in the total grants shared by the centre has declined from 4.52 to 2.88 per cent. Table 9.5 shows that grants as a proportion of SDP range between 1 and 2 per cent for the entire period 1980–2008. The average growth rate is around 19 per cent, which is more than the all states average growth rate of 16 per cent. The per capita grant of Gujarat amounts to Rs. 226, which is higher than that of all states at Rs. 166.5.

The First to Eighth Finance Commissions have confined themselves to the nonplan revenue accounts of the states in terms of determining the grants equal to deficit of each state so that the nonplan revenue accounts of all the states remain balanced or are left with a surplus every year. The Finance Commission has identified Gujarat as a high-income state. Thus grants-in-aid along with shared taxes serve as a levelling up force to promote a balanced development of the region. Therefore, grants given to Gujarat state remain very low as compared to other states.

The state government has strongly argued with the respective Finance Commissions that such a gap-filling approach for sharing grants-in-aid does not facilitate financial discipline among the states. Such an approach, instead, will discourage the deficit states in terms of raising resources of their own and exercising a proper and adequate control on expenditure.

Loans

The proportion of Gujarat in terms of loans shared with other states seems to be quite less. It can be observed from Table 9.6 that the total loan share has declined from 5.4 per cent in 1980–1981 to 2.7 per cent in 2008 (BE). However, for the year 2005, the total per cent of loans shared by the centre is found to have increased to 16.7 per cent. The share of loans as per cent of capital expenditure has also declined from 30 per cent to 0.04 per cent, which is considered a good sign.

However, we cannot deny the fact that the Finance Commission assists the states, with respect to both the development and nondevelopment expenditure. It is a unique feature of the Indian Constitution with no parallel existing in the federal constitutions of the world.

According to Bird (2000, p. 209), 'what is critical about intergovernmental transfers is that who gives them, or who gets them, or what the details of programme design are does not matter so much as their effects on policy objectives. As with user charges, the idea is to get the 'prices right' in the public sector by designing transfers so that they do not weaken the hard budget constraints that exist if local citizens are not only able to determine what services they get but also to pay for them'.

Table 9.6

A Profile of Loans Shared by the Centre to Gujarat State

Year	*Loans Extended by the Centre to States (Cr.)*	*Per cent of Total Loans Given by the Centre to Gujarat*	*Loans as Per cent of Capital Expenditure of Gujarat*
1980–1981	3,021.9	5.41	30.33
1985–1986	8,368.3	5.54	71.10
1990–1991	13,974.3	6.32	63.63
1995–1996	19,599.9	6.67	63.98
2000–2001	107,484	10.6	39.40
2005–2006	178,871	16.7	1.31
2008–2009 (BE)	331,525	2.7	0.64

Source: Handbook of Statistics on State Government Finances, RBI, 2004, Various State Finance Reports of RBI.

Conclusions

1. Gujarat's aggregate receipts and expenditure have increased both in absolute and relative terms, but in comparison with other nonspecial category states, it has not emerged as a good performer state.
2. The Finance Commission is a constitutional body with an autonomous status to which the states represent their case for their just and fair share of resources. From a collective point of view, the states are more interested in vertical justice in the form of greater devolutions from the centre, while an individual state is keen on horizontal justice in the *inter se* allocations.
3. Over the years, however, the transfer of resources from the centre to the states has happened in such a way that the state indebtedness to the centre has gone up resulting in widening fiscal gaps and mounting repayment liabilities. This gap has further gained momentum with liberalization and economic reforms.

4. The most important factor is that the states are not vested with powers to levy taxes that are shared with the centre. All taxes such as personal income tax, corporation tax, customs duties, excise duties, tax on nonagricultural wealth and tax on inter-state trade rest with the centre. The centre collects about 60 per cent of the total tax revenues through states, while states' own collection including the local governments constitutes about 40 per cent. Nearly 56 per cent of the direct taxes and 54 per cent of taxes on commodities are collected by the centre. Approximately, the total expenditure responsibility met by states amounts to 60 per cent. This would indicate that the vertical imbalances work out to about 20 per cent. It is this centralization of tax powers vis-à-vis decentralization of expenditure responsibilities that needs to be addressed by the Finance Commission in determining the respective shares. Gujarat's memorandum to the Eleventh Finance Commission suggested that there was a need to assign more taxation powers to states. The report quoted that this issue was very urgent in the context of the 73rd and 74th Amendments of the Constitution and the consequent appointment of the State Finance Commission whose recommendations were to be taken into consideration while determining new devolutions. Gujarat with its strong local government institutions – both urban and rural – has a special interest in advancing the interests of local governments, because unlike many other states, these bodies have a record of autonomy and regular elections. As of now, almost all such institutions are under democratically elected administration, indicating a high degree of commitment on the part of the state government to ensure their democratic functioning.
5. Over the years, the issue of contribution has been entirely pushed to the background while giving predominance to needs only. This has worked as a disincentive to the states, particularly Gujarat, which is capable of making rigours efforts to support and sustain a greater collection of tax revenues, leading to a greater sharing.
6. Gujarat has suffered badly with respect to the horizontal sharing of resources. The respective Finance Commissions are justified in terms of following a positive discrimination, that is, to reduce the regional disparities. But this is also working as a disincentive

in terms of promoting growth, which alone can augment the shareable revenue pool. The Tenth Finance Commission adopted the criterion 'backwardness' with respect to sharing the divisible pool. Gujarat's share happens to be less both in terms of population and backwardness.

7. Gujarat, particularly, with its forward looking industrial and other economic policies has succeeded in attracting the largest share of investment flows in the post-reform period and would naturally contribute more to the central government in a proportionate manner. If such efforts by the states go unnoticed, it will not only work as a disincentive to the state, but also in the long run, undermine the future tax revenue prospects. It is not now accepted by all that the present design of horizontal sharing has not brought about a greater fiscal discipline among states nor does this method take into account the impact on equity and efficiency.

Thus, the above analysis supports the view that there is a need for evaluating the centre–state fiscal adjustment relationship. This is essential as Gujarat state is now heavily dependent on the centre for financial resources. Second, the devolution formula devised by the successive Finance Commissions shows the discretionary transfer of resources out of the total transfers, and third, there is a tremendous increase in the magnitude of internal debt, which may lead the state into a debt trap.

The implications of the Eleventh Finance Commission with references made to the better performing states such as Gujarat are adverse and have not done justice to the progress achieved by the state so far. It is disappointing that the Finance Commissions have made Gujarat pay a heavy development price for the growth of other less efficient backward states.

Notes

1. See RBI (2004) Reports on Currency and Finances: State Finances.
2. See White Paper on Gujarat Finance (2000).
3. See, Reports of the Sarkaria Commission (1987)
4. Government of Gujarat, Memorandum to Finance Commission, 1977, 1988, 1993, 1999, 2002.
5. See Dholakia (1996).

References

Ahluwalia, M. 2000. 'Economic Performance of States in Post-Reforms Period', *Economic and Political Weekly*, Vol. 34, No. 19, pp. 1637–1647.

Bagchi, 1997. 'Rethinking Federalism: An Overview of the Current Debates with some Reflections in the Indian Context', in Rao. G. (ed.) *Development, Poverty and Fiscal Policy*, India: Oxford University Press.

Bird, R.M. 2000. 'Intergovernmental Fiscal Relations', In M. Govinda Rao (ed.), *Universal Principles, Development, Poverty and Fiscal Policy*, New Delhi: Oxford University Press.

Dholakia, A. 1996. 'Role of the Centre in Fiscal Balances of States: The Case of Gujarat', paper presented at *Prof. L.K. Lakadwala Memorial Seminar* held at M.S. University of Baroda, p. 10.

Dholakia, A. 2000. 'Fiscal Imbalances in Gujarat: Non-Tax Revenue & Subsidies', *Economic and Political Weekly*, Vol. 35, Nos. 35–36, August 26–September 2, p. 3219.

Dholakia, A. 2005. 'Measuring Fiscal Performance of States: An Alternative Approach', *Economic and Political Weekly*, Vol. 40, No. 31, July 30–August 5, pp. 3421–3428.

Government of Gujarat. *Memorandum to Finance Commission, 1977, 1988, 1993, 1999, 2002.* Gandhinagar: Finance Department.

Kishore, A. 2007. 'Indian Sub National Finances: Recent Performances', Working Paper WP/07/205, IMF.

Kochhar, K. 2004. 'India: Macroeconomic Implications of the Fiscal Imbalances', paper presented at NIPFP Conferences on Fiscal Policy in India, IMF.

RBI Report on State Finances: A Study of Budgets, A Various Issues of State Supplements. Reserve Bank of India, Mumbai.

Report of the Sarkaria Commission, October 27, 1987. New Delhi; Finance Commission, pp. 274–276.

Reports on Currency and Finances 2004, State Finances, Reserve Bank of India, Mumbai.

Rao, M.G. 2002. 'State Finances in India: Issues and Challenges'. *Economic and Political Weekly*, Vol. 37, No. 31, August 3, pp. 3261–3271.

Rao, G., Sen, T., and Jena Pratap. 2008. 'Issues before the Thirteen Finance Commission', Working Paper 2008–55, New Delhi: NIPFP.

Vittal, B.P.R. 1988. 'Alternative to Devolutions: Implications of Tenth Finance Commission Scheme', *Economic and Political Weekly*, Vol. 23, No. 40, October 1.

White Paper on Road Map for Fiscal Reforms in Gujarat (2000), Gujarat Chamber of Commerce and Industry, Ahmedabad.

10

Federalism and Regionalism in India

Nagindas Sanghavi

This chapter revolves around two arguments. First argument is that a purely legalistic approach would not be very fruitful in understanding either India or Indian federal institutions as they are under constant evolution. The Constitution is a legal document for the lawyers and for the judiciary. But for students of political developments, the Constitution is as much a political document as it is a legal one. Second, regionalism is not such an unadulterated evil as it is made out to be. Regions and regional interests are part of life in India and can also play a positively contributory role in the development of Indian polity. Federalism is still a rarity among the nations. Only 24 countries out of a total of 193 in the world have adopted a federal form of government. There is still no consensus among political scientists as to what constitutes the essential features of a federal structure. Legally and constitutionally, India is a federation, but its status is disputed and its claim protested by several scholars. This overcentralized Constitution is getting corrected by the political processes that recognize the reality of regional demands.

The Constitution of India is more a product of the pressures and strains of the historical situations rather than a product of the aspirations and beliefs of its people or its leaders. It was a knee jerk reaction to the situational stress that obtained in India during the forties of the last century. The process of drafting of the Indian Constitution is an interesting story with so many unexpected turns and twists. In spite of the flamboyant claims made about its absolute freedom and power to draft any constitution of its choice, the Assembly when it met (9 December 1946) was bound hands and feet by the Cabinet Mission Plan and was handicapped by the absence of its Muslim members. Mr Churchill and Lord Simon denounced this assembly as being an assemblage of caste Hindus (December 1946).

Entrusted with an impossible task of creating a confederation of two-tier federal unions of warring communities, the Assembly was a helpless witness to the events that were happening outside. It also suffered from a continuous flow of members joining and leaving. It was adjourned very frequently, often for months on end and its real work did not begin till November 1947. The Assembly was overwhelmed by the disastrous turn of events and underwent a complete metamorphosis as it were about its purpose and attitude on account of partition and independence. Furious and frustrated by the vivisection of the country and its aftermath and frightened by the cacophony of several fissiparous demands from the regions for Sikhistan, Dravidistan and Dalitstan, the Assembly with a vengeance dumped the Cabinet Mission Plan on a dung heap and went full circle to work for a highly centralized structure for India.

The Assembly had to struggle with stupendous problems of refugees and riots, murder of Gandhi, integration of native states, administrative imbroglios, the looming war with Pakistan and the possibility of India getting broken up into pieces. All these possibilities and a series of catastrophes made the Assembly forge a document that was unitary in nature with a few federal features rather than a federation with a few unitary features. Such a document answered the needs of the day. The regional leaders and regional governments at that moment were incapable of dealing with the Herculean tasks that could be handled only by the collective strength of the entire country through its central government. The overcentralized federation of the forties and fifties was a situational response to the frightful conditions then prevailing. The hostility of the Constituent Assembly to anything even remotely smacking of regional interest, much less to regional autonomy or regional identity, was quite palpable. Those days are over and those circumstances have changed. But there was one regional demand that could not be entirely rejected. Several leaders insisted on the linguistic reorganization of the provinces. This demand was part of a struggle for national independence and was an age-old demand in India even before Gandhi arrived on the scene.

Gandhi had accepted the demand and had reorganized the units of the Congress Party on linguistic basis. The British authorities who had burnt their fingers in Bengal in 1905 were reluctant to openly support any such demand, but both the provinces that were carved out in 1935 – Sindh and Orissa – were linguistic units. The Congress Party in its manifestoes of 1936 and in 1945 had promised the linguistic reorganization of provinces at the earliest opportunity. But the times in 1947 were not propitious for such a drive. It was not possible to cater to any such regional demand in the midst of prevailing fear and anxiety as to where regional pressures might lead. The Linguistic Provinces Commission – the Dhar Commission – issued a grim warning. 'Indian nationalism is deeply wedded to its regional languages ... Indian Nationalism is aggressively attached to its provincial frontiers'. This report was resented by the Assembly and JVP committee tried to assuage the hurt feelings by conceding the legitimacy of the regional demand while pleading unfavourable circumstances. The committee justified the immediate formation of Andhra Pradesh by separating Telugu-speaking areas from the province of Madras.

It was in order to cater to this insistent demand that Articles. 3 and 4 were incorporated in the Constitution giving authority to the Union Parliament which by passing a simple law can make, unmake and remake the states as the units of Indian federation. Such power of life and death is blatantly un-federal if not decidedly antifederal. It is interesting to note that the word federal is nowhere used in the Constitution, the preferred term being the Union. India was to be a Union of States that were non-existent. There were only provinces of a unitary state, as the federal part of the 1935 Act was never implemented. The Republican Constitution of India was imposed from above and was accepted willingly and with acclamation.

Such a centralizing approach was aided by the long and strong administrative traditions under the British regime and the constitutional set-up under the Government of India Act of 1935. The single party domination both in the public life and in the Constituent Assembly reinforced the tendency and made it easy for such a constitution to be accepted without a murmur.

Moreover, the Assembly had to undertake the burden of functioning as a legislative body and this deprived the Assembly of time and energy that could have been devoted to its mission with the result that a large portion of Government of India Act 1935 got incorporated in the Constitution of the Republic making it more an administrative manual rather than a political document. A constitution amending more than 100 times in less than 60 years cannot be rated as a very satisfactory document. Apart from such formal changes, the Constitution has undergone a few formal and nonformal changes. The laws about the Right to Information and the Right to Education have converted Directive Principles into legal rights and the bill for the Right to Food Security is pending. These laws have no constitutional status and are not treated as fundamental rights. But to my mind, they are more basic and fundamental than the entire Part III of the Constitution. A hungry man, an uneducated man and a man without full and proper information can neither claim nor exercise any right.

The judiciary has virtually abolished capital punishment for most of the crimes and for most of the criminals. What I am trying to argue is that the legal form of the Constitution is not a reliable guide to the understanding of the Indian federal polity. No country is or can ever be governed entirely by its constitution. A constitution or a law is a mere document that needs to be humanized and implemented by human activities. The constitutions are mere machines that are worked upon by a parallelogram of political forces. In case of a conflict between such forces and law, it is the law that has to adjust. If we insist too much on legalism, then we have to declare England to be a Monarchy and China a Democracy and Japan a country without any defence organization. What is happening in other countries has happened also in India and several provisions of the Constitution are by now mere legal fictions. We ought to get out of the box to observe and evaluate Indian federalism on the basis of the prevailing and evolving structure of the Constitution.

A federation has been defined as 'a permanent union of the permanent units'. This definition does not apply to India. Here, the Union is permanent, but the units are in a flux. The political map of India is continuously changing and even after six decades, we are not sure that it will not change further. But this is not the only un-federal feature of our constitution. There are many such other provisions.

The governors of the states are appointed by the Union and are expected to act as the agents of the Union sending periodic reports on the affairs of the state. The administrative directives issued by the Union bureaucrats are binding on the state administration. The governments and the assemblies of the states can be dissolved by the Union government at its untrammeled discretion. During the Emergency, the federal structure is converted into a unitary one and can be reverted at the end of the Emergency. Such double convertibility is a unique feature of Indian Constitution. The antiregional bias is clearly the informing approach of the Constitution makers. The Constitution is suffused with a notion that regions are incompetent and unreliable if not positively antinational and that it would be dangerous to trust them with powers and responsibilities.

The Union government in India enjoys primacy in administrative matters and the financial resources are allotted in such a lopsided manner that the Union is a rich Uncle who can make the poor nephews dance to his tune. It is calculated that the Union government collects the revenues that are equal to nearly two-third of the total revenues of all the states put together. All the welfare activities are the responsibility of the states, but they do not have enough revenues. They are totally dependent on the federal funds and grants and loans. The states never have enough, so every state complains of injustice being done to it by the government of Delhi.

The Union government in India is always called the central government though there can be no such centre of power in a federation. The legal provisions of the Constitution were politically reinforced by a dominant and democratic one-party system often referred to as the Congress system. India was fortunate that it had such a party that dominated the political life and provided a shield to the nascent democratic institutions. For the first twenty years of the Republic, the Congress Party dominated the public life from the Parliament to the panchayats and was the only avenue for political advancement. The party rode rough shod over regional aspirations and sentiments and continuously interfered in the states changing its political composition by dismissing governments and leaders at its own sweet will in the name of party discipline and party interests. The efforts to build up a national party as an alternative to the Congress failed as was the case in the efforts of Kisan Mazadoor Lok Paksh (KMLP), the Socialists, the Swatantra and the Communist Party of India (CPI).

The nonfederal features in the Indian federation have been picked up by the political scientists to deny the status of federation to the Indian Constitution. India has been designated quasi-federal – something like a federation, but not exactly a federation, because it is more unitary than federal in its structure and in the division of powers and resources. But such a purist approach is invalid on two counts. There is no exact model of what is federal and what is not federal. As Ronald Watts, quoted by Professor Bhattacharya, said 'There is no single pure model of federation. The notion of evolving a combination of shared rule for some purposes and self rule for others within a single political system so that neither is subordinate to the other has been applied in different ways to fit different circumstances' (New federalism – Experiments in Commonwealth). The circumstances in India are immensely variegated because India is a land of many lands and a symphony of many cultures.

The second objection that can be raised against calling India quasi-federal is that such an approach prevents us from understanding the prevailing ground realities. Let us take one example. The Constitution that came into existence in January 1950 had a state structure that was clumsy, crazy, untenable and unviable. It violated almost every single principle of federalism and was so obviously an unstable equilibrium that it could not be expected to last long. The fact that it could exist for six decades can be attributed to the Congress system.

After some forty Acts and the report of the States Reorganization Commission (1956) that structure has been so completely swept away, nobody now even remembers what it was like. I plead guilty to describe it in some details only for the sake of record.

In 1950, the states were grouped into four categories and there was no uniformity of powers and status among them. Group A consisted of nine former provinces of the British regime (Assam, Bihar, Bengal, Bombay, Madras, Madhya Pradesh, Orissa, Punjab and Uttar Pradesh). They were full-fledged units of the federation enjoying all the powers conferred on the units and working through representative institutions specified in the Constitution.

Class B consisted of the former Indian states or unions created by the merger of such states (Rajasthan, Hyderabad, Kashmir, Saurashtra, Madhya Bharat, Mysore, PEPSU and Travancore-Cochin). They had representative institutions, but they were subject to greater supervision and guidance from the central government and their autonomy was restricted by the directives issued by the bureaucrats from Delhi. More backward areas in British territory and in the Indian states (a total of 11) were grouped into Class C (Ajmer, Bhopal, Bilaspur, Chandranagar, Coorg, Himachal Pradesh, Kachchha, Manipur, Matsya, Tripura and Vidya Pradesh). The conditions in Group C states varied from unit to unit: some states were more free than others, but all were under direct and continuous supervision and control of the Union government. All of them were represented in the Parliament. Andaman was a mere administrative unit under the direct rule by the central government and was designated as a Group D state. It was not represented in the Parliament. Such a ramshackle and weird structure could not and did not last long and started changing since 1953. It received a deathblow in 1956, when the entire structure was altered and given more or less a final shape. After 1956, all states were put on the footing of equality and union territories were under the direct control of Delhi.

How do we evaluate such a changing and evolving structure of Indian federation? The political evaluation should be concerned more with the facts of life rather than with mere legal or constitutional statements. Take, for example, the power to kill or create a state at its sole discretion that is given to the Union Authority. Such power is a blatant denial of the principle as well as the practice of federalism. But the power that represents centralization at its worst has always been a playground for the regional pressures, and the entire process of reorganization of the states is an interesting example of how the Constitution works in actual practice. It is true that the political landscape of India has been and is still under a flux. Several states have been killed and many new ones created and a few are still waiting to be born.

Due to the explosive situation in Andhra (1953), a reluctant, angry and frustrated Nehru had to concede the regional demand to create a new state. Since then, be it in 1956, 1960, 1963,1966, 1988 and 2003 and thereafter, the states have been created, destroyed, reshaped and renamed in accordance with the regional pressures much against the desire and often against the interests of the federal government. Parliament has become a mere registering body rubber stamping what the local leadership had decided. The real power of state reorganization is exercised not by the Union but by the concerned regions. It is Mayawati who advocates the break-up of UP, and Telangana would be created in Hyderabad, not Delhi. Articles 3 and 4 are mere legal fictions.

Of all the political forces that operate on the Constitution and make it tick, the most potent and the most spectacular force is the Political Parties and the nature of polity being federal or nonfederal ought to be determined by examining the prevailing party system. India started with a peculiar party system. One party dominated the political life at all levels, and Nehru was the unquestioned crown of the Congress system. But he had to deal with several stalwarts whose opinions and demands could not be denied. Sardar Patel, Rajendra Prasad, Rajagopalachari, Maulana Azad and several others could not be easily pushed aside or neglected. Even regional leaders – Dr Bidhan Chandra Roy, Pandit Pant, Moraji Desai, Dwarka Prasad Mishra and Anugrah Narayan Sinha – often defied the directives of Congress High Command and did what they wanted to do. Later on Kamaraj, Atulya Ghosh and Yashwantrao Chavan led the second-generation leaders of the Congress Party. This generation started dying in the first and second decade after independence and the Congress Party started dying with them.

Under the aegis of the Congress system, no nationwide alternative party could emerge for two decades. But there were a few regional parties that were strong in their respective areas. Akali Dal in Punjab, DMK in Tamil Nadu, and small parties in Nagaland are some such examples. The Communist Party was active only in Bengal and Andhra. As compared to Socialist Party that claimed a national party status, the CPI, a sort of regional outfit, got less votes but more seats in Lok Sabha (1951–1952). In 1957 elections, the CPI that had only regional presence in Bengal and Kerala emerged as the largest party in Kerala Vidhan Sabha and formed the government. This became a worldwide phenomenon, as for the first time in the world the Communists won a majority in a free election. Unfortunately, this first experiment of a regional party government was short lived with Namboodiripad Ministry dismissed by the Union government by misusing the emergency powers. Nehru felt uneasy as such an action was both undemocratic and unconstitutional.

The Congress domination was challenged for the first time in 1967 not by any national party but by the regional parties. The Congress Party lost power in eight states and was replaced by the ministries of Samyukta Vidhayak Dals that were dominated by the regional parties – Bangla Congress, Jana Congress, DMK, Akali Dal, Haryana Vikas Party and several such other parties. The first step in changing the balance of power between the Union and the states had been taken. The governors were the visible victims of this change with several of them having had to face the music, but what happened to Dharam Vir in Bengal was a clear warning to the Union to behave.

Indira Gandhi threw out the dead wood in the Congress Party (1969); but instead of establishing a collective leadership, she unfortunately converted the Congress into a personal fiefdom and made loyalty the supreme test for distributing power and pelf. This inexorably led to the misuse of authority and a brush with a mild dose of despotism. The Congress suffered a body blow (1977) and has never recovered from the wound. The party needed the bloody sacrifices of its leaders to recover its domination in 1984 and 1991.

The increasing regionalization of Indian federalism can be accounted for by the emerging pattern of the party system. The attempts to build up a national alternative to the Congress Party did not succeed for a long period and the vacuum left by the decline of the Congress has been filled up by the regional parties. All governments at the federal level after 1988 have been multi-party outfits or have been dependent on outside support. Lately, the national parties have willy-nilly entered into coalitions with the regional parties and regional parties have managed to exert a significant pressure on them in terms of adjusting their party-based political ideologies according to the regional pressures. The pre-eminence of the regional parties has been quite assertive during the last two decades and the federal government is feeling the crushing burden of regionalism. A new balance of power is asserting itself and the Constitution has undergone subtle and unnoticed changes towards more and more regionalization of Indian federalism.

The nature of Indian polity depends on the balance of power that would be guided by the shape that our party system would finally assume. This system is still evolving and we have to wait to assess its growth and the resultant scenario. The classification of the political parties by the Election Commission can hardly be accepted. Several parties listed as national by the Commission (BSP, SP, CPI and CPM) have no presence except in the state of their domination.

They should be treated as regional parties together with other parties that profess to be regional in their approach and ambitions.

The political scenario is still largely dominated by the much eroded and much weakened Congress, while BJP is striving hard to match with the Congress. The Congress still rules over 12 states, while BJP enjoys power in 6 states. Ten states including UP, Bihar, Punjab, Bengal, Tamil Nadu, Kashmir and Odisha are under the control of the regional parties. Tamil Nadu has been ruled by regional parties since 1967 and Bengal has gone under regional parties since 1977. What will be the shape of Indian federation in view of the increasing presence and pressures from the regional parties is anybody's guess. The actual authority and the powers exercised by the Union government would depend not so much on the constitutional provisions as on the functioning of the party system.

The emergence of the strongly entrenched regional parties at the state level has already induced several informal changes in the federal relations. The governors have to be acceptable to the regional leaders. The lopsided allocation of financial resources and administrative powers is being increasingly challenged and gradually adjusted to the new environment under the euphemism of grants, aid, subsidies or package deal. The regional pressures are being reflected in the influence exerted by the state parties in what is known as coalitional politics, and the federal government has started confessing helplessness in the absence of regional support. Several policy decisions (e.g. foreign direct investment (FDI) in retail trade, National Counter Terrorism Centre [NCTC]) have to be kept pending for such a long time and to such an extent that the federal government is charged with policy paralysis.

The increasing regionalization of the federation has whipped up a debate about the future of India as a state, and several prophets of doom have predicted that the regional rivalries and antagonisms would lead to disintegration of India in very near future. We were told in 1956 that India had already entered such a dangerous decade and that the elections of 1967 would be the last democratic elections in India. We have been listening to such prophesies since long but after six decades, India is still a thriving and a pulsating democracy despite its persisting inadequacies.

Regionalism has always been projected as a sinister, divisive and disintegrating factor in Indian politics, and some sort of phobia and a lot of prejudices have always been displayed about what was happening at the state level. We always look askance at anything that even remotely smacks of regional identity. The emphasis on regional language or regional interests unnerves us, and we denounce them without any attempt to either understand them or understand their *raison d'etre*. There is no inherent or necessary contradiction between regional and national interests. India is constituted of the regions that are the integral parts of its identity. Many of us are still worried about the linguistic reorganization of the states and the controversies that preceded it. There is no factual data that the linguistic states have in any way harmed Indian unity or loyalty of Indians to the nation.

There is no valid reason to believe that regional leaders are in any way less competent or less patriotic than the so-called national leaders. Except for a few leaders of the Congress and BJP who have no regional basis, most of the national leaders have graduated from the regional politics, and they have played a very significant role in maintaining the unity and integrity of the nation. Many of them have returned from the national level to the regional leadership (Nitish Kumar, Mulayam Singh Yadav, Mamta Banerjee and Prithviraj Chavan). They never seem to experience any contradiction between national and regional interests.

It would be rather absurd to suggest that they were nationalist while at the centre and turned antinational the moment they went back to their regions.

The analysis of Indian politics almost always deplores the increasing potency of regionalism in the form of regional parties or regional loyalties. It is widely assumed that such regional chauvinism as witnessed in Punjab (Khalistan) or in Maharashtra (Shiv Sena) would weaken the national ties, undermine patriotic zeal and would pose a serious threat of balkanization to the Indian polity. Punjab is a special case, but Shiv Sena yields to none in patriotic fervour. We always juxtapose regionalism and nationalism as if they were basically and eternally exclusive and antagonistic to each other. This sounds rather strange in view of the fact that regions have always been the couriers and the crucibles of Indian culture.

It is high time we take a fresh look at the entire issue *de novo*. There is no logical reason and no factual data to believe in such antagonism between the regions and the nation. Devotion to one's region does not necessarily involve any hostility to the national wellness. Regionalism is bound to be a major political parameter in a society as heterogeneous and complex as ours. 'Persistent regionalism often verging on separatism may well be rooted in manifold and complex cultural diversities or in extreme regional unevenness and inequalities in progress and prosperity' (Source unknown). Such factors inculcate 'a sense of enduring deprivation due to long term neglect in development and resource redistribution' (Source unknown).

We are overlooking the fact that devotion and loyalty to smaller units does not necessarily involve any hostility to the larger unit. Man is an animal of several components and is quite capable of being simultaneously devoted to several groups at various levels. Indian culture is largely a summation of regional cultures and it is this culture complex that has preserved the unity of India in spite of multifarious pluralities that have bewildered the observers. Regionalism does not always foster fissiparous tendencies, and such a development may be due to real or perceived injustice felt by the region concerned. The regions can as well be the building blocks for the nation. A chain or a structure is as strong or as weak as the strength or weakness of its components. A prosperous Bihar or a vibrant Gujarat is an asset rather than a threat to Indian unity. The Indian national interests may be best preserved by strong regions and by regionalization of the national polity.

A brief but intense interlude of the supremacy of the nation–states during the nineteenth and twentieth centuries in Europe ought not to blind us to what is happening around us. Even Europe is retrieving its lost multiregion character in the form of European Union. The globalization involves not only global economy but also a global spirit. In the emerging brave new world of supra-national entities, regionalism may well occupy a place of pride.

11

Federalism and Regionalism in India in the Age of Globalization

Harihar Bhattacharyya

> The right of self-determination does not necessarily entail secession; the costs of secession militate strongly against it.
>
> —Michael Keating 2001: 61

One of the reasons why I wanted to start this discussion with the above statement by Keating, one of the leading experts on regionalism in Western Europe (Keating 2001), is to indicate that the lingering doubts surrounding the idea of regionalism, which has received, and continues to receive, in most cases, negative responses from the powers that is prone to consider it a law and order problem, require a Hobbesian solution. The second reason is to draw our attention to the embedded core of regionalism in multiethnic societies, the core being self-determination of communities and peoples, most often articulated in the same language of national self-determination as a Mazzini or a Lenin or even a Wilson would have done for us. Eric Hobsbawm (1992: 163–193), a famous British historian, reminds us that even with respect to the nationalistic break-up of the former USSR, the splitting 'nations' resorted to the same script though the context was so vastly different. To reflect a little further on the issue, by prefacing my discussion, I would like to cite two reasons why such a script is not usually considered as something positive, and also why regionalism is often taken to be something of a taboo, like the 'F' word for federalism.

First, nation–state construction followed since the days of the French Revolution (1798) was ontologically flawed because the informing paradigm was homogenizing when the societies had had strong region-specific social and cultural differences. Second, the whole project was highly centralizing in nature, a hangover of sorts from the days of European absolutism (Anderson 1979) and, hence, would not concede any move for decentralization, or regionalization of political power. No wonder, one hardly hears about regional murmur in Switzerland, ethno-regionally a very complex and diverse country in the West where federalism and regionalism, or region-specific identity have, historically speaking, reinforced each other in a dynamic political equilibrium (Bhattacharyya 2001). The Swiss case, otherwise a late comer in modern state building (post-1848), had then appeared to be an exception when her big neighbours such as Germany, France and Italy were actively engaged in building centralized modern nation–states. However, in hindsight, it is clear that the reverse was in fact the case. As Moreno (2001: 206), a distinguished Spanish scholar on federalism and regionalism, informs us, Spain had begun to confront regionalism in different forms clamouring for the recognition of ethno-regional identities such as the Basque Country, the Catalan, Galicia, Valencia, Andalusia and Asturias from the late nineteenth century onwards, surfacing again and again ever since going further. He informs us that the 'regional autonomy' question also played a fundamental part in the political polarization leading up to the Civil War (1936–39) (Moreno 2001: 207). According to him, Franco's dictatorship was anticommunist and antiseparatism, while seeking to 'extirpate all forms of home rule regionalism and sub-state nationalism' or any form of federalism within a paradigm of 'national unity' which 'brooked no cultural or ethnic diversity' (Moreno 2001: 207).[1] Spain today of course is a unitary state by name but effectively federal, not only by the 1978 Constitution, but also by various informal pressures (Watts 2008: 42).

The above comparative perspective was required to reflect better upon the Indian scenario with regard to regionalism and federalism, and that too, in the era of globalization, or economic reforms in India. The other, more important, reason was to highlight the point that in multiethnic countries, the relations between the federal and the state governments (centre–state or Union–states relations) could not be understood properly to save the regional dimensions, which impinge upon the former. In the Indian context, this aspect has, as we shall see shortly, remained indispensably interlinked because India's regions have provided for the building blocks of Indian federalism.

Indian Perspective

The relation between federalism and regionalism in the Indian context has remained quite complex cutting across such issues as state building, nationhood and national unity and the concomitant centralization, on the one hand, and on the other hand, citizenship (Bhattacharyya et al. 2012), ethno-regional identity and the concomitant devolution, regional autonomy and decentralization. In a multiethnic country like India, characterized as it is by a high degree of with complexity, the notion one forms of national unity, or nationhood, corresponds to one's perspective towards the regions, their contribution to the making of the nation, if any, and finally to regionalism, when regional grievances are politically articulated, and a script of the cultural rights of the community (-ies) is written as self-determination.[2] In other words, a statist notion of national unity, Hobbesian in intent, as the Spanish dictator Franco took and sought to uphold, is inhospitable to regional and ethnic concerns and, hence, regionalism and autonomy.

Luckily, India's top nationalist elites, many of whom sat down on drafting India's Constitution, and also the first-generation rulers of India, were sensitive to India's diversity and heterogeneity, and respectful of the same (Bhattacharyya 2001, 2011a: 55–69; 2011: 102–119).[3] Their nationalist vision encompassed India's ethnoregional diversity. Consider the following famous passage of Jawaharlal Nehru as a representative of that generation:

The diversity of India is tremendous; it is obvious. It lies on the surface and anybody can see it. It concerns itself with physical appearances as well as with certain mental habits and traits ... Yet with all these differences, there is no mistaking the impress of India on the Pathans, as this is obvious on the Tamils. The Pathans and the Tamils are two extreme examples; others lie somewhere in between. All of them have their distinctive features, all of them have still more the distinguishing mark of India. It is fascinating to find how the Benaglis the Marathas, the Gujaratis, the Tamils, the Andhras, the Oriyas, the Assamese, the Sindhis, the Punjabis ... have retained their particular characteristics for hundreds of years, have still more or less the same virtues and failings of which the old tradition or record tells us, yet have been throughout these ages, distinctively Indian, with the same national heritage and the same set of moral and mental qualities (Nehru 1946: 61–62).

Furthermore, Nehru added:

> Some kind of a dream of unity occupied the minds of India since the dawn of civilization. This unity was not something conceived as imposed from outside ... It was something deeper, and within its fold, the widest tolerance of beliefs and customs was practiced and every variety acknowledged and even encouraged. (Nehru 1946: 62)

Shorn of its idealistic shibboleths, the tenor of Nehru's approach to nationhood could not be misunderstood: it was pluralist and region-sensitive that took into account India's ethnoregional and cultural diversity.[4]

Even as a ruler, as the first Prime Minister of India, Nehru was found to be adhering to his pre-independence thought and principles. In his *Letters to Chief Ministers* (henceforth *Letters*) (he resorted to that regularly in order to train them with the art of governance, as it were!) in the 1950s, particularly with regard to the question of Assam and its tribal population, he cautioned:

> It is difficult to treat them by some single formula because they differ greatly among themselves. It seems obviously desirable to grant them some kind of self-government or autonomy. (Nehru 1986: 364)

He simultaneously cautioned against any attempt at homogenization of different culturally specific people (Nehru 1985: 150).

No wonder, as I have argued elsewhere (Bhattacharyya 2001, 2005, 2007, 2010), the Indian Constitution remains centralized yet region-sensitive, and administratively decentralized, at least, up to the level of the states (federal units).[5] Certain specific historical/conjunctural factors apart, the logic of centralization is rooted in the particular mode of federation building/state building in India, that is, by the method of disaggregating a once centralized state built by the British colonial rulers, in phases, or, by the process called 'reorganization of states' provided in Articles 2 and 3 of the Indian Constitution itself.[6] In other words, Indian Union, as it is called, was not the result of a compact of already existing independent states willing to join an alliance for some common purposes, as they had done in Philadelphia in 1789, for instance, when the Americans resolved to transform their loose confederation into a federation. Those so-called provincialists who sat on the Indian Constituent Assembly (1946–1949) (who incidentally had tasted political power at the provincial level following the elections in 1937, according to the Government of India Act 1935)[7] wanted increased revenues for the provinces but then agreed that the Union government should collect the money and then distribute it among the units. For Granville Austin (1966/1999: 187), this can hardly be called a 'traditional defence of provincial autonomy'. Those more familiar with the formative years of the making of the Indian Constitution must be aware that right sizing for the purpose of a federation of a vast yet very complex territory (9 provinces, with Pakistan being carved up, out of 11 directly governed by the British under three Presidencies (Calcutta, Bombay and Madras), and some 560-odd princely autocracies of varying sizes and complexions, and the creation of linguistically homogeneous units to honour the nationalist pledges made ever since the Nagpur Session (1920) of the Indian National Congress (INC) – although efforts had already been made to reorganize the INC, organizationally speaking, along linguistic lines after 1917[8] – were not tasks easy enough! It is not, therefore, surprising that India's federation-building process is yet to be complete even after many phases of 'states reorganization', the latest being in 2000 when the last three states were created and added to the Union (Bhattacharyya 2001. If India's linguistic issues have mostly (around 90%) been resolved in this regard, Indian federation is yet to accommodate all remaining demands of regionalism and subregionalism. Another conclusion that comes out of the above discussion is that Indian federation building has increasingly deviated from the linguistic principle, in favour of ethnoregional concerns in the better sense of the word, although it must be acknowledged that none of the so-called linguistically reorganized states, or for that matter, any state in India, is ethnolinguistically homogeneous. No wonder, there is a growing scepticism about 'states reorganization' thus far followed in India (Sarangi and Pai 2011). However, that is not an argument for not rethinking the relations between the centre and the states within the Indian federation against the vastly changed circumstances, more particularly in the context of India's reforms, which have meant more actions on the part of the states, both constitutionally and by the compulsions of the reforms process (Bhattacharyya 2009: 99–112). It must never be forgotten that, as Morris-Jones (1954) observed long time back, the tensions between the centre and the states in India partly expressed themselves in 'regional awareness' (Morris-Jones 1954: 19). This has to be so since the states are not simply empty territorial spaces, but inhabited by people (s) whose histories, culture, customs, beliefs and manners are often at variance with others.

Changing Meaning of Regionalism and Federalism

What is regionalism? Is it something good or bad? Should it be there? And if so, what relation does it bear to federalism which is often taken to be a taboo as the so-called 'F' word? If regionalism is taken to be something bad, then we are dealing with two devils simultaneously. If that be the case, then to talk of their relation would seem ominous, a recipe for balkanization, or collapse, particularly in a country like ours which is so vast, so complex, besides being beset with varied inequalities and regional imbalances in development, measured nowadays by Human Development Index (HDI), accentuated of late due to 'reforms' (Tendulkar and Bhavani 2007).[9]

To be sure, the issues of regionalism and federalism can hardly be treated separately from that of India's national identity or nationhood;[10] the latter naturally preoccupied the minds of our nationalist elites mentioned above. Bhikhu Parekh (2008) makes a tall claim that among the developing countries, 'India was one of the first to initiate a debate on national identity' (p. 74). He has also drawn our attention to the growing 'national identity' crisis since the 1980s (Parekh: 74–79). But what is missing in such accounts is how does India continue to survive as a 'nation' and a state while such industrially advanced former USSR and its East European satellites failed, and were broken into many pieces in a process which Hobsbawm terms 'nation-splitting', as distinguished from the classical nineteenth-century model of nation building that had followed the principle of 'nation-uniting' (1992: 163–193). Conceptually, we are thus confronted with a triad: 'regionalism', federalism and nationhood/national identity. How do we resolve this triad? What is the desirable relation between the three of them? Are then regionalism and federalism a recipe for national breakdown? Or, does the former complement the latter, by performing a functional role for the latter in a multiethnic country like ours? Before moving on to discuss that aspect, we will make a slight detour here in order to hear a radically different voice for the so-called 'regionalism'.

While the nationalist elites of mostly liberal-democratic-pluralist school (Nehru, Gandhi and others) emphasized an all-Indian/pan-Indian territory-based nationhood that partook both ethnic and civic elements of the phenomenon, the one that sought to accommodate such ethnoregional concerns, they were not ready to accord nationhood status to the movements that arose in the regions of India during the anti-British nationalist movements. Many scholars were ready even to consider them as 'sub-nationalism' (Desai 1948),[11] although the script followed in such cases was no different from that of the pan-Indian level.

The political awakening of the dormant nationalities which these provincial social groups represented, reached such a high level in the thirties of the present century that they felt themselves as distinct entities, as nationalities. It was brought about by a number of factors. These factors were the further economic development of these provinces which led to the appreciable growth of the industrial and commercial classes: the increased in the educated class; and the impact of the great mass civil disobedience movement of 1930–04 which brought sections of the masses of these nationalities for the first time in the orbit of the national movement (p. 387).

There was, however, a different reading of the same situation, a radically different voice to the suppressed, or dominated, as it were, to use the language of the postmodernists. Late Nirad C. Chaudhuri looked at the situation of nationalism in India very differently from many. Making a distinction between two forms of nationalism in India, namely, external and internal – external with respect to the anti-British struggle of the people of India, which was mostly negative in character, and the internal that 'takes full note of the self and is both tenacious and assertive about it' (Chaudhuri 1997: 2). Chaudhuri further argues that there was no correlation between the two but they were 'independent and parallel to each other', and also that they were not antithetical (1997: 1).

One is tempted to quote at some length the apt description of such internal nationalism with its limitations as well.

It therefore has a content and is positive. But instead of being one, it is a collection of many distinct nationalisms, each highly self-conscious and therefore acutely conscious of all the others as rivals and competitors. In simple words, this nationalism is the feeling which the people of each Indian province have of being one as against the people of all the other provinces. Nowadays the provincial organization in India is based only on the unity of language and this linguistic unity is the most obvious feature of comprehensive unity in culture, group behaviour, interests and outlooks that exist within each province (Chaudhuri 1997: 2).

From the above discussion, Chaudhuri made two conclusions. First, he is mindful of the fact that in terms of Western theory, it was not a fully developed nationalism. Second, it was not recognized as legitimate (Chaudhuri 1997: 2). But he was not happy that such a phenomenon was 'deprecated and even abused as regionalism' (Chaudhuri 1997: 2). For him, 'there can be no doubt about its naturalness, its power and its reality' (Chaudhuri 1997: 2).

Elsewhere I have discussed at length the various factors causing regionalism as identified by academic accounts on the subject (Bhattacharyya 2005). The meaning and definition of regionalism has not remained static but has been changing not only in India but also elsewhere. For example, the pre-independence sensitivity to the regions and regionalism maintained by the nationalist elites began to decline after independence, more particularly after 1967 when the so-called 'one-party dominance' of the INC showed its first time ever cracks in the fourth general elections in which various state-based and regional parties posed a serious political challenge to the Congress hegemony. Quite predictably, as Lewis P. Fickett Jr. (1971: 193–221) points out, after 1967, that the rise of regional parties became what he called 'local annoyances to the Congress Party', which was as yet not prepared to accept the fact given India's heterogeneity, 'the politics of regionalism should not be a surprising development' (Fickett 1971: 193). If India has had many regional and state-based parties, the scenario in Western Europe is no better. Hueglin (1986: 439–458) shows, citing various surveys done, that there were as many 50 active regional movements in Western Europe, and 187 active ethnic associations in France alone! So much for the so-called homogeneous West/Europe and its nation–states![12]

Two points that I would like to raise here are: first, given India's deeply rooted heterogeneity, the fact that her cultural identities are regionally rooted, that her regions are actually cultural regions, regionalism of sorts is unavoidable, and is likely to persist. Second, since India's nationhood could not be thought of in isolation from its regions, regionalism per se should not ring an alarm bell to the powers that be, and invite a Hobbesian solution. On the contrary, regionalism in many cases has been complementary to the nation (Mitra 1999). The only important caveat here is that India's regions are not equally placed in developmental terms, an issue that gets accentuated in the current days of reforms when a social interventionist state gives way to a free-market economy and a 'regulatory state' (Rudolph and Rudolph 2001: 127–163).

As far as federalism is concerned, the conventional meaning of federalism as simply a territorial distribution of powers and authority between the two layers of government is long passé. As Ronald Watts (2008), the world famous authority on the subject of federalism, point out, even in the formation of US federation, considered thus far a 'model' for others, the distinctive regional political culture of the federating states was a central concern too (Watts 2008: 29). Following Daniel Elazar (1987), Watts (2008) offers the new definition of federalism as a compound polity that combines within a single polity shared rule (for general common purposes) with regional self-rule (for specific purposes). Watts (1996: 1) quoted:

> There is no single pure model of federalism that is applicable everywhere. Rather the basic notion of involving the combination of shared rule for some purposes and regional self-rule for others within a single political system so that neither subordinate to the other has been applied in different ways to fit different circumstances.

Keeping the above definition in view in our case, it is not difficult to see that federalism as a political principle and federation as a descriptive institutional arrangement are by themselves capable of providing for the institutional space for accommodation of ethnoregional identity provided that democracy informs the institutional arrangements. The experiences have shown (Bhattacharyya 2010) a federal design failing in the absence of democracy. It has also been found that federations failed not because they were federations (Watts [2008] said, Federations as modes of government are in any case difficult to govern) per se, but because the design was defective in the first place. The above definition, however, serves to demolish the two-tier model of federalism as the ideal one. In this connection, Riker's observations are noteworthy. According to Riker (1996), federalism is a 'constitutionally determined tiered structure', a form of government which implies arrangement of tiers of government 'in permanent agreement' (p. 10). The constitutional guarantee precisely serves to ensure their permanency, as is the case with Swiss federalism (Bhattacharyya 2001).

From the above discussion, I would like to stress the following points. First, there is no necessary conflict between federalism and regionalism; the relation between the two may be conflictual or compatible depending upon the context. Second, federations, properly so-called rather than the nation–state, though ideal typically, provide for a better accommodation of regional/ethnoregional identity, as the nation–state overemphasizes homogeneity at the cost of diversity. Third, a two-tier structure may not be sufficient enough to accommodate regional or subregional identities, (Bagchi 2012) but such identities may have to be accommodated at multiple levels (Arora 1995). Finally, regionalization by itself and be a tool for ethnoregional accommodation provided both the constitutional inputs and the ethnic pressures from below are brought to bear upon it. This helps minimize the spillover effects of regional discontent.

Impact of Globalization: The Era of the States, or India of the Regions?

In this concluding part of the discussion, I would briefly reflect upon the impact of India's reforms on her regions, or the states. In the recent context of Indian politics too, we come across such expressions as 'the rise of the States' (Rudolph and Rudolph 2008: 313). Is there such a ground in India to argue along that line? Are the states in India enjoying more freedom of action and autonomy than before (i.e. before 1991)? It is true of course that in India, the 'one-party dominance system' has gone; the national parties have suffered a relative decline (Arora 2000; Hasan 2010) as evident in their decline in popular voting share relative to the regional parties, which have been playing a more important role at the national level in multi-party coalitions of various brands. While summing up the 'New Dimensions of Indian Democracy', Rudolph and Rudolph (2008: 312–326) find, among others, a 'prominent role for federal states in India's political system', and the rise of a multi-party system with a significant role for regional parties in the coalition governments at the centre – both together serve, they argue, 'to keep cultural and ethnic differences within peaceful bounds', and to 'soften extremism'.

That may be taking too optimistic a position, as we shall see shortly. India's reforms regime, with its thrust on market economy, and a declining role of the social interventionist state, do not augur equally well for all her regions/states and, in fact, have prepared the bases for newer ethnoregional tensions and conflicts. When looked at the issue comparatively, in Europe, as Michael Keating (2002: 39–61) argues, new regionalism is confronted with a new reality given the 'fragmented nature of the European Community structure' in which many 'stateless nations' do not have a slot to fit, but a 'variety of channels to be used as appropriate'. He observes,

> What is more important is, however, the role of Europe in fostering a new nationalist discourse. It provides a fairly neutral political space within which a variety of channels can be articulated, challenges to the idea of absolute sovereignty, and facilitates nation building by allowing stateless nations a field of action. (Keating 2001: 61)

Two points merit our attention from the above comparative knowledge. First, India's regions, or the people (s) inhabiting the region (s) do not confront such a supra-national structure, and the channels of communication, although the nationalist discourses, as we have pointed above, have never been in short supply for India's ethnoregional identities for a long time until today (Baruah 2010). Second, despite the centre's reluctant willingness since the mid-1990s (Bhattacharyya 2009: 99–112) to involve the states in the reforms process, by the fiat of executive federalism, the Indian state's absolute sovereignty, internally speaking, is not impaired at all.

The existing researches and the official data available show that as a result of India's reforms, newer regional disparity has been created in terms of HDI so much as that a distinction nowadays is made between what is called 'forward states' and 'backward states' in India (Tremblay 2003: 341–342). Rao and Singh (2005: 370) find a deterioration in fiscal deficit mostly at the state level since the onset of reforms. Saez (2002), one of the early observers of India's political and economic reforms on federalism, points out that it was not true that all the regional forces had liked India's reforms. On the contrary, 'most regional forces provided an alternative model of federalism' (Saez 2002: 14) more or less on the lines of the Sarkaria Commission recommendations. However, as we all know, that was not to be! As a result, Saez noted a new development in Indian federalism with respect to intergovernmental relations: a marked shift from interstate cooperation to interjurisdictional competition (Saez 2002: 14) for more foreign direct investment (FDI), special economic zone (SEZ) and all that. Bagchi and Kurian (2005: 336) note widening regional disparities during the 1990s in India in terms of investment flows to the extent that the so-called Group I states were also the hot spots for FDI. Five states – Andhra Pradesh, Gujarat, Karnataka, Maharashtra and Tamil Nadu – altogether account for about 75 per cent of the total FDI in India since liberalization (Bagchi and Kurian 2005: 336–339). The HDI indicators, when disaggregated region-wise, are also very dismal: the public expenditure as per cent of GDP remains stationary (3.1% in 1995 to 3.2% in 2008); public health (0.7% to 0.9%) and the increase in gender disparity (3.9% in 1994–1995 to 5.3% 2004–2007) (Haq 2010). When viewed from the perspective of 'resource federalism',[13] the states find increasingly themselves in difficult situations in the development of resources, the mineral-rich states are not the 'forward states' or the Group 1 states.

No wonder, 'regional development, imbalances in centre–state relations' figures as a section in the Common Minimum Programme (CMP) of UPA (1) in which imbalances in regional development and regional disparities are seen as a matter of grave concern (Bhattacharyya 2012: 30–31). The CMP has identified some 250 'backward districts' in 27 out of 28 states of the federation while expressing a grave concern for their development. This seems hardly adequate to cut much ice because the growth model followed now is market oriented.

Quite predictably, the tenor of the recommendations of the Second Commission (known as the Justice Punchhi Commission) on centre–state relations (submitted in 2010), appointed to review the working of the federation in India in the wake of the reforms, is also a united market (Article 301) for the freedom of trade, commerce and intercourse, and hence to retune Indian federalism to these needs! This is in sharp contrast to those of the Sarkaria Commission (1983–1987), which were more prone to a social welfare state with further devolution and decentralization. The Punchhi Commission has, however, noted,

> The onset of the coalition governments, at the federal level in particular, expanded the political space of regional entities for participation in the federal functioning in addition to facilitating their involvement in the national economic and social policy formulation (Government of India 2010: 98).

In the 'summary' of its recommendations, the commission (2010: 99) remains tied to 'economic growth', not redistribution! The commission recommends also the cooperation of the Union and the state governments 'for the successful implementation of PPP Projects' (Public-Private Partnership), another instrument of globalization (Punchhi Commission Report, Vol. Vl, point 6.5.18). The so-called 'populist' social sector spending of the UPA (I & II) through such programmes as Mahatma Gandhi National Rural Employment Guarantee Scheme (MGNREGA) and Social Security for unorganized workers (SSUW) amounting about 18.32 per cent of the total central government expenditure (Tendulkar and Bhavani 2007: 200) does ensure popular votes for the UPA (Manor 2012: 13–26), but not higher income employment for the unskilled and less educated workers because the manufacturing sectors are hardest hit (Tendulkar and Bhavani 2007: 199). Needles to comment, the above paves the way for further tensions in Union–state relations in India because the so-called 'backward states' will have reasons to feel deprived.

Finally, I would conclude by saying that if federalism is a dynamic political equilibrium and also if that is to be maintained in conditions of India's deeply rooted social and cultural diversity for national unity, accentuation of regional imbalances, and the resultant frustrations and deprivations of the peoples living in those regions would pave the way for a major crisis in federal governance. Ruefully, unlike Europe, India is nowhere near to re-emerging as the 'India of the Regions or the States'. Also, since regions are inhabited by peoples who are unequally placed in the social, economic and cultural scales, an unqualified defence of regionalism does not provide the answer to the need for a political equilibrium.

Notes

1. Spain has since accommodated much of the 'ideology of atonomism' and the state structure has been made politically decentralized. The near federalization of Spain is reflected in a decreasing share in public expenditure and a simultaneous increase in the same by regional and local governments. For example, during 1981–1999, the following was the break-up patterns: central government (1981: 87.3%; 1987: 72.6%; 1997: 59.5% and 1999: 54%); regional governments (1981: 3%; 1987: 14.6%; 1997: 26.9% and 1999: 33%) and local governments (1981:

9.7%; 1987: 12.8%; 1997: 13.6% and 1999: 13%) (Moreno 2001: 209). Spain today (after its 1978 Constitution), after about four decades of hard dictatorship, is only formally a unitary parliamentary federal (monarchy), but effectively a federal state with 17 autonomous communities with more or less symmetrical spheres of jurisdiction, engaged, following Ronald Watts (2008: 4, 12 and 41–42) in a dual process of federalization internally (by the process of devolution and recognition of regional autonomy) and externally, by integrating within the European Union, and exhibits innovative steps in federalizations.

2. Such ethnicity-based home rule or self-determination discourses abound in India's northeast. For further details, see Baruah (2010). Interestingly, in many cases, as Baruah (2010) shows, such discourses are exclusivist in nature, based as they are in tribal ethnic identity, creating in its wake, deprivations for the nontribals living there for ages, resulting in a distinction between what he calls citizens and denizens.
3. The Dar Commission appointed by the Constituent Assembly of India (1946) recommended: Indian nationalism is deeply wedded to its regional languages; Indian patriotism is aggressively attached to its provincial frontiers (quoted in Bhattacharyya 2001: 256). The Report did not shy away from recommending a 'Federation as an absolutely government for such a vast country is neither desirable nor practicable (quoted in Bhattacharyya 2001: 257). Not that it did satisfy the founding fathers in toto; thus the INC's JVP committee report sought to exercise some caution with respect to the formation of linguistic provinces, another political expression of regionalism in India and nationalist pledge since 1920.
4. This pluralist and even synthetic approach to nationhood is maintained by other thinkers of modern India starting with Raja Ram Mohun Roy, Bhudev Mukhopadhyay and Rabindranath Tagore (Bhattacharyya 2011a: 55–69 and Bhattacharyya 2009: 15–29). Interestingly enough, Nehru himself seemed not to have been so enthusiastic about the linguistic provinces, as he had said in his speech in Parliament on 7 July 1952 'if the state is multilingual, it should encourage all the different languages, whatever they are. I do not quite see why the political boundary should necessarily be a linguistic one. I feel that behind the demand for linguistic province there lies something a little more difficult to deal with than the problem of language' (Nehru 1946/1983: 40).
5. Now, with the passage of the 73rd and the 74th Constitutional Amendment Acts for panchayats and municipalities, respectively, in 1992, the substate level governments also enjoy some autonomy, and are responsible for implementing many of the state-sponsored social welfare programmes.
6. The 5th and the 6th Schedules of the Constitution may also be cited in this connection.

7. Morris-Jones, W.H. (1957). *Parliament in India*, Westport, CT: Greenwood. As Morris-Jones aptly remarked, 'Not only the holders of ministerial office during 1937–39 but also the members of the provincial legislatures during that period came to appreciate the scope and importance of government at the provincial level. It was unlikely that these men, when they came to form a significant proportion of the members of the Constituent Assembly in 1948–49, would allow much talk of a purely unitary constitution (p. 17).
8. The Soviet Revolution of 1917 apart, this move nearly coincided with the rise of M.K. Gandhi into prominence in the nationalist politics who realized the immense democratic potentials in such a move as far as building mass bases for the INC (see Bhattacharyya 2008: 169–175 for further details). Thus, Bombay Provincial Committee apart, Maharashtra and the Gujarat Provincial Committees were also formed in 1917.
9. In this book, based on a thorough statistical analysis, the myth of India's growth post-1991 is demolished. They show that before 1991, even before the 1980s, there were many years when India's annual GDP growth rates were above 8 Per cent (Appendix, pp. 208–209)
10. This nationhood is understood here not entirely as an ethnic category, which is an impossibility in such a vast multiethnic country, but as a critical space for both the ethnic and civic elements constantly in interactions with each other at many levels. Depending upon a particular moments, ethnic/or civic elements get thicker/or thinner. This approach to nationhood is slightly different from Benedict Anderson's idea (1987/1991) of nationhood as a political community which is for him a possibility in conditions of diversity. For further details on the approach that I have developed, see Bhattacharyya (2007), Chapter 4: 5–68, and Chapter 11: 212–225, and Bhattacharyya (2011b: 55–69).
11. Following mechanically a Stalinist approach to the nationality question, A.R. Desai (1948) considered such urges for self-determination as 'dormant nationalities', as subnationalism, and also as a problem of Indian nationalism. (See for further details, *Social Background of Indian Nationalism*, 381–431)
12. Quite rightly, he points out that the scholars failed to recognize regionalism and the concomitant decentralization drives because of their preoccupation with centralization of the nation–state and the modernization hypothesis (p. 439).
13. See for further details, Nioronha, L., Srivastava, N, Datt, D. and Sridharan, P.V. (2009) 'Resource Federalism in India: The Case of Minerals', *Economic and Political Weekly*, Vol. XLIV, No. 8, February, 51–69.

References

Anderson, P. 1979. *Lineages of the Absolutist States,* London: Verso.

——. 1983. *Imagined Communities: Reflections on the Origin and Spread of Nationalism,* London: Verso.

Arora, B. 1995. 'And Verney', in Douglas V (ed.), *Multiple Identities in a Single State New*, Delhi: Konark Publisher.

——. 2000. 'Coalition and National Cohesion', in Frankel, F. et el. (eds.), *Transforming India: Social and Political Dynamics of Democracy*, New Delhi: Oxford University Press.

Austin, G. 1966/1999. *The Indian Constitution: The Cornerstone of a Nation*, Delhi: Oxford University Press.

Bagchi, R. 2012. *Gorkhaland: Crisis of Statehood,* New Delhi: Sage Publications.

Bagchi, A. and John Kurian. 2005. 'Regional Inequalities in India: Pre-and Post-Reform Trends and Challenges for Policy', in Jos Mooij (ed.), *The Politics of Economic Reforms in India*, New Delhi: Sage Publications.

Baruah, S. 2010. Ethnonationalism in India: A Reader, Delhi: Oxford University Press.

Bhattacharyya, H. 1989. 'The Emergence of Tripuri Nationalism, 1948–50', South Asia Research, London, Vol.9, No.1, May, pp. 54–72.

Bhattacharyya, H. 2001. *India as a Multicultural Federation: Asian Values, Democracy and Decentralisation* (In Comparison with Swiss Federalism), Fribourg: Helbing and Lichtenhahn.

——. 2005. 'Federalism and Regionalism in India: Institutional Strategies and the Political Accommodation of Identity', Heidelberg Papers in South Asian and Comparative Politics, Working Paper No. 27, May 2005 (ISSN 1617-5069), available at: www.hpsacp-hd.de.

——. 2007. 'Federalism and Competing Nations in India', in Michael Burgess and John Pindey (eds.), *Multinational Federations,* London and New York: Routledge.

——. 2009. 'Globalization and Indian Federalism: Reassertion of States' Rights', in H. Lofgren and Prakahs Sarangi (eds.), *The Politics and Culture of Globalization: Indian and Australia,* New Delhi: Social Science Press.

——. 2010. *Federalism in Asia: India, Pakistan, and Malaysia.* London and New York: Routledge.

——. 2011a. 'Sensing and Acknowledging India's Cultural Diversity for Nationhood: Budev Mukhopadhyay, Rabindranath Tagore and Jawaharlal Nehru', *The Calcutta Review,* Vol. Xlll, Nos. 1 & 2, pp. 102–119.

——. 2011b. 'Nation-building in Multicultural Contexts and Beyond', *Journal of Social and Political Studies*, Vol. 2, No. 1, pp. 55–69.

Bhattacharyya, H., Kluuge, A. and Koenig, Lion (eds.). 2012. *The Politics of Citizenship, Identity and the State in South Asia,* New Delhi: Samskriti.

Choudhuri, D.N. (ed.). 1997. *Nirad C., Chaudhuri: From the Archives of a Centenarian,* Calcutta: Mitra and Ghosh.

Desai, A.R. 1948. *Social Background of Indian Nationalism,* Bombay: Popular Prakashan.

Elazar, D. 1987. *Exploring Federalism,* Albama: The University of Albama Press.

Ficketr, L.P. Jr. 1971. 'The Politics of Regionalism in India', *Pacific Affairs,* Vol. 44, No. 2.

Government of India. 2010. *Report: Evolution of Centre-State Relations in India,* Punchhi Commission, March, Vol. 1.

Haq, M. Ul. 2010. *Human Development Centre, Human Development in South Asia 2009,* New Delhi: Oxford University Press, pp. 72–175.

Hasan, Z. 2010. 'Political Parties', in Gopal, N.J. and Mehta, P.B. (eds.), The Oxford Companion to Politics in India, New Delhi: UP, pp. 241–254.

Hobsbawm, E. 1992. *Nations and Nationalism since 1780: 'Nationalism in the Late Twentieth* Century', Cambridge: Oxford University Press.

Hueglin, T.O. 1986. 'Regionalism in Western Europe', *Comparative Politics,* Vol. 18, No. 4 July.

Keating, M. 2001. 'So Many Nations, So Few States: Territory and Nationalism in the Global Era', in Gagnon-Alain,-G and Tully, J. (eds.), *Multinational Democracies,* Cambridge: Cambridge University Press, pp. 39–65.

Manor, J. 2012. 'Did the Central Government's Poverty Initiatives Help to Re-elect it?', in Saez, L. and Singh, G. (eds.), *New Dimensions of Politics in India: The United Progressive Alliance,* Oxon: Routledge, pp. 13–26.

Mitra, Subrata K. 1999. *Culture and Rationality: The Politics of the Post-Colonial State in India,* New Delhi: Sage Publications.

Moreno, L. 2001. 'Ethnoterritorial Concurrence, Multinational Societies: Spanish Communidades Autonomas', in Gangnon, A. and Tully, J. (eds.), in *Multinational Democracies,* Cambridge: Cambridge University Press, pp. 201–222.

Morris-Jones, W.H. 1954. *Parliament in India,* Westport, Connecticut: Greenwood Press.

Nehru, J. 1983/1946 orig.. *The Discovery of India,* Calcutta: The Signet Press.

——. 1985. *Nehru's Letters to Chief Ministers, Vol. 1*, Delhi: Oxford University Press.

——. 1986. *Nehru's Letters to Chief Ministers, Vol. 2,* Delhi: Oxford University Press.

Parekh, B. 2008. A *New Politics of Identity,* London: Palgrave Macmillan.

Report of the Second Centre State Relations, Punchhi Commission, Government of India.

Riker, W. 1996. 'European Federalism: The Lessons of Past Experience', in Wright, Jeans and Wright V. (eds.), *Federalising Europe: The Costs, Benefits and the Preconditions of Federal Political Systems*, Oxford: Oxford University Press.

Rao, M.G. and Singh, N. 2005. *The Political Economy of Federalism in India*, New Delhi: Oxford University Press.

Rudolph, L. and Rudolph, S. 2011. 'Redoing the Constitutional Design: from an Interventionist to a Regulatory State', in Kohli, A. (ed.), *The Success of India's Democracy*, Cambridge: Cambridge University Press, pp. 127–63.

Rudolph, L. and Rudolph, S. 2008. *Explaining Indian Democracy: A Fifty-Year Perspective, Vol. 2,* The Realm of Institutions, New Delhi: Oxford University Press.

Saez, L. 2002. *Federalism Without a Centre: Impact of Political and Economic Reforms on India's Federal System,* New Delhi: Sage Publications.

Sarangi, A. and Pai, S. (eds.). 2010. *Interrogating Reorgansation of States: Culture, Identity and Politics in India,* New Delhi: Routledge.

Tendulkar, S.D. and Bhavani, T.A. 2007. *Understanding Reforms: Post-1991 India*, Delhi: Oxford University Press.

Tremlay, R.C. 2003. 'Globalization and Indian Federalism', in Dua, B.D. and Singh, M.P. (eds.), *Indian Federalism in the New Millennium*, New Delhi: Monohar, pp. 335–350.

Wats, R.L. 1996. *New Federations: Experiments in the Commonwealth*, Oxford: The Clarendon Press.

Watts, R.L. 2008. *Comparing Federal Systems* (3rd ed.), Montreal and Kingston: Queen's McGill University Press.

12

Regions in Nation or Nation in Regions

Regionalist Aspirations and Federalist Dilemma in Postcolonial India

Sajal Nag

In a national seminar at Teen Murti House, New Delhi, in response to a query to my presentation, I had proposed that instead of one capital for India in Delhi, there be many capitals in each region. While Delhi remains the political capital, Mumbai can be declared the financial capital, Kolkata, the cultural capital, and so on. In this chain, I Proposed that Imphal in Manipur (northeast India), which supplies a huge number of sport persons to the pool of national sports, be declared the sports capital of India. It would be an example of perfect adherence to the principle of federalism in terms of implanting a bit of the nation onto the regions. It would also nullify the obnoxious concept of mainstream and periphery and make regions feel part of a nationhood. The idea roused a pale of laughter and participants not only scoffed but also ridiculed the proposition. The national capital and its intellectuals were not even ready to share their space of hegemony and control over the regions even if it had the potential of reducing centre–region conflict and competition. This is interesting considering that India was conceived as a federation only to accommodate its regions and regional aspirations.

Region, Nation and Federalism

Regions have been the essence of Indian political evolution. Indian civilization was a conglomeration of cultural communities. Intermittently, there emerged empires that unified regional units into one single political unit through conquests and subjugations. The centripetal pull, resulting from such unifying attempts, had often tended, in a greater or lesser degree, to encompass the entire subcontinent. However, almost as a rule, these periods of political unity were followed by its disintegration into small kingdoms. After the Mauryas, the imperial control of the subsequent empires including the Guptas was confined to one or two great regions. The Pallavas, Chalukyas and Cholas despite all being powerful kingdoms were regional powers. Under the Tughlaqs in the fourteenth century, much of the subcontinent was brought under the Delhi sultanate. So was under the Mughals. However at the end of the seventeenth century, Aurangzeb's conquests upon the already massive Mughal Empire brought formal unity to most of the areas, but within 50 years of his death, the disintegration of his empire was followed by the rise of the Sikhs and Marathas, again strong regional powers. In fact, this has been the pattern of Indian history. Strong monarchies rose at regular intervals and attempted to bring about the political unification of the subcontinent. But the decline of these monarchies was followed by the fragmentation of the empire and the rise of regional kingdoms and powers (Embree 1985: 19ff). The regions were not just political entities, but also mostly well-defined cultural areas. With historically evolved cultural communities manifesting themselves in their arts, language, literature and even territorial vision. While Sanskritic language and culture, Brahmanic ideology, Epic traditions, etc., had acted as the unifying thread, regions for all practical purposes remained autonomous as culturally demarcated areas. It is this very visible diversity that distinguished the foundation of Indian nationhood from that of Europe. While Europe produced ethnically cohesive, culturally homogeneous polities to emerge as nation–states, India was ethnically, culturally and linguistically diverse, (Kumar 1985: 1ff) which made the Europeans scoff the claim of Indian nationhood. However, the Indian nationalist had to carve out a modern nation out of these diversities only. It had been appreciated early that India was a historically evolved land of continental proportions where diversity in language, religion, culture, traditions, practices and autonomy was not only the norm but also often created conflict situations. Therefore, they had to recognize the historical reality of regions by accommodating them in their concept of nation. For Indians, the emotionally charged, and the politically significant issue other than independence, was community rights and status (Austin 1966). Hence, when the Constituent Assembly met to discuss the Constitution, accommodation of this diversity was one of prime concern. Nehru had said as early as in 1936 'it is likely that free India may be a federal India though in any event there must be a great deal of unitary control' (Ibid). Hence, when a constitution was actually drawn up, it conformed to the principle of federalism. While introducing the Draft Constitution, B.R. Ambedkar said, '(it) is a federal constitution in as much as it establishes what may be called a dual polity (which) ... will consist of the Union at the Centre and the States at the periphery each endowed with sovereign powers to be exercised in the field assigned to them respectively by the Constitution ... the proposed Constitution is a dual polity with a single citizenship. There is only one citizenship for the whole of India ... there is no state citizenship' (*Constitution Assembly Debates* 1948: 33ff). Yet Indian Constitution does not even mention the word federation. It just states in its Article I (1), 'India, that is Bharat shall be a union of states (2) the states and territories thereof shall be as specified in the first schedule'. Earlier, they had toyed with idea of federation as practices in certain European and American nations and even preferred to call it cooperative federalism (Austin 1966). Even those who had attempted to theorize India's nationality question did it in the light of this multiplicity of culture (Nag 2000). Regions are, therefore, a political reality in India and unlike many other countries, the existence of these diverse regions and their political aspirations forced India to constitute itself as a federal polity and not the other way around. It was not really a concession to the region. Indeed, it is this federal polity that saw India through many crises and saved it from disintegration. But neither federalism as a principle can be absolute nor regional aspirations can be curbed to a limit. There has been a debate regarding how much autonomy India can afford to grant to its federal units and whether the right to secede to the regions should be incorporated in the Constitution or does federalism mean only a certain degree of autonomy to its federal units or should touch upon other aspects of bilateral relations.

Regional Movements in India

Contemporary Indian politics is characterized by two sets of politics: national and regional. National Politics is determined by the politics of power at the centre, while regional politics is for the state-level politics. While the national politics is the zone of activity of the central political elite, regions are the areas where regional political elite with regional aspirations play a dominant role. Similarly, central politics is the stronghold of national political parties, whereas the regions are of regional political parties. They often crisscross each other but within a limit. Strong regional parties may send their representatives to the centre, but only by forming a coalition with national political parties and national political parties might have regional units but will give preference to regional issues and aspirations, and leave the field to regional political leaders. India is a vast land – a conglomeration of habitats of different people settled here at different periods of time. Despite the pan-Indian civilization traits it has evolved, each had historically developed its own culture and tradition too. As a result there have always been two identities for the Indians – one Pan-Indian and the other regional based on race, language, religion and such cultural features. Indian nation-making process also experienced these two streams of coeval processes. One was based on its pan-Indian identity and the other on its regional linguistic-cultural identity. The period of Indian freedom struggle coincided with the period of awakening of these dual identities. Such an awakening manifested itself in the form of agitations and movements for the recognition of their respective vernaculars, formation of unilingual provinces and separation from large and dominant nationalities. In the colonial period, these movements flowed under the shadow of anticolonial movement, but after independence, they surfaced with a greater degree of intensity. These movements were not isolated movements or contradictory to each other. The movements based on regional identities and aspirations have been variously termed as regionalism, subnationalism and little nationalism. Although they are called regional movements, they are actually confined to a particular state boundary mainly concerned with the aspirations of the communities whose interests are not adequately represented either at the national level or by the central elite. The main theme of the regional aspirations has, in general, been identity and autonomy of the region – cultural, political and economic. What it amounts to, in other words, is that the region should have the autonomy to perpetuate its distinct identity and culture unhindered; the government of the area should be run by them and economic development of the region should be commensurate with the particular needs of the people of the region. Needless to say all three are interdependent. Without self-rule, the regional cultural practices cannot be perpetuated. Again most of the peripheral regions are marginalized and underdeveloped. Their resources are drained out to the metropolitan areas for processing, depriving the region, in the process, of its resources, resulting in an acute uneven regional development. The peculiar economic needs of the region are mostly not understood by the nonindigenous planners making it imperative that the region should have the political power to decide the nature and configuration of its development. It would ensure coeval, complementary and even a balanced economic development of all the regions of the nation.

Regionalism as Autonomy Movements

The British conquered India by taking advantage of the disunity that followed the decline of the Mughal Empire. The empire-building process and the Constitution of provinces by the British were arbitrary and meant to meet the needs of growth of the British power. They overlooked the systematic cultural demarcations of the regions and in fact disturbed them by combining several cultural groups within one administrative unit in some cases and distributing one cultural group among several units in other cases. The colonialists consistently ignored the demands of communities to ensure that they were united under one administrative boundary. The government in fact finalized this arrangement by enforcing the Act of 1935 on this very structure without the required modifications. The Indian National Congress, as the major representative of Indian peoples' aspirations, recognized the Principle of Linguistic Provinces as the basis for creating provinces. When it inherited power, it constituted State Reorganization Commission to investigate the problem. After its report was implemented in 1956, the process of state formation began. The Indian Union which started with 14 states had 25 states and 7 union territories over the next 50 years. After the carving out of Uttaranchal, Chhattisgarh and Jharkhand in November 2000, the number of states has risen to 28. Still there are more demands for elevating Delhi from a union territory to a state and movements for statehood in Telangana, Vidarbha, Harit Pradesh, Bodoland, Gorkhaland, Kamatapur, Dimaraji and Karbi Anglong. Most of the states created since 1956 are the manifestation of the overwhelming people's desire expressed through regional movements. Since India is a union of multiple identities, developed or dormant, federal units were created on the basis of cultural features of which language was the most prominent one. The rise of regionalist aspirations was also visible when Hindi was sought to be made the official language of India in 1960.[1] The regional communities felt that the move would entail the suppression of their mother tongues. The entire non-Hindi speaking region rose in a violent rebellion against the move forcing the government to reconsider the decision.

Regions in Flames: Jammu & Kashmir

Regional aspirations and the consequent regional movements are the strongest in the states of Kashmir, Punjab and the states of northeast India with historical roots. The regions where regionalism had the strongest historical roots were Kashmir, Punjab, Tamil Nadu and northeast India, each with a distinct cultural identity. Jammu, Kashmir and Ladakh are the three districts which form the state of Kashmir. An overwhelming majority of Kashmiris are Muslims who speak Kashmiri language. The people of Jammu, however, are predominantly Hindus, while Ladakh is inhabited by people who are Indo-Mongoloid professing Buddhism. Each of these regions has had its own distinct past besides being inspired by different historical events. They came to form part of a single political entity only in 1846 when the British East India Company acquired Kashmir through an agreement called the Treaty of Amritsar. The regional movement in Jammu & Kashmir centred mainly around the issue of Kashmiri identity known as *Kashmiriyat* and autonomy. Kashmir, a princely state during the British rule, was, for all practical purposes, outside the control of the Government of India. After the British withdrawal, like all princely states, Kashmir also had the liberty of either merging with India or Pakistan or remaining independent. The King Hari Singh wanted to remain independent, but the most powerful leader of the Kashmiris, Sheikh Abdullah wanted Kashmir to merge with India considering India's secular polity and multicultural identity. As a goodwill gesture, the Government of India granted constitutional guarantees embodied in the Article 370 of the Indian Constitution. The Kashmiris felt it would ensure the protection of their national identity and autonomy. The Government of India, on its part, guaranteed full autonomy for Kashmir besides committing itself to a plebiscite. The Kashmiris appreciated the recognition accorded to them as it came in the form of their being allowed to a have a separate constitution, a flag of their own and even a separate national anthem. The Srinagar Radio Station was permitted to identify itself as Radio Kashmir.

However, the new state of Pakistan could not reconcile itself to the loss of Kashmir to India. It continued to make efforts to separate Kashmir from India by instigating violent secessionist movements as well as making aggressive postures. In view of this the Government of India could not continue with the quantum of autonomy given to Kashmir. The integrity of this frontier state necessitated the dilution of some of the commitments made earlier. Hence, through a Constitutional Order (Application to Jammu & Kashmir) 1954, the jurisdiction of the central government was extended from the original three subjects of Defence, Foreign Affairs and Communication to all subjects coming under the Union List. On 29 March 1956, the order of a plebiscite was withdrawn on the following grounds: (1) for a plebiscite to take place under, the UN terms, Pakistan had to first withdraw its forces from Jammu & Kashmir: (2) Kashmiri Constituent Assembly had already approved the merger with India and accepted the Indian Constitution making a plebiscite redundant. But the perpetuation of the plebiscite demand by Sheikh Abdullah through his *Plebiscite Front* compelled the Government of India to arrest him from 1953 to 1964 on grounds of antinational activities. His son and successor Farooq Abdullah, though a popular chief minister, faced frequent dismissals from the centre causing widespread discontentment among the Kashmiris.

The state has witnessed sustained insurgent activities since then, mostly sponsored by Pakistan. It has kept up its demand for secession from the Union of India apart from inciting violent insurgency activities and instigating communal divide. A large number of Kashmiri Hindus have been displaced by the divide and violence. The development also affected the people of Ladakh adversely. There have been autonomy demands from both these regions as well as a result of this. Although the regional aspirations of Kashmir have all along centred around the question of autonomy, the situation is getting further aggravated by the centre's perpetual neglect of the state. Kashmir is one of the poorest regions of the country. There is huge unemployment and deterioration in the living conditions of the people. In the absence of industrial growth, the government is the only provider of employment. The traditional sources of livelihood of the people – agriculture, horticulture, handloom and textile and tourism – have got badly affected because of insurgency leaving young men easy preys to the recruitment drive of militants. Added to this is the centre's frequent interventions in the democratic process of the state. Elected governments were frequently toppled by the party in power at the centre. Unwanted governors were sent to rule the state and a potent opposition was not allowed to develop. This made the people of the region feel that the government created by their vote was not allowed to continue by the authoritarian centre and that their democratic rights and autonomy were not being honoured.

The alienation of Kashmir is thus a result of unfulfilled promises to protect the identity and autonomy of the people, derailment of democratic processes, conscious creation of communal divide, imposition of puppet governments against the will of the people, military interference at the behest of the government even when the situation did not warrant it and a pathetic level of economic development. The lack of initiative on the part of the centre towards promoting economic development of the state, the failure to ensure its emotional integration with the rest of the nation and its reliance on the armed forces for maintenance of law and order have only further aggravated the problem. The demand for federal autonomy has thus been allowed to grow into a demand for sovereignty. Yet, a majority of the Kashmiris are not averse to the idea of being an integral part of India if their desire for protecting identity, autonomy and development is seriously addressed.

Punjab

Like the Kashmiris, the Sikh history also has been a chronicle of a long struggle. From the beginning, the Sikhs have tried to establish themselves as a separate entity – as followers of a new faith – by themselves. Despite having distinct cultural identity based on religion, language, script, territory and consciousness, the Sikhs had been consistently denied a separate identity. The Hindus considered

Sikhs part of Hindu community, while the Muslims, a majority in Punjab, denied them of their legitimate political rights. During the colonial period, this fear of losing their identity increased as the powerful Arya Samaj claimed Sikhism to be only a branch of Hinduism. The Sikh intelligentsia asserted that they were not Hindus and that the Sikhs had a distinct identity. Since then there was a conscious move to establish its independent identity. The Singh Sabha Movement (1870) started a reformist movement to spread literary, education and religious awareness among the Sikhs. The Chief Khalsa Diwan was formed to coordinate the Singh Sabha Movement and to unite the Sikhs. The Singh Sabha and the Khalsa Diwan dominated Sikh public life for 50 years and laid the foundation for the political movements of the 1920s when the religious and political leadership of the Sikhs was taken over by the Shiromoni Gurdwara Reform Movement. The Akali Dal was also formed (1920) as a political wing of the Sikhs. The emergence of Muslim League brought recognition to the Muslims as a minority community and their demands for separate electorate was given a fair weightage by the British Government, while the Sikhs were perpetually ignored both in the 1909 Act as well as the Lucknow Pact (1916). Despite making a representation to the Montagu–Chelmsford committee, even the Act of 1919 refused to accord them any minority status. Despite the presence of a Sikh representative, the Motilal Nehru Report also ignored the demands of the Sikhs. In fact, the communal award of 1932 granted the Muslims a permanent majority status in Punjab, whereas Sikhs continued to be denied of their political rights. The alienated Sikhs led by the Shiromoni Akali Dal countered the Muslim League demand of Pakistan by a demand for 'Azad Punjab' – an independent Punjab state, in 1943. In the All Party Sikh Conference of August 1944, Master Tara Singh declared that Sikhs too were a nation by themselves and that if there was a division of the country they would refuse to be the slaves of either Hindustan or Pakistan. A sovereign Sikh state was seen as the only solution to the vexed Sikh nationality question. The resolution demanding a sovereign Sikh state was officially adopted by the Akali Dal on 22 March 1946. The British government was, however, not inclined to concede it. Moreover, the partition and the resultant communal riots submerged the Sikh state issue. The issue of a Sikh state reappeared again after independence. In the wake of the creation of Andhra province in 1953 and the State Reorganization Commission Report in 1955, the Sikhs of Punjab became restive again. Two committees,

Sardar Hukum Singh committee and Shah Commission were formed to look into the matter. The government agreed to reorganize the state on the basis of the census 1961. The Punjab state was bifurcated into Punjab and Haryana with Chandigarh as the common capital in 1966 through an act adopted in the Parliament. As a reward of the struggle, the Akalis came to power, but twice over a span of five years the government was dismissed by the centre. The dismissal plunged Punjab into a chaos once again. The dismissal of the Akali government was a display of suppression of regional autonomy by the centre. This brought the entire centre–state relationship and the question of regional autonomy to the fore once again. It was felt that there should be an adequate guarantee against the dominance and authoritarianism of the centre over the states. The Akalis came up with the Anandpur Sahib Resolution on the basis of their struggle. From a struggle for the regional autonomy, the movement grew in size, proportion and intensity, demanding an independent state of Khalistan, while the leadership of the movement passed from the moderate Akalis to the terrorists and fundamentalist elements who had witnessed the marginalization of the Sikh Panth in Indian polity. Because of the political instability, the development of Punjab also suffered. It was the first Indian state to have witnessed successive green revolutions. Although the state occupied only 1.54 per cent of the total geographical area and with a population accounting for only 2.54 per cent, it contributed 40–50 per cent of the total rice and 60–70 per cent of wheat production to the central pool. However, the Green Revolution was not followed by a substantial Industrial growth and the surplus generated through Green Revolution went waste as the centre did not facilitate any infrastructure development to usher in an industrial revolution. Despite this, Punjab has on its own emerged as one of the leaders of India's industrial sector, manufacturing industrial spare parts and machine tools. Even the agricultural sector has suffered in view of the long pending Ravi–Beas interstate water sharing dispute, which the centre is yet to resolve. All these developments have brought forth the issue of regional autonomy for deciding on its development requirements.

The North-East of India

The northeastern region of India is also marked by its distinctive culture and history. In fact, it falls under that politico-cultural zone inhabited predominantly by non-Hindu, non-Hindi speaking ethnic communities with myriad tribes being in primitive stages of development. Despite their seclusion for ages, they were part of the Indian civilization and had regular exchanges with people from the plains developing in the process, a syncretic culture. But the British, afraid of their violent uprising and vulnerability to the influence of the Indian nationalist ideology, prevented their traditional mutual intercourse with the people from the plains belonging to the neighbouring Bengal and Assam. They even fed them with racist and separatist ideas since most of the tribes of northeast India were Indo-Mongoloid, Indo-Aryans, speaking Tibeto-Burman languages and were either animists or Christians. They had been debarred from participating in the socio-economic and political processes of the rest of India through various constitutional devices such as the Excluded Area, Partially Excluded Areas and Inner Line Regulation. Thus, a hundred years of isolated existence and fed up with separatist ideas, the northeastern tribes, such as the Nagas and Mizos, were not sure of their Indian identity at a time when the British decided to withdraw from India. Since they belonged to the excluded area, these tribes felt that they could exercise their right, like the then princely states of India, to decide their future identity status. Although they did not enjoy such a right, they deliberated among themselves and finally decided to merge with India; the Mizos, on the other side, felt merging with India would rid them of the oppressive chiefly rule, while the Nagas toyed with the idea of remaining independent, but later decided to try the option of joining India for a tentative period of 10 years and accordingly signed an agreement with the Government of India. However, the interpretation of the 'period' clause had led to a disagreement following which they declared unilateral independence, which the Government of India rejected. After a period of violent insurgency, a section of the Nagas signed a 16-point agreement with the government which granted them a maximum constitutional autonomy and a separate statehood. The twenty-five Khasi states and the princely states of Tripura and Manipur signed the Instrument of Accession to join India. Assam had no such problems except that a large number of Muslim immigrants from Bengal district encouraged and settled by the British created a perceived threat among the indigenous Assamese that these immigrants would reduce them to a minority and rob them of their political hegemony. The partition of India had reduced the northeast to a land locked region with only about 22 km corridor to link it to the rest of India. Cut-off from the rest of India, the region was not only ignored by the centre for economic development, but also its politics was insulated.

Assam was the largest province in the region where the majority were the Assamese surrounded by a number of tribal population. The British government developed a huge tea plantation industry with a number of gardens in the province, while importing a massive number of labourers from outside the province to work in them. They also encouraged a massive migration and the settlement of Bengali Muslims across the wastelands of Assam. After independence, however, the presence of such a massive number of outsiders posed a problem to the Assamese. There was a fear that these immigrants would become a majority, and takeover political power from the indigenous Assamese. Therefore, there were repeated demands from the Assamese for detecting and deporting these 'foreign nationals'. In fact, most of the elections were fought over this issue in Assam and whichever party promised to act on this was voted to power. But once the large immigrant Bengali Muslim community had got assimilated into Assamese society, it started concentrating on establishing its political hegemony over the myriad tribes and other minorities. It announced the official language bill of 1960, which sought to make Assamese the official language of polycultural Assam. It sparked opposition, protest riots and violence through the state. The major tribes demanded a hill state carved out of Assam. After the official language bill, all the tribal leaders who had formed the Eastern India Tribal Union transformed it into a more comprehensive All Party Hill Leaders Conference in 1960. This was further compounded by the demand for Kamatapur state in Goalpara and an Ahom homeland in Sibsagar and Lakhimpur. There was a famine resulting from bamboo famine in Mizo hills state, which the state government mishandled causing starvation deaths and alienation of the Mizo tribals. The Mizos demanded separation not only from Assam but also from India itself through a secessionist political organization named Mizo National Front (1958). The central government was compelled to carve out Meghalaya, Mizoram and Arunachal Pradesh from Assam. Tripura and Manipur were upgraded to states too. Nagaland had already been made into a state in 1960.

There were other economic issues as well. Despite the presence of a small population, there was widespread poverty and unemployment in Assam. Its natural resources such as oil, tea and coal were drained out without any commensurate benefits to them. Due to the repeated failures of the government in tackling the issue of 'foreign nationals', the antiforeign national movement was launched by the All Assam Students Union in 1979. The centre responded by signing an accord in 1985 following which the Student Union and the Assam Gana Sangram Parishad organized themselves as a political party called Asom Gana Parishad (AGP). It came to power with a thumping majority in the general elections of 1985 with the main promise of resolving the 'foreign nationals' problem as well as building a 'Sonor Asom'. However, in the five years of its rule, it failed to ensure any economic prosperity or solve the vexed problem of infiltrators. But it is not the end of problems for Assam. It is plagued by internal crises also. On the one hand, there is the United Liberation Front of Assam that wants to secede from India through violent means. On the other hand, a number of tribes living in Assam such as the Bodos, Karbis, Dimasas and Ahoms desire autonomy in the form of a statehood. Some smaller tribes have already been given autonomous councils and some others such as Gorkhas, ex-tea garden population too aspire for autonomous councils.

In Tripura, the contest had always been between the Congress and the CPM. The former was known as the champion of the immigrant Bengalis who had reduced the indigenous tribal groups into a minority, while the CPM had a long history of association with the tribal struggle for land and political rights. Although both Congress and CPM were the national parties in Tripura, they fought on issues that concerned the tribal communities and the immigrants. The tribal groups resented the fact that the immigrant Bengalis had wrested political power from them.

In the state of Meghalaya, Khasi-Jaintia were the majority and educationally much advanced communities than others in the state, but it mostly had a Garo Chief Minister which the Khasis resented. On the other hand, despite having a number of ministers, the Garo hills remained neglected in terms of development. The two tribes, therefore, sought separation from each other and the formation of their own states.

Nagaland remained plagued by the prolonged insurgency. Its demand for autonomy had graduated to a demand for complete sovereignty. While a majority of the Nagas desired peaceful existence within India, a section of the extremists under the banner of National Socialist Council of Nagalim continued to fight against the Indian government for independence. The 50 year long insurgency has affected the economic development of the state adversely while making the Nagas feel further neglected.

Manipur resented the forceful integration of the state with the Indian Union in 1949. The subsequent economic neglect by the centre only further alienated them. There are a number of insurgent groups operating in the state for independence. It also has a number of tribal groups such as the Nagas who desire merger with the state of Nagaland and Kukis who want a home state. This has threatened the territorial integrity of the state. The centre's tactics of carrot and stick in quelling the situation has only aggravated the problem further.

Cultural Context of Regionalism

An interesting feature of the autonomy movements is that these emerge in the regions which are either located in the periphery or not strongholds of the majority populations. The regions described above – Jammu & Kashmir, Punjab and northeastern region – where regionalist movements have been strong come under the peripheral regions where dominant communities of India do not have a significant presence. It will be clear if we divide India into three circular zones. In the core circle, are some of the large states such as Uttar Pradesh, Madhya Pradesh, Rajasthan and Bihar occupying the so-called Indian mainland with predominantly Hindu. Hindi-speaking belt has been identified as the core Indian mainstream (Chaube 1984)[9] with no fissiparous movements either for sovereignty, autonomy or for regionalist movements observed. The new state movements that have emerged here are the cumulative effect of autonomy movements or regional movements taking place elsewhere. Even the small parties that have currently come to power in these states are the remnants of old national parties. In fact, these states were once the traditional fortresses of the Congress Party.

In the second circle lying outside the core circle, states such as Gujarat, Maharashtra, Karnataka, Kerala, Tamil Nadu, Andhra Pradesh, Orissa, Haryana and West Bengal, most of which are not Hindi-speaking, yet are home to a predominantly Hindu population subscribing to the Brahmanic ideology and Ramayana–Mahabharata tradition. This cultural political zone may be seen as associated with the core or mainstream.

On the outer fringe of these two zones are states such as Jammu & Kashmir, Punjab, Assam, Goa, Lakshadweep, Andaman Islands, Mizoram, Nagaland, Meghalaya, Arunachal Pradesh, Tripura and Sikkim. These units are inhabited by a predominantly non-Hindu, non-Hindi speaking cultural communities. Heavy concentrations of tribal population are observed in these states except Goa and Punjab where a huge proportion of the depressed classes is an integral part of the population. It may be pointed out here that Jammu & Kashmir and Lakshadweep are the two Muslim majority units of India. Punjab is the only Sikh state, Sikkim the only predominantly Buddhist state and Nagaland, Mizoram, Meghalaya and Arunachal Pradesh have a predominantly scheduled tribe population. Among them, the first three are Christian majority states, while the last one has various forms of animism. Assam has less Hindus and more tribal faiths, Goa has a large Christian population and the rest of the states mentioned in this group have a similar tribal population with both tribal faith and non-Hindu religion dominating. All these states have a strong tradition of regional parties or state-based parties. As a broad generalization, most of the large states can be said to be the mainstream of Indian states, while the smaller states are located in the periphery. Regionalist sentiments and demands for autonomy are the strongest in this region. There are sovereignty demands leading to secessionist insurgency in most of these states too. As a result, there is a heavy deployment of army by the state in most of these states. Draconian laws such as Armed Forces Special Power Act, Disturbed Area Act and such similar laws are still in operation in some of these states.

Tangent in National Politics

Another significant feature is the political context of the regional movements. The areas where regionalist movements have been generated are just a tangent in national politics. It is evident that the regionalist movements are stronger in the region that has a feeble political voice base in the Parliament. The first category states mentioned above account for 40 per cent of the seats in the Indian Parliament; the second category states mentioned above share 52 per cent of the seats in the Parliament and the third category states constitute only 8 per cent of the members of the Parliament (Ibid).[10]

It is quite clear that the first and second category states which the Indian state itself recognizes as the mainstream control a larger share of parliamentary seats and hence control political power. The share of the third category states is so less that they are actually inconsequential in national politics. The cultural and demographic marginalization has a significant political implication: that northeast India plays the role only of a tangent in Indian parliamentary democracy. Their voices are lost in the cacophony of the majority. Even if they raise their voices, they are never heard because, as tiny minorities, they do not count; they never matter. It is this dimension of Indian democracy that we propose to highlight in this chapter in the context of the political participation of seven states of northeast India vis-à-vis the federal polity of India. It is obvious that these MPs, divided by race, ethnicity, nationality and party ideologies are hardly found in a position to influence the decision making of the majority. They occupy only a marginal space in the Indian political system (Nag 2003: 336ff). Overwhelmed by a vast majority of MPs, these tangents hardly get an opportunity to express themselves in the Lok Sabha as it is futile unless it concerns their own state. Most of the time, they justifiably go through the formalities mechanically. There were, however, some exceptions who, due to their personal charisma, had risen to higher levels. G.G. Swell, Santosh Mohan Deb and Purno A. Sangma are such examples. As a stalwart from Jammu & Kashmir, Farooq Abdullah is given an insignificant portfolio in the Union Ministry. Although Punjab has contributed a number of Sikh leaders to the national pool, Giani Zail Singh could become the President of India only because of the patronage of Indira Gandhi. Despite being such an important state, Punjab has had to fight for its language and most of the demand for the implementation of Anandpur Sahib Resolution still remains unfulfilled. The state of Punjab does not yet have a capital of its own. To extract their pound of flesh, these MPs from the small states of northeast India generally adopt an alternative method outside the Parliament. They form a lobby on issues concerning the region and meet the concerned minister or the Prime Minister personally to impress upon their concern. That is why the Lok Sabha elections are virtually unimportant to these states, whereas the Assembly elections are generally far more intense. During the Parliamentary elections National Parties are given high importance, whereas in the state elections region and state-based parties assume a bigger role.

Development Agenda

Besides identity and power, the common complaints of the regionalist forces concern deprivation, discrimination and underdevelopment. Indeed, Jammu & Kashmir, for example, still survive on tourism and horticulture even after 60 years of independence. There is no industry, no investment and no infrastructure worth its name. There is extreme poverty and unemployment especially in the rural areas. The only available employment avenue is government services, mostly police, which too can absorb only a fraction of the unemployed youths. The major infrastructure is power sector with a potential, as per one assessment, of 20 megawatts or say 18 megawatts, yet the state is deficient in its power requirements to the tune of 65 per cent. The total strength on the live register of the employment exchange seeking employment increased from 51.28 thousand in 1980 to 114 thousand in 2005. Unlike many other states in the country, Jammu & Kashmir has a few natural disadvantages such as being a remote terrain economy, to be able to support industries. It has a sufficient potential and an assured domestic market for promoting a consumer goods industrial sector for gainful economic opportunities and also for producing for domestic absorption and exports. The state intervention programmes from time to time particularly in the form of subsidy and tax incentives have failed to attract investment to the extent they could have to set a pace for industrial development. The state has witnessed the growth of industrial units in the small-scale sector to the extent of 49.43 thousand in 2006–2007 as against 2 thousand in 1973–1974 and 9.43 thousand in 1980–1981 providing employment to about 43 thousand people in 1980–1981 and 2.2 lakh persons in 2006. In the so-called large and medium industrial sector, the number of units have gone up to 132 with an investment of about Rs. 2392 crore, while providing employment for more than 19 thousand till 2006. Another category of industries are state public undertakings, minerals, handicrafts and other enterprises, with an annual production worth Rs. 28.44 crore and an average daily employment of 3600; but among these undertakings, most of them suffer revenue losses annually, possibly due to a higher revenue expenditure. A number of industrial estates have been created through the state intervention programmes such as industrial growth centres, but the share of their production and employment generation is very less in the total secondary sector. The growth of Small Scale Industries (SSI) units works out to 2.5 per cent, while the growth of employment generation in these units is 3.1 per cent for 2006–2007 (Ali 2012; Mohapatra and Pathak 2013).

Conflicts have affected important sources of livelihood and discouraged private investment in the state, resulting in increased unemployment and poverty. Losses to the tourism industry, one of the Kashmiri's main occupations, have been monumental. The state has lost out on 30 million tourists over a span of 15 years since 1989, causing a loss of Rs. 15 billion per year – an amount equal to 25 per cent of the state's annual outlay of 2010. Considered one of the best tourist destinations of the world, the picturesque state today is no longer among the top Ten Indian States that jointly account for 90 per cent of the international and domestic tourist traffic. It has been reduced to competing with the rest of the states for the left over 10 per cent tourists. The central home ministry has shown that a huge amount of Rs. 3583 crore was spent on security-related expenditure in Jammu & Kashmir since militancy began in the late eighties. The figures in the ministry's annual report pertain to the period between 1989 and 2011.The Planning Commission has finalized the annual plan outlay for the development of Jammu & Kashmir for the year 2012–2013 to the tune of around Rs. 7300 crore but again a good part of this money would go towards maintaining law and order in the province.

Similarly Punjab has been one of the first provinces to have ushered in a Green Revolution with a great hope that it would propel the region towards becoming a giant industrial power. Unfortunately, it did not happen. Punjab provided food to the rest of the country, but depended on the rest of the country for its industrial goods. The total central investment in the public sector was about Rs. 70,000 crore in 1988–1989 of which Punjab's share constituted only Rs. 700 crore. Until recently, except for a Railway Coach factory at Kapurthala, there was no heavy industry in the state. There was a huge disruption even during the secessionist uprising in the 1980s. But the situation according to experts did not change even when peace returned. In fact, there has been a deceleration of growth in Punjab (Singh and Singh

2002: 9ff; Mohapatra and Pathak 2013). The rates of growth in the post-reform period (1991–1992 to 1997–1998) reveal an interesting phenomenon. The rate of growth of the Indian economy accelerated at 6.89 per cent per year, much higher than that in the 1980s. However, the rates of growth of Punjab economy as also of Haryana decelerated at 4.71 per cent and 5.02 per cent per year, respectively. The analysis of 'Punjab economy shows that these factors especially capital accumulation, technological breakthroughs and human capital are constraining further growth and the sustenance of the earlier growth momentum of the state economy. This is evident even in the crisis of the farm sector especially at the technological plane and in the rising costs to maintain the existing level of productivity. Similar is the case of the industrial sector so far as levels of capital investment and human capital up gradation are concerned' (Ibid).

The condition of northeastern region is one of a historical neglect. The World Bank describes conditions in the region as a low-level equilibrium of poverty, nondevelopment, civil conflicts and lack of faith in the political leadership. According to the Ministry of Development of North Eastern Region, a sum of more than 426 billion rupees was kept apart for the development of northeast between 1998 and 2006. The Deputy Governor of the Reserve Bank of India informs that funds to the northeastern states add up to more than what India gets from the World Bank and the Asian Development Bank. Also, the central government ministries have been allotting 10 per cent of their annual budgets as a nonlapsable pool for northeastern states since 1998. Yet, there are no signs of improvement.

Agriculture is the mainstay on which 80 per cent of the population is still dependent on it. But the total rice output of the region constitutes one-third of Punjab's output. Except Manipur and Tripura whose agriculture productivity (per unit of land) is higher than the All India average, in the rest of the states in northeast, agricultural productivity is dismal. In 1991–1996, Assam's agricultural growth rate was estimated at 1.2 per cent, much below the rate of growth of population and that of Meghalaya (0.8%) and Tripura (0%). Despite the fact that agriculture and allied sectors contribute more than 31 per cent to the state GDP and has the potential to grow, the state budget allocation to this sector is meagre. Assam spends only 7 per cent of a total Rs. 6000 crore budget on that sector. The Shukla Commission estimated that Rs. 2500 crore worth of consumables are imported from outside every year. Assam imports 74 per cent of its milk products, 94 per cent of eggs and 98 per cent of its meat requirements. The region is endowed with abundant water resources, yet about half of its fish requirements are imported from outside. The credit deposit ratio is very low in the region. The banking sector transfers about Rs. 5000 crore from this region to other regions for investment. The lack of infrastructure, particularly, communication (northeast constitutes 8% of the total geographical area of the country but has only 3.2% of its railway track, makes transportation and power critical. Together with the lack of inevitable capital, the lack of entrepreneurship has slowed down the pace of development (Dutta 2013: 179ff). The local entrepreneurship is absolutely small in view of a stagnation in investment growth. Only the service sector, that is, the government construction sector, due to government investment mostly on border roads in some states, is growing. Because of the prolonged insurgency in the region, despite the abundance of natural resources (oil, gas, coals, granite, limestone, water and forest wealth), no outside investment has taken place despite the government announcement of a long tax holiday on such investment. Indeed, there was a flight of capital in the last decades from the region. Unemployment, particularly, educated unemployment, is very high. The growth rates of all the NER states have actually increased during the 3 five-year plans with Manipur and Tripura registering persistently higher growth rates. Sikkim and Manipur grew fastest among the Indian states during the ninth and tenth plans. However, this growth has not been adequate enough to catch up with all India per capita income. The challenge of growth before the northeastern states is, therefore, how fast these states can grow to catch up with the per capita GDP of the country by 2020 (Singh and Kumar 2009: 36ff).

A sense of urgency has been aroused in response to the people's pursuit for a place in the sun to ensure that the region catch up with the country by including it in the process of development. The most important thing is to identify the matrix of policy variables impinging on target variables such as per capita income, employment, expectancy of life at birth, literacy rate and poverty ratio. However, unfortunately economic policies have either failed to deliver or delivered an unrecognizable baby due to the simple fact that economic policies used to base on fleeting glimpses of the northeastern reality are seen through parted clouds. There is a persistent denial to recognize the constraints to growth in the region. The issue of interstate disparities in income growth has become more prominent in the post-reform era. The question of convergence or divergence has not been answered unequivocally. The eleventh plan notes a widespread perception all over the country that disparities among states and regions within states, between urban and rural areas and between various sections of the community, have been steadily increasing in the past few years. This has been vindicated by the available statistics with respect to a number of indicators. The northeastern region has always remained at the other side of the divide (Ibid).

There is a perception that 'the union government deliberately neglects north eastern region. The evil forces of regionalism in north eastern region grew faster due to the problem of economic and social development. Although different provisions are made in the Constitution of India to bring socio-economic progress, all these went in vain ... the states of north eastern India are far behind these other states of the Indian union so far as the basic amenities of life such as health, education, safe drinking water, food security, banking facility, communication are concerned. All these created the seeds of contention amongst the people of NER for which the feeling of regionalism is growing more and more ... an important cause of regional tension which led to popular agitation and at times militant activities are such regional disparities in economic and social development' (Dutta 2013: 179ff).

Regionalism and Federalism

As has been seen, regionalist movements emerging in areas that fall under the cultural outer circle of a Hindu-Brahmanic ideology dominated nation have less access to political control besides being economically deprived. However, it has to be said that the economic backwardness alone is not responsible for the growth of region-centric sentiments. Otherwise the BIMARU states of India would have a forerunner in such movements. However, with regard to identity question, the political parties power in these states control the Indian statecraft. Hence, when the nation is at their disposal, backwardness of the region does not create any concern. However, the areas where regionalist movements are strong, the economic backwardness coupled with cultural and identity questions and the lack of political power create a strong sense of alienation, which forms the foundation for the emergence of regionalist movements. Hence, regionalist movements are not just for autonomy and further federalization of the polity, but also the recognition of the cultural identity of those communities as well as demanding the economic care of their region. Thus, the federal units demand a more equitable share in the financial resources, more royalty on local resources, more central aid in building infrastructure, protection of regional economic interests, land policy, resolution of water conflicts, royalty issues on resource sharing and centre's aid in mitigating natural disasters and so on. Indian federalism, unlike others, has shown an incredible flexibility. Responding positively to various regionalist demands, the Indian polity has so far created 28 states, a number of autonomous areas, district councils and autonomous councils. There are provisions such as Article 370 for Kashmir, Article 370 A for Nagaland, a provision of 90 per cent central aid for northeastern states, which make the federalist structure stronger. It has also been quite prompt in sanctioning cash packages than actually investing in the regions. However, the areas still remain 'regions' and not part of 'national' space. There is hardly anything in the region that would make the people identify with the nation. In all the areas-mentioned above, the only symbol of nation–state is the army men who have been sent there for controlling a 'hostile' people. Hence, even the army men view the people in the region with suspicion. The army atrocities including fake encounters and rape and indignity to women have further alienated the regions. In Punjab, the counter insurgency measures in the in the 1980s were so severe that a whole generation of young Sikhs who dared revolt got paralysed. Operation Bluestar and the demolition of the Golden Temple have alienated the Sikhs permanently. All these have alienated not only the regions, but also strengthened their identity vis-à-vis India. The declaration of parts of Haryana and Uttar Pradesh as National Capital Region and the huge investment that has gone into transforming them show the prejudiced stance of the Indian state. The state of Punjab does even have a capital of its own. While regions are still in their extreme primitive state in terms of development, zones around Delhi thrive in the luxury of modern amenities comparable to the metropolitan cities of the world. Unless the regions feel the presence of nation in them, regionalism would grow in strength. The creation of states and autonomous space by the Indian state is apparently in pursuance of the federal principle, but actually it is an attempt to create a local power base rather than devolving power. The unending state-centre conflicts in India are a testimony to the aspirations of the regions. Despite being federal, right from the beginning, the Indian state has insisted on a strong centre. This is mainly because of the recognition of the inherently fragile character of the nation and frequent threats of secession. This makes the centre more insecure about the integrity of the nation. It continuously is trying to strengthen the centre through discourses on national integration, mainstream-periphery, extremist and hostile threats to the integrity of the nation and so on, but at the same time, refuses to concede anything more substantial to the regions.

Conclusions

As per the Constitution, the Union government is committed to preserving and protecting the integration of the nation. At the same time it cannot ignore the aspirations and demands of its regional communities. Therefore, it has evolved a structure of federal polity. India is a multiethnic and multicultural country. Each of these communities with a twin identity – Indian and regional – are coeval and cherish a desire for self-rule. The nationalist aspirations for self-rule of these communities remain either satisfied or neutralized in the context of a federal structure. It means that most of these communities have been granted autonomy in the form of statehood or district councils or autonomous councils. The Indian state has been declared as the Union of these states with governments functioning at two different levels: one at the centre and the other at the state. There are certain areas that remain designated as union territories. It is further subdivided into districts, subdivisions and panchayats. Although the term 'federation' is not used in the Constitution, the Constitution of India is regarded as Federal Constitution with the authority commanded by the state governments deriving directly from the Constitution. Although the states can have a maximum autonomy, the Constitution does not permit the right to secede from the federation. In fact, not only are there no rights granted to secede, but also the advocacy of secessionism has been ruled out under the Sixteenth Amendment of the Constitution. However, it is possible for the Union Parliament to reorganize the states or to alter their boundaries by a simple majority. It is through this provision that so many new states have been created since independence. The states, however, do not have an equal representation in the upper house of the legislature. It is determined on the basis of population. Thus, bigger states with massive populations have a large number of representatives, while smaller states such as Nagaland, Mizoram and Sikkim have just about one Member of Parliament, while some populous states such as (undivided) Uttar Pradesh and Bihar have 85 and 54 representatives, respectively. Hence, MPs from these states alone could determine the party which would come to power at the centre, whereas the MPs of smaller states remain as mere tangents. Due to their weak numerical strength, the MPs of smaller states are not only less heard, but also their influence on the making of national policies is the least. There is a clear cut distribution of powers between the central and the state governments. The Constitution has laid down clearly where the residuary powers will rest within this dual system of governance. Any state government also could be dismissed by the centre under Article 356 of the Constitution. The responsibility of guarding the distribution of powers between the centre and states has been vested with the Supreme Court of the country, which could invalidate any action by either party that violates the constitutional provisions. It is the Constitution that has the supreme authority. There is a provision provided for in the Constitution for declaring an Emergency during which the state could become unitary. A state of Emergency can be declared in the context of an internal crisis or external aggression by the Union government with the assent of the President of India.

Note

1. Although the anti-Hindi movement was the strongest in Tamil Nadu and had threatened to secede from India on the basis of this movement, it did not experience any regionalist movements. It only started as an anti-Hindi, anti-Brahmanic movement, which gave rise to a regional party DMK, and its offspring AIADMK and settled down to being a prominent Indian federal unit. It has since then been a regional party in power with no regionalist ideology.

References

Ali, Nisar, 2012. 'Potential and Constraints in Jammu Kashmir Economy', in *Kashmir Speaks*, downloaded from http//.Kashmirspeaks.com, on 26 July 2012.

Austin, G. 1966. *The Indian Constitution: Cornerstone of a Nation*, Bombay; Oxford University Press.

Chaube, S.K. 1984. 'Cultural Frame and Dynamics of Federalism in India', *Social Science Probings,* Vol. 1, No. 2.

Constitution Assembly Debates, 1948. Vol. VII, No. 1, pp. 33–34.

Dutta, Paritosh C. 2013. 'Regional Disparity and Its Consequence in North Eastern Region of India', in A.C. Mohapatra and Chitta Ranjan Pathak (eds.), *Economic Liberalisation and Regional Disparities in India with a Special Focus on North Eastern India.*

Embree, A.T. 1985. 'Indian Civilisation and Regional Cultures: The Two Realities', in Paul Wallace (ed), *Region and Nation in India*, New Delhi: American Institute of Indian Studies and Oxford University Press.

Kumar, Ravinder. 1985. 'Nationalism and Social Change', in *Essays in Social History of Modern India*, Delhi: Oxford University Press.

Mehra, Ajay K.D.D. Khanna, and Gert W. Kweck (eds.), 2003. *Political Parties and Party Systems*, New Delhi: Sage Publications.

Mohapatra, A.C., and Chitta Ranjan Pathak (eds.). 2003. *Economic Liberalisation and Regional Disparities in India: Special Focus on North Eastern Region*, Shillong: Star Publishing House.

Nag, Sajal. 2000. *Nationalism, Separatism, Secessionism*, New Delhi and Jaipur: Rawat Publications.

Singh, Lakhwindar and Sukhpal Singh, 2002. 'Deceleration of Economic Growth in Punjab: Evidence, Explanation and a Way Out', in *Economic and Political Weekly*, Vol. 37, No. 6, February, pp. 9–15.

Singh, E. and Bijoy Kumar. 2009. 'Understanding Economic Growth in North Eastern India', in *Dialogue*, Vol. 10, No. 3, January–March.

Wallace, Paul (ed). 1985. *Region and Nation in India*, New Delhi: American Institute of Indian Studies and Oxford University Press.

13

Cooperative Federalism, Competitive Regionalism and Regional Parties-led Coalition Governments

Roles, Rights and Responsibilities

Biswajit Mohapatra

In the words of 'William H. Riker, the strength of any federal system depends not so much on the constitutional structure, but rather the political and economic culture, that may be prevailing within the country at any given time. According to him, two equilibrating features can be said to be necessary for the survival of federalism: '(1) centralization, which allows the central government to exploit the advantages of a larger base for taxes and armies, and (2) maintenance of guarantees to the constituent units, which prevents the transformation of federalism to a unitary government' (Riker 1969). Riker was careful to point out that these features should not simply be thought of as a structure guaranteed on paper in a constitution; instead, they must be based on actual incentives and abilities of politicians in key institutions. If the American federal system has at all succeeded, it is due to the very fact that, (i) the American system is a very centralized federal system, and has been from its beginning and (ii) the main peripheral zing institution checking the numerous pressures toward centralization is the political party system. Simply said political centralization rather than any fiscal or economic policy centralization is the key for an everlasting federal structure in any country.

'The essence of federalism is the political feature: (1) the political bargain that creates it and (2) the distribution of power in political parties which shapes the federal structure in its maturity'. Everything else about federalism is accident: the demarcation of areas of competence between central and constituent governments, the operation of intergovernmental relations, the division of financial resources, etc.'

If we were to ponder over the question, over the years if federal systems have proved its efficacy more than unitary governments in promotion and maintenance of political freedoms for their population, there have been views that as far as the honoring of guarantee of such freedoms, its argued that the federal systems have proved to be better as they provide double security as if under any condition, these freedoms tend to get abridged or limited by government, by way of any policy imposition, federalism does offer multiple layers of restrictions.

In 1996 piece, Riker wrote: 'Considering all the federations there have been in the world, I believe that federalism has been a significant force for limited government and hence for personal freedom' (Riker 1969). It's pointed out that as federalism has been proved to have its origins in some kind of a fundamental bargain struck amongst political leaders when threatened with territorial expansion and military threats, in the newly decolonized states, they remain steadfast in supporting the fundamental principles of an evolved federal structure. Further any desire for centralization of power in one's hand or in the central institution gets effectively checked by the existing political parties in a democracy, who by their very nature all the time seem to be showing their insistence on peripheral zing the power and decentralized political structure.

Likewise in India, the success of federalism can be said to be due to the nature of democratic politics in our country besides our constitutional provisions, which have ensured the spirit of federalism, respect for diversity and national unity as far as people are concerned. Over the years as the regional parties have gained due to the gradual decline of the Congress Party and disappearance of Congress dominant system, in our body politic, the centre and state governments' relationships has come under severe challenges, not merely that the political parties remain accountable to people for various issues that they are entrusted to govern at their respective level of administration, but more so when two different parties or coalitions are leading governments,at the centre and at the states. Besides the era of single party since 1989, coalition governments have not only continued at the centre but also in different states too. Besides after 1990, there has been a significant rise in the number of regional parties in many states of the country.

This complex combination of regional parties and national parties forming coalition government at both the levels has made the era of 'coalition governments' very challenging. This has also marked a new culture of power sharing and is responsible for the autonomy of state governments. Their coexistence though have often been marked with high degree of tensions at times, yet its reflective of the trend, that Coalition governments are here to stay and that the broad spectrum of political parties have also accepted this to be some kind of truth. Further over the years it has been markedly seen that there is a progressive reduction in the number of cases where Art 356 has been used by the Centre to dismiss the government at the level of states, howsoever they may have proved their incompetence in carrying out the mandate of governance at their level rather the fact that the Central Government has undertaken several development schemes for these states so as to build their capacity of governance and also to swiftly deploy required paramilitary forces for maintenance of law and order in their areas are indicative of their appreciation of the role that these state governments headed by regional parties play in the socio economic progress of the country and in the strengthening of the federal structure by extending cooperation to the Centre when it is in need of.

Rise of Coalitions

The birth of a coalition-based state governments marked the rise of a new phase in the context of state politics as much smaller and regional parties compared with the nationalist parties, were able to not only win the popular support of the masses at the time of election to state assemblies but also were able to combine themselves with each other despite their differences in political ideology and form the government at the level of various states. It's true that their common anti-congress ideology came to the fore in such activity but there is more to it than simple the much touted anti congress ideology.

The 1990s is quite significant also for the fact that the national government again came to be consisted of regional parties who provided not only the much needed numerical support base for any government to have a majority in the Indian Parliament but also the ideological unity in the shouldering of the burden of governance and new policy initiatives.

Regional Parties: Rising Actors in National Politics

If we look back in our history of Indian Politics, one but sees the desire on the part of regional parties to be prominent actors in the national politics of the day given the fact of much politicized allocation of financial resources to the states by the Central Government, both in the times of distress and also in normal times including at the level of the Finance Commissions, which have often aroused the ire of the state governments. As the regional parties developed a stable role for themselves in their respective states, then they very rightly stepped out to essay a possible and albeit meaningful role for themselves in the national level politics. The time also was right as the hold of the Congress party which had dominated the national scene for far too long was weakening along with the rapid socio economic changes and a weak central leadership within the Congress Party.

The formation of the Janata Dal Government at the Centre, as was crafted out of a veritable of regional non Congress parties acted as a booster for the regional parties to play a much more important role for the fulfillment of their political and regional aspirations, even though in the words of some commentators, was a short-lived example of a unlikely cohabitation. As far as that experiment goes, though the life of the government at the Centre was indeed short, yet the treatment meted out to the regional parties both at the level of government and at the level of states was something which was both honorable and didn't smack of any partiality, be littleness or any kind of politicking, something unparalleled in the political history of our country. Anoop Sadanandan has demonstrated as to how India's regional parties, by having entered into opportunistic alliances with national parties and joining coalition central governments, have indeed become very effective barriers against central dominance (Sadanandan 2012: 247–269). He has further shown how the central government interference in the state governance being effected through President's Rule, which had happened for about 100 times since the proclamation of our Constitution has declined since the mid-1990s after the participation of regional parties in the Union government (Sadanandan 2012: 247–269).

The year of 1988, which is well known for the formation of National Front government at the Centre again, brought to the fore many regional parties like, Telgu Desam Party, DMK, and Asom Gana Parishad etc. who were part of the Union government and participated effectively in the system of governance. Even in the 1991 government formation, though the regional parties were not so much directly involved, yet they were being courted by the national parties as they by virtue of their numerical strength in the Parliament, in the formation and continuation of the Central Government at those times. The partnership between the National parties and the Regional parties that was seen from the Janata Dal experiment of 1977 became a permanent and a unique feature of Indian federalism as was witnessed again from 1996 onwards given their essentiality in the formation of any kind of Government at the Centre.

As in the 1996 elections, while both the Congress and the BJP didn't succeed in winning about fifty percent of total votes polled in the election, the regional parties taken together had been able to muster the support of people by way of winning almost one fourth of the votes. Further in the election held in 1999, the regional parties are said to have even increased their vote base, making them more significant players in any kind of a given situation facing the Central Government. The political arrangement at the Centre came to be dominated by a conglomeration of regional parties. This new development showed the interesting change that had come about in the context of Indian body politic and more particularly in the context of Indian federal set up.

Regionalism: Cause for Rise of Regional Parties?

Regionalism in India has been rooted in India's manifold diversity as India, by demographic factors is the second largest country after China and also socially and culturally the most diverse in the world (Bhattacharyya 2005). For a diverse country like India, Indian federalism has been a proven method of accommodation of rising regionalism in various parts of India. Further Federalism is very well perceived as much in the manner of a political equilibrium, striking an appropriate balance between shared rule and self-rule. In the aftermath of the Second World War period, it was witnessed that many newly independent countries embraced federalism as a model of governance in their multi-ethnic and multilingual societies to guard the national unity.

According to Watts, there is no pure model of federation that can be applied everywhere. The need for federalism is enhanced in countries with ethnically distinct regions where the territorial accommodation of distinct groups of people is of paramount importance (Watts 1996). For this purpose, some kind of mixture of shared rule and some kind of self rule, for maintenance of regional diversity serves well the purpose of unity and integrity.

Granville Austin offered the strongest ever defense of Indian Federalism, from a constitutional-legal perspective (Austin 1966: 186–87). He has shown the pragmatic character of Indian federalism, which, according to him, was a 'new kind of federalism to meet India's peculiar needs' and which is what he calls 'a co-operative federalism' that 'produces a strong central government yet not necessarily resulting in weak provincial governments (Austin 1966: 186–87).

Dr B.R. Ambedkar, the Chairman of the Drafting Committee of the Indian Constitution had said: 'The Draft Constitution can be both unitary as well as federal according to the requirements of the time and circumstances. In normal times, it is framed to work as a federal system. Even K.R. Bombwal has also noted the Indian federalism's success as an institutional solution to intra-societal conflicts and tensions in a diverse society (Bombwal 1967).

In line with these commentators, Carl Friedrich (1968) also has recognized the burgeoning strength of Indian federalism. He has noted, 'India is clearly undergoing a federalizing process in the course of which federal diversity is increasing. It is, a recurrent feature of this process that in the course of democratizing of a society, regional and linguistic-cultural communities become more articulate and demand recognition in the form of a set of political institutions, including safeguards for the identity of the particular community' (Friedrich 1968).

Rajni Kothari, has argued that,the federalism we have, is 'an ambivalent federalism which gave the Centre much scope and initiative, a major share in resources and all residual functions, but simultaneously gave the states considerable powers and scope for manoeuvre' (Kothari 1970: 91–92).

The period of Emergency rule,which stretched for about 18 months between the year 1975–77, as witnessed concentration and centralization of powers in the Centre, during the time when Mrs Gandhi was the then Prime Minister of India. This was also the time where India had gone away from the federalism route as it emphasized more on centralization and concentration of power, as the political regime had felt crippled due to many challenges it was facing at that time. In the words of Rajni Kothari, 'The political constitutional sphere has itself become prone to the same tendencies of centralization, domination and inequity' leading to 'institutional disorder' (Kothari 1970: 91–92).

To Rudolph and Rudolph, the federal system had come under severe strain having been sandwiched between the growing centralization and concentration of powers, on the one hand, and the growing strength of regionalism, on the other hand (Rudolph 1987: 98–99). The Janata Experiment (1977–1980) had very distinct federalist implication as India's existing cultural heterogeneity had found its clearest explanation in the 'federal organization of power' (Ray 1987). The Janata government, itself as was an agglomeration of many regionally based groups and parties, also demonstrated a balanced operation of the India's federal system during the its rule (Rudolph 198.157).

The 1980s and 90s however came to be marked with a sense of renewed vigour and hope as no sooner had the Emergency been lifted, democracy got restored with full strength and the federalism got a new lease of life and legitimacy.

States' Rights and Regional Identities

Apart from the issue of states' rights, regional and local identities, which have been persistently stressed by the various state governments, the question of decentralization also got added to the agenda and it also was continuously focused in any kind of centre and State Governments meeting. The Administrative Reforms Commission (ARC 1966)[1] and Sarkaria Commission (Sarkaria Commission 1983)[2] had also recommended further state autonomy and decentralization, both at the federal or state levels for a harmonious relationship and co-operative spirit between the Centre and the States and among the States themselves. Its indeed true that harmonious and cooperative relations between the Centre and the States are as important as that between different States, for the healthy functioning of our federation. Rasheeuddin Khan held forth that, decentralization of real power to these local institutions would thus help defuse the threat of centrifugal forces, increase popular involvement all along the line, broaden the base of our democratic polity, promote efficiency and improve the health and stability of intergovernmental relations (Khan 1992: 212).

E.M.S. Namboodripad, prominent Marxist leader stressed through regionalism, the case for assertion of rights of the federating units, and strongly advocated for expanding states 'rights (Namboodripad 1981). The West Bengal Government also demanded greater powers to the states in its Memorandum on Centre–state Relations of December 1, 1977, submitted to the Union government. They also further asserted: 'We are definitely for strong states, but on no account do we want a weak centre. The concept of strong states is not necessarily in contradiction to that of a strong centre, once their respective spheres of authority are clearly marked out' (Kurian and Varughese 1981: 204–14).

Rasheeuddin Khan strongly advocated about the need for simultaneous practice of urban and rural grassroots democracy as a devolutionary measure and for provision of space for the various regions and sub-regional identities in his proposal for a new federal balance, and identity in India (Khan 1992: 15). He described Indian federalism as a 'bouquet' that exhibits different flowers, each with its individuality yet tied together as a single whole (Khan 1992: 13). He wrote: 'The process of infrastructuring of the Indian federation is not yet over. Therefore, political demands of viable regions for new administrative arrangements are not necessarily antithetical to the territorial integrity of the country. For, every urge for autonomy is not divisive, but most probably a complementary force; it would not lead to balkanization but to the restructuring of nation identity' (Khan 1992: 16).

Nirmal Mukherji, former Union Cabinet Secretary and former Governor of Punjab, has stressed on the need for a more federal India as also for linking decentralization with sub-nationalism. According to him, the starting point for fresh thinking in regard to devolution has to accord due recognition to sub-nationalism as a growing reality. The federal centre would, as a first inference, have to be viewed as the focal point at which various sub-national identities converge rather than as a source from which power is exercised upon them. As such devolutionary measures would require to be coordinated in a spirit of partnership between the federal and sub-national levels rather than unilaterally by the dominant centre (Grover and Arora 1994: 399).

According to Paul Brass (Brass 1990/1992: 66), 'Insofar as Indian federalism and the question of decentralization is concerned, there had never been a case of continuous centralization on a long-term basis, rather across institutions and policy areas in India, the directions or the underlying patterns point towards pluralism, regionalism, and decentralization' (Brass 1989: 225). He nonetheless has talked about immense capacity of the Centre to build a stable power as according to his studies, power in India is inherently regional and local in character (Brass 1989: 227).

In an article, Rajni Kothari, noted the growing federal political reality in India in the late 80s in recognition of the persistent diversity in the society and said, 'Never before has the Indian polity been more multi-centric than now. With so many states being run by various opposition parties and with each of them becoming more assertive vis-a-vis the centre than was earlier the case, with the wide spread of regionalism and the upsurge in so many places of regional identities' (Kothari 1989: 13).

When we look back into our past we can easily see that while there has been a constant demand for honoring the federal features of the Indian polity, there has also been the so called demand for decentralization of power and resources, both for the states and to grass root levels under the backdrop of gross inability of the Centre to deliver public services in an efficient manner all through this vast country. Further the sudden upsurge of ethnic identities, and their constant struggle for more autonomous spaces as reflected in the demand for separate statehood for themselves, within the federal set-up complicated the task of a centralized governance from any level.

According to Rajni Kothari, these developments hold much more significance for a more federal democratic India. He says, 'The battle for federalism in India is fundamentally a battle for greater democracy in which the people come into their own through social identities, organizational forms and institutional frameworks with which they feel comfortable and through which they can find their potency and self-respect' (Kothari1989: 13).

Conclusion

As far as our understanding about Indian federalism is concerned, the debate about more power for the states in the context of federal India is usually seen as a problem of 'centre–state relations', i.e. strong central authority versus states' rights, when the governments on both sides are being led by ideologically opposite parties or group of parties but it stands reduced to non issue when the same party or group of parties do rule on both the sides of the spectrum. The failure of the Centre in redressing the regional disparities in the context of allocation of resources by way of plans seems to be the important contributor to the growth of a feeling of much malignment and deep neglect on the part of the people and various state governments, who are then forced to take up the issue at the political level, which often have serious consequences for the political system. The inept handling of the questions of nationality and homeland in the remote North Eastern India has been responsible for the continuation of militancy movements for over fifty years. This has also often not only complicated the centre State relations as Assam got divided into further six states over the years,which were carved out of it and with new movements raising their demands, it stands further to be cut into more smaller states,thus becoming a truncated state.

Elections held periodically in the country though may have proved as a commitment to resolving differences peacefully and democratically and attempts to transform diversity into a source of strength (Kohli 2001: 1). Yet the policies often inspired by politicization of issues can endanger India's rich diversity and turn it into a fireball leaving a trail of disaster and unresolved grief challenging the unity and integrity of our country and becoming an obstacle towards assured socio economic progress and mutual prosperity.

Notes

1. First Administrative Reforms Commission was set up by the Government of India on 5 January 1966
2. Sarkaria Commission was set up in June 1983 by the Government of India, for details: interstatecouncil.nic.in/Sarkaria_Commission.html

References

Bhattacharyya, Harihar. 2005. 'Federalism and Regionalism in India: Institutional Strategies and Political Accommodation of Identity', *Heidelberg Papers in South Asian and Comparative Politics*, Working Paper No: 27.

Bombwall, K.R. 1967. *The Foundations of Indian Federalism*, Bombay: Asia Publishing House.

Brass, Paul. 1989. 'Pluralism, Regionalism and Decentralizing Tendencies in Contemporary Indian Politics', in Wilson A J and Dalton, D. (eds.), *The States of South Asia: Problems of National Integration*, London: Hirst and Co.

Friedrich, Carl. 1968. *Trends of Federalism in Theory and Practice*, London: Pall Mall.

Granville Austin. 1966. *The Indian Constitution: The Cornerstone of a Nation*, Delhi: Oxford University Press.

Granville Austin. 1999. *Working of a Democratic Constitution*, Delhi: Oxford University Press.

Grover, V.V. and R. Arora (eds). 1994. *Development of Politics and Government in India,* Vol.10, Delhi: Deep and Deep Publications.

Khan, Rasheeuddin. 1992. *Federal India: Design for Change*, New Delhi: Vikash Publications.

Kohli, Atul (ed.). 2001. *The Successes of India's Democracy*, Cambridge: CUP.

Kothari, Rajni. 1970. *Politics in India*, New Delhi: Orient Longman.

——. 1989. 'The Problem', *Seminar*, No. 357, p.13.

Nambudripad. E.M.S. 1981. 'National Political Background of Indian Federalism', in Kurian and Varughese (eds). *Centre-State Relations in India,* Delhi: Macmillan, pp. 65.

Ray, Amal. 1987. 'Tension Areas in India's Federal System', in T.C. Bose (ed.), *Indian Federalism*, Calcutta: K P Bagchi and Co.

Riker, William, H. 1969. 'Six Books in Search of a Subject or Does Federalism Exist and Docs it Matter?, *Comparative Politics,* Vol. 2, No.1, pp. 443.

Rudolph L. and Rudolph, S. 1987. *In Pursuit of Lakshmi: The Political Economy of the Indian State,* Chicago: Chicago University Press.

Sadanandan, Anoop. 2012. 'Bridling Central Tyranny in India: How Regional Parties Restrain the Federal Government', *Asian Survey*, Vol. 52, No. 2, pp. 247–269, California: University of California Press.

Watts, R.L. 1966. *New Federations Experiments in the Commonwealth*, Oxford: Clarendon Press.

14

Federalism, Regionalism and States' Paradiplomacy in India

Prakash Chandra Jha

Broadly speaking, the term 'paradiplomacy', that is, 'parallel diplomacy' is used in academic literature for the involvement of subnational governments in foreign affairs with a view of promoting their own interests.[1] Subnational paradiplomacy, especially in economic sphere, has become a worldwide phenomenon in the recent times. As the global trend shows, central governments often try to accommodate the transnational economic interests of their constituent units. India is a federal system where states enjoy a considerable degree of autonomy. The economic globalization and regionalization have made it possible for the constituent units of India to interact with their respective investors in foreign countries in a *de facto* sense if not in a *de jure* sense (Jha 2004: 164, 2011). Compared to other countries, including some of our neighbours (China, Japan, etc.), subnational paradiplomacy in India is still at an incipient stage. However, paradiplomatic initiatives by states, of late, have begun gathering momentum. It is evident from the states' high-profile investment-promotion activities abroad. Such activities indeed have helped some states in their economic development besides reducing their economic dependency on central government. States in India so far have adopted a host of instruments that fall under paradiplomacy. They include putting pressure on the central government to sign or not to sign a treaty affecting their region/interests, pressing the centre for facilitation of their trade negotiations with external bodies, negotiating loans directly with the World Bank, International Monetary Fund (IMF) and Asian Development Bank (ADB), showcasing states' achievements, providing incentives to attract foreign investments, participating in international forums such as World Economic Forum, visiting abroad for trade prospects, hosting foreign diplomats, ministers and even heads of state and organizing conferences and seminars, wooing NRIs using their diasporas and setting up sister cities and twin cities, border *haats*, among others.

Aside from economic gains, states' paradiplomatic activities can arguably also be useful for the purpose of addressing some of the long-standing problems with our neighbouring countries such as water-sharing, terrorism, and illegal cross-border migration, environmental protection, among others. Further, it can also be used by the centre as part of soft diplomacy that can complement the national foreign policy. Nevertheless, paradiplomacy presents challenges too. It is taking place in unplanned and scattered manner without the central government coordinating with states in systematic way. For example, some state governments may lack the skills to exercise responsible foreign policy; they rather may complicate national foreign policy making.

Given the increased subnational international activities, no systematic study has, so far, been conducted to assess the extent of the forays made by states into Indian foreign policy in the recent times. There is hardly any debate or discussion either in academia or government over the need for a greater role of states in India's foreign policy. The study examines the factors responsible for the development of paradiplomacy in India. It also focuses on responses of the centre towards subnational diplomacy. Further, it also underlines the potential gains not only in economic terms but also in political and cultural terms from paradiplomacy. Furthermore, the study also highlights challenges to national foreign policy on account of states' international activism. It calls for an institutionalized mechanism for states' paradiplomacy.

Federalism and Paradiplomacy

The studies on subnational paradiplomacy began in the 1970s in the form of case studies on the external activities of constituent units of the federal countries such as Canada, United States and Australia. Theoretical works on paradiplomacy were carried out by scholars with a predominantly academic background in federalism. Therefore, most of them understand in the first place the subnational governments' diplomacy as a result and attributes of the vast transformations that are taking place within federalism and intergovernmental relations. Thus, they primarily study the impact of paradiplomacy on federalism and intergovernmental relations rather than paradiplomacy as a new political phenomenon. Notwithstanding the fact that subnational paradiplomacy also takes place in nonfederal countries, until today this federalist dimension has played a leading role in studies on paradiplomacy (Duchacek et al. 1988; Hocking 1993; Aguirre 1999; Kincaid 2002; Michelmann 2009; Cornago 2010). With this respect, it is imperative to examine the following questions:

Does being part of a federal system help the subnational governments to engage in paradiplomacy? In other words, does federalism as an institution help subnational governments in their quest for paradiplomacy? Indeed federalism helps because it constitutionally divides power between the central government and its constituent units. But not necessarily subnational governments participate in foreign policy only in the federal country (Cornago 2010: 17). Even in federal countries, foreign policy is normally one of very few areas, along with defence and monetary/fiscal policy that does not come under the jurisdiction of subnational governments. However exceptions do exist such as Argentina and Spain, among others. In a federal system, the state enjoys an absolute autonomy in several areas well protected by the Constitution. Thus, federalism, as an institution, may help the constituent units of a country influence/participate in foreign economic policy (Kincaid 2002; Hocking 1993). Constitutionally speaking, however, states and local governments are not legitimate international actors in most of the federal countries in the world including India.

As per the constitutional division of subjects under the Constitution of India, most of the sectors that are important for liberalization process fall within the jurisdiction of state governments. They include industrial infrastructure, power, development, agriculture and irrigation and social sectors such as education and health. Indeed, while the central government has a primary role in the formulation of liberalization policy, the implementation of the policy, however, cannot be feasible without seeking the support of states. Thus, states become important actors and without their support the centre cannot reap the benefits of the foreign economic policy. Despite the adoption of India's new economic policy (NEP) in the early 1990s with some state governments playing an important role in the foreign policy formulation in the form of paradiplomatic activities, however, states' role appears to be quite limited as compared to other countries. Leave aside countries with federal set-ups, Indian states are playing weaker role in this regard than provincial/subnational governments even in unitary countries such as China, United Kingdom and Japan, among others. It can, however, be argued that subnational international activism is gaining momentum in India and that India's federal structure would, in fact, prove to be an asset in helping the constituent units in terms of developing paradiplomatic activities.

Globalization, Regionalism and Development of Paradiplomacy in India

Aside from federalism, globalization and regionalism remain important factors behind the rise of states' paradiplomacy in India. First, once coalition governments became dominant at the national level in India, the influence of states on national government became increasingly pronounced. Second, the adoption of economic liberalization in the early 1990s gave the Indian states unforeseen opportunities to engage in activities that fall under paradiplomacy (Chelliah, 1996).[2] The quest for trade and investment forced them to look across the border. Further, coalition formation at the national level led to the empowerment of the states at the expense of the centre. On the other side, economic globalization has provided with conducive environment for the states to play a key role in foreign economic policy, particularly with regard to seeking foreign direct investment (FDI) and the promotion of foreign trade. However, it would not be wrong to say that the centre is still constitutionally strong, but it has become politically weak.

During the pre-liberalization era, industrial development of the states was largely determined by the central government, often in a partisan manner. Sarkaria Commission, which was constituted to examine the centre–state relations in the 1980s, observed that this was a major complaint of states. Karnataka, a state not governed by the Congress Party when the commission was making its inquiries, cited instances of industries not being located in Karnataka for political considerations. The most glaring example was the relocation of the Indian Telephone Industries, a public sector unit factory that manufactures electronic telephone exchanges, to Gonda in Uttar Pradesh. The move was pursued by the central government despite the fact that the best infrastructural facilities for producing the exchanges were available in Karnataka. The relocation of the public sector unit was influenced by political considerations, and Karnataka government also noted that private sector corporations, such as Glaxo, the Tata Electric Locomotive Company and Tractors India wanted to set up their industrial units in Karnataka and were asked by the centre (led by the Congress Party) to locate their plants elsewhere. Kerala government argued that no objective criteria had been followed in deciding regarding the location where the investment in the public sector by the central government would occur (Chhibber and Kollman 2004: 139–140). Contrast this to the post-liberalization period, one can at once notice a paradigm shift in the centre–state relations in India.

Regional parties led by charismatic and in some cases development-oriented regional leaders have become important national players, while the central leadership can no longer take them for granted. Leaders openly admit that 'regional parties are not only looking after the problems of their respective regions, they are also involved in deciding the national problems'.[3] A foreign policy analyst has observed,

> With the Delhi *darwar* at its dysfunctional worst, power is flowing away from Delhi to state capitals, where some strong men and women are ruling. India's external partners tend to see this with much greater clarity than the domestic observers ... If Mamata has the last word on India's policy towards foreign direct investment in the retail sector, why won't outsiders go to Kolkata? If Gujarat and Bihar are places where you can get things done, aren't the Chinese communist leaders smart enough to woo the chief ministers of the two states? (Rajamohan 2012a)

There is a growing tendency among some state governments that have some broad motives for developing stronger external economic relations, such as the need to project their image abroad, growing pressures to compete in the international economy and the desire to assert their autonomy vis-à-vis the central government (Agarwal 2012).[4]

Defining Moment in Paradiplomacy

The 'defining moment' in paradiplomacy occurred in 1993 when the Government of India's most industrialized state Maharashtra entered into negotiations with Enron, Texas energy giant. It signed the largest contract in history with the company on a power purchase agreement. Here, a weak central government played a supportive role because it was compelled by Maharashtra to provide the sovereign counter guarantee against its own better judgement. This is considered as a paradigm shift in the centre–state relations in India as the lead player happened to be the state rather than the centre, and this was the result of the opening up of the Indian economy, which enabled the state to exercise a considerable control over the issue. This is, however, not to say that the decision was a rational one (Rudolph and Rudolph 2001: 1542). During the United Front government's term in office, West Bengal Chief Minister, Jyoti Basu played an unprecedented role in the resolution of the Ganges water issue between Bangladesh and India. His six-day official visit to Bangladesh and the negotiations he held there finally paved the way for the water sharing treaty between the two countries in December 1996.

Growing Tendency among States for Paradiplomacy and the Centre as a Facilitator

Historically, some states in India – implicitly or explicitly – influenced the foreign policy making of the central government occasionally. Recently, there is a growing tendency to involve relevant state governments in diplomatic discussions, which were previously conducted mostly between the central government and the country in question. The centre has now realized that regional leaders can help provide a greater understanding because of the common cultural ties between their states and the people across the border. On his trip to Bangladesh, the Indian PM was accompanied by a number of chief ministers of northeast regions. Recently, at the International Labour Meet at Geneva, Labour Minister of India was also accompanied by his state counterparts from Bihar, Haryana and Andhra Pradesh (*Times of India* 2012).

The central government is encouraging border states to take measures such as opening border *haats* for making border villages more prosperous through an improved market accessibility to their locally produced goods. The centre has also facilitated states' direct financial assistance related negotiations with overseas banks. In the 1990s, the World Bank officials decided to develop lending relationships directly with select states such as Andhra Pradesh, Karnataka and Tamil Nadu. This was a significant change from the bank's earlier practices. In order to encourage the states to pursue market-oriented reforms, the centre asked the World Bank to provide financial aid to lagging states that were performing poorly with respect to human development indicators. As a result, the World Bank shifted its focus to Bihar and Uttar Pradesh, among India's economically weakest states. Explaining this, Kirk (2011) underlines the central role that New Delhi played by encouraging the World Bank to make its lending available to states that were being left out of India's growth trajectory. The World Bank President claimed that the bank was directly dealing with some Indian states, a major departure from the established norm and has caused some concern within India because it is seen as violating Article 292 of the Constitution, which allows for a state to borrow only within the territory of India. However, this is apparently being interpreted flexibly by the centre, because it has endorsed and accepted the loan proposals forwarded by states and has requested the bank to sanction them. Sridharan (2003: 476) argues,

> When I spoke to state-level policy-makers in India they pointed to a noticeable change in the attitude of the Central government – the Department of Economic Affairs within the Ministry of Finance is now encouraging the states to take the initiative in accessing external assistance. There is no doubt that the responsibility for providing the sovereign guarantee for the loans still rests with the Centre, and these negotiations have to adhere to certain basic norms, but the states have been empowered to negotiate with the multilateral institutions. In other words, in their negotiations with the external agencies the presence of the Finance Ministry official is not seen as overbearing, as was once the case.

The centre has established India Trade Promotion Organisation (ITPO) and it has also encouraged states to set up regional trade promotion centres in state capitals and major cities. This has led to the intensification of paradiplomacy relations at vertical levels, anchored in bilateral agreements, between Indian states and foreign countries. States have come to acquire an important say in the national government's negotiations with World Trade Organisation (WTO). The Union government has advised all the state governments/union territories to set up WTO cells and appoint nodal officers to effectively coordinate various WTO-related matters. Accordingly, a number of states have established WTO cells. The main objective of the cells is to carry out research and provide inputs to the state governments for taking up state-specific issues with the Government of India to be negotiated with WTO. The centre is also encouraging northeastern states to open border *haats*.

In short, the central government has recognized and, to some extent, favoured this increasing international activism of states. These developments can be seen as an act of legitimizing subnational paradiplomacy by the central government.

Aggressive Promotion of States Nationally and Globally

When it comes to the question of aggressive promotion of a state, both nationally and globally, Gujarat has perhaps no parallel in India. The state is leaving no stone unturned to showcase its achievements on various fronts to the global investors. A glance at the Gujarat government's website (www.vibrantgujarat.com) (which is daily updated) shows how aggressively the state is projecting itself as the best possible FDI destination in the world.[5] Diplomatic delegations from several other countries, including the United Kingdom, United States, Australia and Singapore, have already visited the state in the run-up to the event and expressed interest in intergovernmental and business partnerships.

A number of states are taking a leaf from the book of Chief Minister Narendra Modi in terms of promoting a pro-business atmosphere and showcasing their states' achievements. Recently, chief minister of Madhya Pradesh had gone on a tour to Japan, South Korea and Singapore for inviting industrial investment and promoting exports from the state. Trying to capitalize on its surplus government acquired land, P.K. Dash, additional chief secretary of Commerce, Industry and Employment, Government of Madhya Pradesh, argued: 'Land acquisition is not a problem in our state. The government is sitting on 20,000 hectares which would be available for industry' (Bhattacharya 2012). Till recently, Bihar, Madhya

Pradesh, Rajasthan and Uttar Pradesh were known as the 'Bimaru' states. But these states are trying hard to leave this image far behind by seeking external investment. They compete with each other in providing potential investors with numerous incentives such as special economic zone (SEZ), some guaranteed return on investment and reimbursement of value added tax.

Aggressive promotion of states for seeking investment was perhaps nowhere more visible than at Pravasi Bharatiya meet. As one newspaper reported 'the third Pravasi Bharatiya Divas congregation in Mumbai would be remembered more for chief ministers than NRIs'. The chief ministers from Uttar Pradesh, Rajasthan, Punjab, Gujarat, Chhattisgarh, Maharashtra, Kerala and Karnataka had literally queued up to woo prospective investors to their states (*The Economic Times* 2005).[6] Kerala surprised the Gulf Diaspora with its plans to start a budget airline to the Gulf region. According to Chief Minister Oommen Chandy, the state is in the process of seeking centre's permission for starting it. With about 15 lakh Keralites in the region, the cash-strapped Kerala government hopes the airline will be a profitable venture (*The Economic Times*, 2012).

Some chief ministers have become very popular with foreign investors and they are being accorded honour provided previously only to the head of a nation. These CMs head several business teams abroad several times in a year. They are aggressively pitching in their states not just nationally but also globally for the sole purpose of attracting more and more capital investment and promoting states' exports. Several forward looking states are organizing global business Summits to advance their business interests.[7]

States are becoming increasingly aware of the fact that in the present globalized market economy, they cannot be solely dependent on the centre for generating resources to achieve their developmental goals. They are, therefore, looking for external sources to meet their needs. In order to reap the benefits of the market economy, states require huge financial resources to develop sound infrastructure base. But they are constrained by revenue raising limits, given that they do not have independent borrowing powers. No wonder, therefore, states are forced to look for foreign investment. This has turned most chief ministers of the states into salesmen who advertise their state's unique endowments to their foreign audience (Sridharan 2003).

State governments signing memoranda of understanding (MOUs) with external agencies have become a regular affair. Some states have gone to the extent of inviting foreign companies to take over and run some municipal services, for example, in Andhra Pradesh and Tamil Nadu. Some states have also been exploring the possibility of boosting tourism-related business with foreign countries. For instance, Kerala tourism officials have finalized plans with Singapore Airlines subsidiary Silk Air to bring tourists from the Australasian region to India. The state, of late, has floated the idea of having its own airlines.

The increasing clout of states is understandable from the fact that recently Secretary of State, Hillary Clinton chose Chief Minister Mamata Banerjee's Kolkata as the first stop of her India tour to advance US foreign policy interests. In a televised interview, before meeting with Banerjee, Clinton had urged that India permit FDI in multibrand retail trading and for an 'amicable' water-sharing arrangement with Bangladesh regarding Teesta River – issues stalled by Banerjee's opposition (Chellaney 2012).

Chief Ministers of Bihar and Gujarat visited China to explore trade and investment opportunities.[8] They were accorded a red carpet welcome by the Chinese government. Their visits attracted a huge media attention in India. Chief minister of Gujarat was received at the Great Hall of People, where normally heads of national governments are received and accorded such honour. As per media reports, Gujarat CM was not only invited by Japan but also treated him almost at par with the head of a nation.

State Leaders at International Forums

Through their participation in international gatherings such as the World Economic Forum held annually in Davos, Switzerland, developments taking place in some reform-oriented states are being brought to the attention of international audiences. Maharashtra CM, Chavan, recently headed a high-level delegation to the World Economic Forum's annual event at Davos. In November 2010, Chief Minister Prem Kumar Dhumal of Himachal Pradesh had been invited by the Governor of California, Arnold Schwarzenegger, for participation in 'Governors' Global Summit on Climate Change' (*Tribune* 2010).

States have acquired a considerable say in WTO negotiations. They have persuaded the centre to be more transparent and inclusive in its deliberations with external entities such as WTO (Jenkins 2003). Recently, at the International labour Conference hosted by the International Labour Organization (ILO), Geneva, Union Labour Minister of India was accompanied by Labour Ministers of Haryana, Andhra Pradesh and Bihar (*Times of India* 2012). These developments indicate the emergence of parallel diplomacy, in which states have become additional players in a sphere that is usually the preserve of the central government.

In November 2011, speaking at the World Economic Forum's 'India Economic Summit' hosted by Maharashtra, Chief Minister Chavan said that he would sign memoranda of understanding with 32 companies that were ready to invest over 500 crores each in two months before the end of the year (*The Economic Times* 2011). At the summit on 'The New Role of the States: Catalyst for Growth', chief ministers of Maharashtra, Kerala, Madhya Pradesh and the Premier of British Columbia, a Canadian Province, discussed a host of issues concerning paradiplomacy.[9]

Foreign Trade Offices in India

Increasingly, there is a realization among the investors that the states in India are becoming autonomous players in crafting foreign economic policies suited to their own needs and that the old way of approaching the central government to pursue trade relations at the state level is no longer useful. Not surprisingly, therefore, various state capitals have witnessed the setting up of a number of foreign trade offices in major cities such as Mumbai, Delhi, Bangalore, Ahmadabad, Chennai, etc. Several subnational governments of foreign countries are also setting up foreign trade offices in India.

Taiwan has a trade office in New Delhi rather than a full-fledged embassy. Some years ago, it had sought permission from the Ministry of External Affairs (MEA) to open a subsidiary office or consulate in Chennai because several Taiwanese companies have substantial investments made in Tamil Nadu. Worried about the reaction of Beijing, MEA backed off. Finally, Taiwanese government asked the then DMK government in Chennai to use its political clout with UPA (Malik, 2012).

City Twinning/Sister Town

'Sister town'/'twin cities' is a recently evolved concept. It is when two cities are considered to be in an agreement with respect to promoting cultural and commercial ties. Bangalore, Jaipur, Delhi, Mumbai, Chennai, Lucknow, etc., have sisters/twins abroad (Wikipedia). Government of India is encouraging Indian cities to develop twinning link with other cities (Government of India). Twinning agreement signed on 20 December 1996 between Leicester and Rajkot was first such twinning undertaken by a city in India. The Leicester–Rajkot twinning association is one such voluntary organization that aims to further a link between two cities. City twinning supports exchanges between cities, it can be business, culture or education. Under this agreement, both sides agreed to carry out, promote and support exchanges and cooperation in a wide range of areas of common interest in the public, private, voluntary and community sectors aimed at deepening links between local people in the two cities in the fields of education, training, culture, leisure, economy, science youth and women's issues, voluntary and grassroots developments and civic management. Recently, there was a proposal put forth by the Vadodara Municipal Corporation (VMC) to sign a twin city agreement between the Chinese city, Chengdu and Vadodara under the aegis of United Cities and Local Government (UCLG) (*The Times of India* 2012).

States' Paradiplomacy and Development in India

States' paradiplomacy has the following gains: In the economic sphere, it can lead to international funding, as well as foreign investments and increased exports of locally produced goods. In the political sphere, agreements can empower state public policies and disseminate best practices as well as carry the needs of subnational governments to the international system – through networks of cities and bilateral agreements, for example. In the cultural sphere, subnational governments can seek/sign agreements with foreign countries to increase tourism.

The implications of paradiplomacy on the economies of some states such as Gujarat, Maharashtra, Tamil Nadu, Andhra Pradesh, Haryana, Delhi and Karnataka, among others, are unquestionably immense. Various industries in these states have grown, developed and also expanded. FDI in various states has led to a growth in trade and exports. With increased volumes of FDI, these states have registered phenomenal growth rates in the recent times. The success stories of some of these states have been globally acclaimed. States are competing with each other in terms of attracting investment – domestic as well as foreign. In their competitive horizontal federalism, they are adopting a number of strategies such as organizing global summits, making foreign trips, showcasing their growth stories to their potential investors and providing a number of incentives. These strategies have helped states such as Maharashtra, Karnataka, Andhra Pradesh, Gujarat and Tamil Nadu tremendously. Other states such as Bengal Bihar, Orissa, Kerala, Madhya Pradesh, Haryana and UP are also resorting to these paradiplomatic activities to woo foreign investors (Srivastava 2012). FDI giants such as Maharashtra are facing a stiff competition from several states that are vying each other to attract investments.[10] States are busy formulating new industrial and investment policies. A number of states have set up a single-window clearance systems. They are trying to upgrade the infrastructure bases of their less developed regions so as to attract investments.

Although most of our states are engaged in the so-called paradiplomacy, they exhibit differential capacities to do so. Gujarat, Tamil Nadu, Maharashtra and Andhra Pradesh represent coastal states that are particularly crucial for promoting external trade. There exist multiple factors that make these states attractive destinations for FDIs:

(i) They are strategically located, providing easy access to external markets.
(ii) These states possess the most robust infrastructure with an extensive network of railways and roads, and the highest number of airports (international and domestic) in the country.
(iii) A large pool of high-quality manpower is abundantly available in these states across various sectors.
(iv) The governments in these states have also been proactive in introducing sector-specific policies for the promotion of investment and growth.
(v) They have also witnessed the establishment of foreign trade offices by various countries for facilitating mutual trade.

Tourism is one of the biggest industries in the world with a capacity to employ 200 million people worldwide. A projection of tourist inflow around the world will be in the range of 1.6 billion spending US$ 5 billion a day by 2020. It goes without saying that India has an immense tourism potential that has not been effectively exploited so far. States' paradiplomacy in this regard can play a significant role. A subnational paradiplomacy can help an FDI laggard state such as Bihar to realize its tourism potential. In 2011, CM of Bihar visited China. During his meeting with provincial leaders, it emerged that China was keen to establish its relationship at a level where a province of China can have a relationship with a state in India. Culture can be one of the most important areas for regional cooperation between Bihar and China. It is felt that Chinese provinces can provide a considerable support for projects aimed at preserving historical patrimony (including numerous buildings of historical value in Gaya, Bodh Gaya, Rajgir, Nalanda, etc.), and thus contributing significantly to Bihar's tourism potential development. Countries such as China, Japan and other Asian countries have recently promised to invest in Bihar to develop its religious tourism.

In short, states in India are involved in foreign economic policy, particularly with regard to seeking FDI and the promotion of foreign trade. Under the previous command economy model, this subnational economic paradiplomacy was not possible. The relationship between the centre and the states, notwithstanding the dominant position enjoyed constitutionally by the centre, has been neither confrontational nor can it be considered cooperative. Of late, the centre has informally allowed states to engage in economic paradiplomacy.

Border States and Paradiplomacy

India shares its geographical borders with Pakistan in Kashmir, Punjab, Rajasthan and Gujarat in the north and west and with China and Nepal in the north-central states of Uttar Pradesh and Bihar. With Bangladesh, it shares its boundary in the eastern state of West Bengal and the small northeastern states to the east of Bangladesh and with Sri Lanka in Tamil Nadu in the south (a littoral border) (Dossani and Vijaykumar 2005). Considering the commonalities existing with respect to ethnicity, religion and stages of economic development, border states have a great incentive to undertake paradiplomatic initiatives.

Northeast India shares 98 per cent of its geographical border with Myanmar, Bangladesh, China and Bhutan. Thus, building transport and trading corridors at various border points can make essential subsistence items much cheaper in this region. It has been observed that due to higher transport costs, people in the region pay a very high price for goods coming from the industrial metros such as Delhi, Mumbai and Kolkata. The opening of transport connectivity and trading routes within the Forum of Bangladesh, China, India and Myanmar (BCIM) neighbourhood can substantially relieve the burden in the frontiers of northeast India, whose market turnover is estimated at US$ 50 billion. India's willingness for closer trade and economic ties with its eastern neighbours has opened up possibilities for the entire northeast states to engage themselves in paradiplomacy. India can draw lessons from China, which has taken full advantage of Yunnan's geographical location and its cultural affinities with China's neighbours, in its efforts to strengthen ties with Southeast Asia. Baruah (2005) has critiqued the role of central government for not facilitating northeast region's paradiplomacy.

It was in Yunnan's capital Kunming that experts, scholars and business people from China, India, Myanmar and Bangladesh got together for initiating the BCIM forum. Yunnan's provincial government plays a far more active role in attracting foreign investments to the province than northeast Indian states. It plays a role in the institutions of the Greater Mekong Subregion. But there is little room for India's northeastern states in the Mekong–Ganga Cooperation forum or BIMST-EC (Bangladesh, India, Myanmar, Sri Lanka, Thailand Economic Cooperation). The difference is quite ironic given that China's political system remains centralized and authoritarian while ours is democratic and federal.

India can take advantage of the history and culture of the northeastern states and their shared cultural ties with Southeast Asia as a soft power resource. In Southeast Asia, there is a growing awareness of the Indian northeast. It has been reported recently that 3,200 km trilateral highway linking India, Myanmar and Thailand, funded by Asian Development Bank (ADB) and the World Bank will become a reality by 2016. It will play a crucial role in boosting trade and investment flows between the three countries, creating jobs and other benefits (*Times of India* 2012).

It has long been recognized that subnational paradiplomacy has a huge potential to address some of the long-standing problems ranging from water sharing to terrorism, and illegal migration to environmental protection that confront India and its neighbours such as Afghanistan, Pakistan, Sri Lanka, Bangladesh, Myanmar and China. A foreign policy analyst argues that the central government in

India must get its chief ministers involved more actively in the pursuit of foreign policy interests. Some chief ministers of states bordering sensitive neighbours have already acquired an indirect role in the shaping of India's regional policy. Instead of treating this as an exception to the rule, the central government should consider it as an opportunity to make India's regional policy morc cffcctivc (Raja Mohan 2011; 2012b).

There is a demand for closer economic interactions between Tibet and India's Ladakh regions of Jammu & Kashmir and of China's Yuan province with northeastern states. Horizontal paradiplomacy between subnational governments of India and China can help generate a great deal of goodwill and also reduce tensions between the two countries. Indian markets to China's south provide Tibet and indeed other western Chinese provinces with additional options. Indian states of Uttar Pradesh, Bihar, Jammu & Kashmir, Himachal Pradesh, Uttarakhand, Sikkim and northeastern provinces will have numerous opportunities for economic growth if they are linked to Chinese economy overland through Nepal and Tibet regions. States such as Bihar and UP have very little opportunity for external linkages except equally weak and even smaller economies of Nepal and Bhutan (Jacob 2011). In Arunachal Pradesh, there exist several traditional routes for trade but are not accessible on account of security considerations. In Tripura, many projects related to irrigation, flood control and embankment building have been stopped since 2007 following objections from Bangladesh. These are some areas where states' paradiplomacy can be successful, given the failure of national diplomacy to sort out the differences.

Myanmar is considered a significant part of India's Look East Policy for the simple reason that it is the only Southeast Asian nation with which India shares its land border. Four of our sensitive north-eastern states (Arunachal Pradesh, Nagaland, Manipur and Mizoram) share 1,600 km of land border with Myanmar. Cross-border ethnic links with Naga and Mizo tribes inhabiting both sides of India–Myanmar border can be an asset for paradiplomacy.[11] Concerted efforts directed towards integrating the northeast provide innumerable possibilities in terms of bringing about a significant economic transformation. The vast hydroelectric resources can be harnessed for exporting electricity to the neighbouring countries. An integrated plan for harnessing hydrocarbon resources with a grid of pipelines to move gas and petroleum products into the entire region is another possibility (Khanna 2005). Similarly, two Punjabs can benefit immensely from cross-border trade. There is a growing awareness that subnational governments' involvement in paradiplomacy can also contribute to an enhanced regional security and eliminating trust deficit between hostile neighbours (Raja Mohan 2012b).

In brief, border states especially the northeastern states of the country share their borders with various countries such as Myanmar, Bangladesh, China, Bhutan and Nepal and their proximity to countries east of India demands that their economies benefit more from cooperation between the economies across their borders. In this manner, states could play a role in regional diplomacy. Regional leaders have been suggesting that New Delhi take them on board while conducting economic diplomacy, particularly with respect to the neighbouring countries. Often it has been observed that the centre acts on the views of 'specialists', intelligence officials and members of the foreign policy and defence establishments. It would be appropriate to design a foreign policy unit comprising the Minister for External Affairs and his representative as well as the chief ministers of the northeastern states that can advise New Delhi on how to move forward on a host of issues, ranging from trade and security to migration and navigation. It is also noteworthy that the centre has encouraged an open approach to borders with respect to both the east and west. In the East, there has been a push for enhanced connectivity between the northeastern provinces and Bangladesh. In the west also, there is some progress made regarding the opening up the borders with Pakistan, for example, in Kashmir and the two Punjabs located in India and Pakistan respectively (Maini 2011).

Border Haats

Opening of border *haats* (local marketing centres) between India's border states and Bangladesh has been quite successful. There is a proposal to establish more border *haats* to foster trade relations between India and Bangladesh. These *haats* would benefit both countries, especially the people living along the border areas. Recently, Tripura traders have demanded more such border *haats* (*Business Line* 2012). *Haats* would permit people to sell locally produced vegetables, fruits, spices, fish, poultry, minor forest produce, products of local cottage industry, small agricultural household implements, second-hand garments, melamine products and processed food items. According to Commerce Minister of India, 'an estimated $20 million worth trade will take place annually between India and Bangladesh through border *haats* (*Business Line* 2011). There is also a proposal to establish border *haats* between Myanmar and India.[12]

New Trends

Subnational paradiplomacy can take place both vertically and horizontally. Indian states are new to this (horizontal) intersubnational cross-border trade. Several foreign countries including subnational governments have begun establishing trade offices in India's developed states. Visits of state/provincial delegations led by their governors/premiers to states' capitals in India are becoming a regular affair in the recent year. Last year, a 12-member delegation from Gansu province of China visited Bihar for exploring trade and other opportunities. However, states in India are not allowed to open trade office abroad. But given the global trends, days are not far when states in India will also have trade offices abroad. However, states are allowed to host representatives from subnational/national governments of foreign countries.

Chief minister of Bihar, after his return from a four-day official visit to Bhutan in 2011, put forth a proposal before the centre to make the state a partner in the hydel power projects of Bhutan and sought permission to have an equity stake in them so that the power-starved state can get an assured supply of power from the neighbouring country. The upcoming institution such as Nalanda University (NU) in Bihar, like in the past, can become a prominent promoter and facilitator of cultural exchanges and bonding between India, especially Bihar, and East Asian and Southeast Asian nations. Recently, Thai Prime Minister has talked of a Chennai–Dawei corridor, which will connect India's emerging industrial hubs in southern India with the continental Southeast Asia, China and other thriving East Asian markets (Raja Mohan, C. 2012c). These developments are an indication that Indian states in future will engage in interprovincial diplomacy abroad. A number of countries in the world including China and Japan have taken full advantage of states' paradiplomacy in their efforts to strengthen ties with Southeast Asia. India could do the same with the northeast.

Challenges from Paradiplomacy

Paradiplomacy also presents challenges. For example, states may lack the skills to exercise responsible foreign policy especially in the political sphere, given the fact that states do not have trained diplomats; regional influence moreover may complicate national foreign policy. The irony is that most of India's neighbours are hostile. Thus, states' paradiplomacy is likely to pose a threat to the country's sovereignty and integrity from forces of terrorism, insurgency and separatism often supported by some of India's hostile neighbours. How to reconcile the demands of a globalizing economy that relies on greater elbowroom to security concerns is a policy dilemma we face today.

States' paradiplomacy especially in the political sphere can affect the national foreign policy negatively. With respect to both Teesta river treaty and the US-led resolution on UN General Assembly, the national interests were subordinated to regional interests and the centre abdicated its national responsibility by keeping its alliance partner in good humour. Bhambhri (2012) maintains, 'India is likely to pay a very heavy price if it makes foreign policy a football game where 'regionalists' begin to dictate and decide the directions of policy'. Here association of the federalism with populism is responsible for two foremost states in prevailing over the centre to toe their lines. But the danger is that centre can do a great disservice to the nation by allowing itself to be dominated by parochial regional interests. Thus, states' political paradiplomacy has evoked negative reactions. Singh and Mishra maintain that it is important that demands of states on the foreign policy front should be seen in a larger perspective. They argue,

When West Bengal demands that the Central government cannot conclude an agreement on the issue of waters of a river that flows through the state to Bangladesh, it also needs to consider the implications on other states and related security issues. The North Eastern States could have benefitted with more river water transport from the north eastern region of India to Bangladesh, opening the gates for more commerce. Bangladesh has proactively cooperated in controlling militant activities in North East, particularly Assam, which now gets compromised over the rift on Teesta waters (Singh and Mishra. 2012: 8–9).

Paradiplomatic activities motivated by nationalism can inflict a greater harm on our national interests. As some policy analysts have stated, 'There are regions and sub-nationalities in the country that have not yet fully accepted the unity of the country. Under such circumstances, it might be rash to grant constituent units such freedoms' (Mattoo and Jacob 2009: 185).

While there is euphoria and media hype over FDI-induced development, there are also concerns that it is resulting in an uneven development. For example, despite impressive growth rates, Gujarat has failed to reduce malnourishment levels, while Uttar Pradesh and Bihar, among the most backward in the country, have done better in improving the lot of their marginalized Dalits and tribals.[13]

Conclusions

In this chapter, I have argued that paradiplomacy is a multifaceted phenomenon; it can both complement and contradict our national foreign policy. It has become a worldwide phenomenon no longer confined to the developed countries alone irrespective of the existence of federal or unitary structure because of the twin forces of globalization and regionalization. However, states/provinces/constituent units in federal countries have advantages to engage themselves in paradiplomacy as compared to their counterparts in unitary countries.

Paradiplomacy has indeed made some states especially developed states in India economically more fiscal independent. Huge gains have been registered with respect to the flows of FDI. Maharashtra, Karnataka, Andhra Pradesh and Gujarat are the examples. Border regions would arguably gain as their economies benefit more from the economies across their borders. Paradiplomatic activities of states can lead to potential gains not only in economic terms but also in political and cultural terms. It can perhaps also be useful for the purpose of addressing some of the problems with our neighbouring countries such as water-sharing, terrorism and illegal cross-border migration, environmental protection, among others. Further, it can also be used by the centre as a form of soft diplomacy that can complement the national foreign policy.

Subnational paradiplomacy in India, however, takes place in an unplanned and scattered form without the central government coordinating and collaborating with states in a systematic manner. Despite the fact that there is a felt need for the centre to respond to states' international activism by creating coordinating agencies, thereby legitimizing the states' paradiplomatic acts, the centre in India has so far supported states informally without creating institutions meant for facilitating or promoting states' paradiplomacy. Indian states thus have adopted quite a distinct form of subnational paradiplomacy (Mattoo and Jacob 2009: 185). Instead of overseas representation and mission around the world, states' paradiplomacy has been largely the result of a variety of informal economic schemes which have helped the rich states.[14] There have been commendable attempts of late by some of the economically backward states in creating a pro-business environment leading to competitive federalism. On the one hand, there is a euphoria over investment-driven growth and on the other hand, there are also concerns that FDI-induced economic growth has not been inclusive. An increasing urban–rural divide and the ever widening gap between the rich and poor in some of India's developed states are a glaring testimony to this fact. This calls for a more pro-active role on the part of the central government in terms of accommodating regional interests in national foreign policy in a systematic way and at the same time ensuring interstate as well as intrastate inclusive growth. While states' economic diplomacy has been informally supported by the centre, political paradiplomacy practised by some of the states has often put the centre in an embarrassing situation. There are two ways through which states' economic paradiplomacy can be supported by the centre. First, a constitutional amendment can be made in order to incorporate states' role in foreign economic policy making. However, this is not a very practical approach as very few countries in the world practise it. Second, delegation of powers to states as in China, United Kingdom, Japan, Brazil and so on and setting up institutions meant for cooperating and coordinating with states in their paradiplomacy. The centre could invent a system where safeguards can be placed so that any untoward happening in the name of paradiplomacy affecting national interests could be checked. States should be made agents and partners of the national government in foreign policy formulation.

The overall argument of this chapter is that rather than seeing paradiplomacy as a threat, the central government in India should embrace it as a means (soft diplomacy) and an opportunity to manage and ultimately resolve some of the major cross-border problems. The potential of paradiplomacy especially with respect to the border regions of northeast India remains untapped, given the lack of political will at the central level. China has, since long time, been using its provinces to establish interprovincial relationships with their counterparts in other countries.[15] It has shown a great deal of interest in the internationalization of the vast majority of its provinces, not only through market integration, or the establishment of informal relations across the border, but also by authorizing its governors to sign international agreements and to receive and send international missions all over the world (Zhimin et al. 2010). The experiences of provincial governments in Japan reveal that they can serve as valuable arms of the national government for accessing external markets (Jain 2005). The centre in India can delegate to states a number of foreign economic policy making powers and responsibilities, which states can undertake with their own resources. This, in turn, can also reduce Delhi's workload. Trade and investment promotion activities of states and transnational economic engagement of state-owned companies albeit of their own economic interest would deepen India's relations with foreign nations. 'Despite the moderately increasing role of the states in decision making on foreign policy, it is curious that there is hardly any discussion of the need to give a greater role to the state governments in the country's foreign relations' (Mattoo and Jacob 2009: 185).

A systematic study of the paradiplomatic activities of various states in India is overdue. This study could only hint briefly changes brought about by states through their international economic activities. A more thorough examination is still awaited.

Notes

1. The term 'paradiplomacy' was introduced by a Canadian scholar Soldatos. The US scholar Duchacek further developed it (Duchacek et al. 1988, Michelmann and Soldatos 1990). Paradiplomacia.org is an online magazine designed to promote the international projection of provincial and local governments. It seeks to enhance the international relations of local governments in order to connect cities, towns and regions for an enriching and sustainable trade. The term paradiplomacy was not used until recently in India (*Indian Express* 2012). There is no consensus among the academia as to which term is more convenient for defining the subnational governments' external activities. Paradiplomacy, state diplomacy, constituent diplomacy, subnational diplomacy, regional

diplomacy, subnational foreign policy, etc., are used as synonyms for the involvement of subnational governments in foreign policy. I prefer the use of paradiplomacy in this chapter for it has become a very popular term today.

2. The NEP opened up new vistas for creative and innovative activities by the subnational governments.
3. *Times of India,* 13 April 2000
4. Narendra Modi's speech in Japan recently is a testimony to the fact.
5. The Gujarat government has/is tried/trying hard to tell its success story to external investors through 'Vibrant Gujarat Global Investors' Summit'. In January 2013 the state government started posting advertisements on the websites of international publications such as *Washington Post* and *Wall Street Journal*. The state government has been using social media websites such as Facebook, and search engines such as MSN and Yahoo for promoting and showcasing its achievement. US-India Business Council in Washington and Australia–India Business Council based in Sydney are the official partner organizations, while Japan and Canada are the official partner countries of the Vibrant Gujarat Global Investors' Summit', 2013.
6. Mulayam Singh Yadav, who was CM at that time, announced the setting up of an investment commission headed by himself in order to bring all government departments under one umbrella to provide a single-window clearance for potential investors. He invited NRIs to participate in the development of Kanha Kunj in Brindavan and build international convention centres at Agra and Varanasi. Rajasthan CM, Vasundhara Raje Scindia, requested NRIs to contribute to the state's development through adoption of monuments, villages and schools. She also intended to make Rajasthan a year-long tourist destination.
7. Kerala organized 'Emerging Kerala 2012', the flagship global connect programme of the state government at Kochi from 12 to 14 September 2012. Other states that have organized/are organizing state summits in 2012 to promote states globally include Bihar, MP, Maharashtra, Karnataka and Haryana, among others. World Economic Forum meet that was being held in national capital is being held in state capitals. In 2013, Gurgaon, national capital region of Haryana hosted the annual World Economic Forum meet. The first-ever 'Goa Investment Forum 2012', to attract industries to Goa, was held in Panaji on 30 June 2012.
8. The Government of the People's Republic of China and the ruling Communist Party of China (CPC) accorded an unprecedented importance and the highest level of protocol to the chief minister going beyond the established norms.
9. Over the last 26 years, the World Economic Forum India Summit was held in India's capital, Delhi. Maharashtra became the first state to host the summit in 2011. In 2012 Haryana hosted WEF India Summit. The shift

from the national capital to state capitals is clearly mentioned on the website of WEF: 'Last year's summit in the state Maharashtra validated our model going forward to incorporate the important role which states are playing in shaping India's political and economic landscape' (WEF, India Summit, 2012).

10. Even when Maharashtra succeeded in attracting an investment of Rs. 1 lakh–crore since April last year till date, it lost big-ticket investments – including Maruti and Peugeot – to neighbouring Gujarat. Even smaller states such as Chhattisgarh and Uttarakhand besides Orissa are giving a run to Maharashtra (*Business Standard*, January 14, 2012).
11. Dean (2005) gives the example of a community known as Kachin in Upper Myanmar, Singpho in Assam and Arunachal Pradesh and Jingpo in Yunnan, China. According to her, the community has 'creatively adjusted to the dominating international system of the states' by incorporating into their self-definition references to the three 'host' states of China, Myanmar and India. Despite being citizens of three different states, they are 'united through a tight unique kinship lineage network of various spatial trajectories and social bonds, a commonly recognized *lingua franca* and a variety of tangible ethnic features'.
12. The chief ministers of Meghalaya and Arunachal Pradesh, Minister for Industry and Commerce of Tripura and Minister for Public Health Engineering of Assam along with delegation members separately called on Foreign Minister of Bangladesh, Dipu Moni and discussed strategies for enhancing cooperation in trade, border management and other areas of mutual benefit.
13. These are some of the conclusions of India's human development report. 'Human Development Index: Gujarat worst', *Indian Express*, 21 October, 2011.
14. However, there is a silver lining as some of the poorer states are also trying to catch up with developed states.
15. Chinese provinces have developed a sophisticated provincial foreign affairs management system. It is usually led by a small leading group on foreign affairs, headed by either the governor or the provincial party secretary. Under the provincial leadership, the provincial Foreign Affairs Office (FAO) and the Foreign Trade and Economic Cooperation Commission (FTEC) are the two major bureaucratic organs dealing with provincial foreign relations. FAO, which is under the dual leadership of provincial leaders and the Ministry of Foreign Affairs in Beijing, deals with political affairs at subnational levels and coordinates the overall provincial foreign relations. FAO is responsible for implementing the national foreign policy locally, arranging the reception of foreign VIPs and for the overseas visits of provincial leaders, administering passport and visa matters of provincial official business travel abroad, organizing and promoting activities with sister cities and provinces of other countries,

administering consular affairs and foreign media affairs, and guiding foreign affairs-related work of other local government departments (Zhimin and Junbo, 2009).

References

Agarwal, V. 2012. 'Narendra Modi's Look-East Policy', *The Wall Street Journal*, 22 July.

Aguirre, I. 1999. 'Making Sense of Paradiplomacy: An Intertextual Enquiry About a Concept in Search of a Definition', *Regional and Federal Studies*, Vol. 9, No. 1, Spring, pp. 185–209.

Baruah, S. 2005. 'The Problem', *Seminar*, Vol. 13, No. 11.

Bhambhri, C.P. 2012. 'Indian Foreign Policy: Foreign or Provincial?', *The Economic Times,* 31 March.

Bhattacharya, P. 2012. 'Another Chief Minister Comes Seeking Investments', *The Wall Street Journal,* 2 August http://blogs.wsj.com/indiarealtime/2012/08/02/another-chief-minister-comes-seeking-investments/.

Business Line. 2011. 'Potential of India-Bangladesh Trade via Border Haats put at $20 million', 21 July.

——. 'Tripura Traders Demand more Border Haats', January 8, 2012.

Business Standards. 2012. 'Chavan to Woo Investors at Davos', 14 January.

Chellaney, B. 2012. 'Water Treaties & Diplomacy: India Faces Difficult Choices on Water', *The Economic Times,* May 10.

Chelliah, R. 1996. *Towards Sustainable Growth: Essays in Fiscal and Financial Sector Reforms in India,* New Delhi: Oxford University Press.

Chhibber, P. and Ken Kollman. 2004. *The Formation of National Party Systems: Federalism and Party Competition in Canada, Great Britain, India, and the United States,* Princeton, Oxford: Princeton University Press.

Cornago, N. 2010. 'On the Normalization of Sub-State Diplomacy', *The Hague Journal of Diplomacy,* Vol. 5, pp. 11–36.

Dean, K. 2005. 'Territorialities Yet Unaccounted', *Seminar*, Vol. 13, No. 11.

Dossani, R. and Srinidhi Vijaykumar. 2005. 'Indian Federalism and the Conduct of Foreign Policy in Border States: State Participation and Central Accommodation since 1990'. http://iis-db.stanford.edu/pubs/20858/Dossani_Vijaykumar_2005.pdf.

Duchacek, I.D., Latouche, D. and Garth Stevenson. (eds.). 1988. *Perforated Sovereignties and International Relations: Trans-Sovereign Contacts of Subnational Governments,* New York: Greenwood Press.

Government of India, urbanindia.nic.in/programme/lsg/Twinning_Guidelines.pdf

Hocking, B. 1993. *Localizing Foreign Policy: Non-Central Governments and Multilayered Diplomacy,* London: Macmillan.

Indian Express. 2012. 'Modi's Parallel Diplomacy', 4 January

Jacob, J.T. 2011. 'The Sino-Indian Boundary Dispute: Sub-National Units as Ice-Breakers', *Eurasia Border Review,* Vol.2, No.1, pp. 35–45. http://eprints.lib.hokudai.ac.jp/dspace/bitstream/2115/50850/1/EBR2-1_003.pdf Jain, P. 2005. *Japan's Subnational Governments in International Affairs,* Oxon: Routledge.

Jenkins, R. 2003. 'India's States and the Making of Foreign Economic Policy: The Limits of the Constituent Diplomacy Paradigm', *Publius: The Journal of Federalism*, Vol. 33, No. 4, pp. 63–81.

Jha, P.C. 2004. 'Emerging Issues and Challenges in Brazilian Fiscal Federalism: Some Lessons for India', *India Quarterly*, Vol. LX, Nos. 1 and 2, January–June, pp. 144–170.

——. 2011. 'Paradiplomacy in Federal Polities: Sub-national Governments in Brazil and India as International Actors', in the International Conference, 'India-Brazil Dialogue' organized by Goa University from 28–30 October.

Khanna, S. 2005. 'Economic Opportunities or Continuing Stagnation', *Seminar*, Vol. 13, No. 11.

Kincaid, J. 2002. 'Foreign Relations of Sub-National Units: Constituent Diplomacies in Federal Systems', in Raoul Blindenbacher and Arnold Koller (eds.), *Federalism in a Changing World: Learning from Each Other,* Montreal: McGill-Queens University Press, pp. 74–96.

Kirk, J.A. 2011. *India and the World Bank: The Politics of Aid and Influence,* New York: Anthem Press.

Malik, Ashok. 2012. 'A Twist in Diplomacy', *The Asian Age*, 30 July.

Maini, Tridivesh. 2011. 'The Politics of Centre-State Relations and the Formulation of India's Foreign Policy' 24 November http://www.futuredirections.org.au/publications/associate-papers/313-the-politics-of-border-regions-in-the-formulation-of-indias-foreign-policy.html#sthash.IbbOmODN.dpuf

Mattoo, A. and Happymon Jacob. 2009. 'Republic of India', in Hans Michelmann (ed.), *Foreign Relations in Federal Countries,* Montreal and Kingston: McGill-Queen's University Press and Forum of Federations, pp. 169–187.

Michelmann, Hans. 2009. *Foreign Relations in Federal Countries*, Kingston & Montreal: McGill-Queen's University Press.

Michelmann, H.J., and Panayotis Soldatos. (eds.). 1990. *Federalism and International Relations: The Role of Subnational Units,* Oxford: Clarendon Press.

Rajamohan, C. 2011. 'India's Regional Diplomacy: Getting the States Involved', *Indian Express*, 20 June.

——. 2012a. 'To Delhi via Kolkata', *Indian Express*, 8 May.

——. 2012b. 'Across the Radcliffe Line: Reconnecting the Punjab', *Indian Express*, 1 October.

——. 2012c. 'Thai PM for Chennai-Dawei Corridor', *The Indian Express*, 26 January.

Rudolph, L.I., and Susanne Hoeber Rudolph. 2001. 'The Iconization of Chandrababu: Sharing Sovereignty in India's Federal Market Economy', *Economic and Political Weekly*, Vol. 36, No. 18, pp. 1541–1552.

Sridharan, K. 2003. 'Federalism and Foreign Relations: The Nascent Role of the Indian States', *Asian Studies Review*, Vol. 27, No. 4, pp. 463–489.

Srivastava, A. 2012. 'Bihar Enters the Industrial Age', *India Today*, 16 June. Available at http://indiatoday.intoday.in/story/bihar-nitish-kumar-big-business-houses-queue-up-to-establish-industries/1/200866.html.

The Economic Times, 2012. 'Kerala Government to go ahead with Air Kerala Project to Operate Flights to Gulf Sector', 21 November.

——. 2012. 'Air Kerala May Fly Overseas on FDI', 15 October.

——. 2011. 'Maharashtra to Sign 32 Global Investment MoUs in 2 Months: Prithviraj Chavan', 10 November.

——. 2005. 'Ministers Line up to Woo Investors', 10 January.

The Times of India. 2012. 'Bihar to Figure in International Labour Meet at Geneva', 27 May.

——. 2012. 'Vadodara Eyes "Twin City" Status with China's Chengdu', 12 July.

——. 2012. 'India-Thailand Highway to be Ready by 2016', 13 August.

Tribune News. 2010. 'CM Invited to Climate Summit in US', 3 November.

Wikipedia, http://en.wikipedia.org/wiki/List_of_twin_towns_and_sister_cities_ in_India

World Economic Forum, 2012, http://www.weforum.org/news/first-world-economic-forum-india-set-gurgaon-6-8-november-2012?news=page

Zhimin, C., Jian Junbo and Chen Diyuc. 2010. 'The Provinces and China's Multi-Layered Diplomacy: The Cases of GMS and Africa', *The Hague Journal of Diplomacy*, Vol. 5, pp. 1–26.

Zhimin, C. and Jian Junbo, 2009, 'Chinese Provinces as Foreign Policy Actors in Africa', *Occasional Paper No. 22*, South African Institute of International Affairs, http://www.saiia.org.za/occasional-papers/chinese-provinces-as-foreign-policy-actors-in-africa

15

Resource Federalism in India

The Case of Minerals*

Ligia Noronha, Nidhi Srivastava,
Divya Datt and P.V. Sridharan

While natural resources are spatially located, their development is of a wider national interest. Gains from their development accrue to a large common market, though the process affects local lives and environments. The distribution of powers and functions across levels of government and the way they play out determine the effectiveness with which various policy goals are met. The need to examine these becomes important, given the increased demands from resource-bearing states for a more 'fair' distribution of resource rents in buoyant commodity markets, and from local people in resource regions for greater recognition of their rights and compensation for the effects of resource development. This chapter examines the federal structure in India in the context of minerals and suggests ways in which this can be strengthened through expanding the space and institutional capacity for local governance and by improving compensation and the sharing of resource revenues.

Buoyant commodity markets and liberalized investment rules are attracting foreign and Indian capital to resource-rich states in India. Given their financial and development problems, these states see the resources – minerals, oil, natural gas and hydropower – as key

---

* This paper was first published in *Economic and Political Weekly* Vol–XLIV No. 08, February 21, 2009.It is being published here with due permission from the publishers.

revenue and development handles, and are demanding a greater share of the economic benefits of their development. While the centre and states are proactively engaged in creating investment opportunities in resource development, the local people in resource-bearing states are concerned that the authorities may overlook local environmental and social responsibilities. It is against the backdrop of the states demanding a more 'fair' distribution of resource rents and of the local people demanding a better recognition of rights and compensation for the adverse effects of resource development that we undertook an analysis of compensation issues and the way 'resource federalism' plays out in India. The present chapter focuses on mineral resources, drawing from a larger study on 'Compensation to Resource Bearing States' done for the Inter-State Council (TERI 2007, 2008), which covered the oil and gas, hydropower and the minerals sectors.

It is evident that while natural resources are spatially located, they have a wider national significance. Gains from their development accrue to a large common market though the process of their development affects local lives and environments. A discussion on resource federalism in India thus needs to focus on the following issues:

- How are the powers and functions over resources and resource development assigned among various levels of government?
- Do governments at different levels respect the constitutional assignment of powers and functions, or is there an encroachment into each other's domain?
- How does the functioning of the institutions of federalism in the context of resource development balance the government goals of economic efficiency, political participation and protection of rights?[1]
- How can federalism be strengthened, given the developments in the area of natural resource development?

An analysis of resource federalism needs to recognize the three perspectives on resource development: agency, spatial and temporal. Resource development has an agency perspective because there are a number of actors involved in the production and marketing process, those impacted and those charged with regulation and oversight. It has a spatial basis because resources are 'located' and have a 'place'. Their exploitation affects local lives and other resources that are found conjointly.[2] For example, a discussion on the development of minerals cannot be independent of the land below which they exist, forests where they are often located or rivers, which may get polluted or used up in the process of development. And there is a temporal perspective given that these are long-term projects and that being finite, they involve intergenerational issues, since extraction today implies development opportunities foregone tomorrow.

Thus, mining minerals is not just about minerals, but also about all these attendant issues. The complexity for resource development policy and, consequently, for sharing costs and benefits from the development of a particular natural resource, say minerals, arises not just from issues related to this resource, but also from the roles and functions that other affected resources perform and the values attached to them. Apart from material value, resources can also have a cultural or an existence value and are sometimes seen as 'resources for collective representations that exceed the concern with immediate material use' (Baviskar 2003: 5052). Demands made by various stakeholder groups reflect the different meanings and values that are attached to resources. These demands can most often be traded off against each other, but in some instances values are not comparable and no exchange is possible.

This multifunctionality of resources and the multiple dimensions of resource development create three key policy issues. One, balancing the interests of the wider constituency (say, the mineral consumer) with that of the more vulnerable, local groups that have insufficient information and voice. Two, seeking to understand and include the interests of different stakeholder groups, particularly the marginalized. And three, addressing the aspirations to modernity of indigenous (tribal) groups (in areas where minerals are found) while providing them with the option of remaining or being able to return to traditional ways of living, given that people have multiple affiliations that are intrinsic to their lives and that these create contradictions to what they want at different points of times.[3] This, of course, is part of the larger development debate.

This chapter is organized as follows: Section 1 reviews the minerals potential of resource-rich states, their economic and fiscal condition; Section 2 examines the constitutional provisions that regulate centre–state relations in this sector; Section 3 focuses on decentralization as it is key to resource development, given its spatial and local impacts; Section 4 briefly examines resource revenue assignments and sharing in India and the final section concludes with a commentary on how we see resource federalism playing out in the country.

Minerals and Mineral-Rich States in India

India produces about 90 minerals, including major fuel (coal), metallic (iron-ore), nonferrous (bauxite) and industrial (limestone) minerals. Internationally, India is a leading producer of coal and lignite (fuel minerals) and iron ore, bauxite, chromite and manganese ore (metallic minerals). The country is also an emerging world player in industrial minerals such as baryte, steatite and kyanite. The mining and quarrying sector constituted about 2.8 per cent of the gross domestic product (GDP) in 2005–2006. Coal occupies an important position among minerals, as about 60 per cent of India's energy needs are met through it. The index of total mineral production in 2004–2005 was 153.8 (1993–1994 = 100), which went up to 155.25 in 2005–2006.[4] In 2005–2006 the country exported (including re-exports) Rs. 79,790 crore worth of minerals, an increase of 13 per cent from the previous year. Diamonds and iron ore constituted 64 per cent and 21 per cent of the value of exports.[5] The mineral-rich states of India are Andhra Pradesh, Chhattisgarh, Gujarat, Jharkhand, Karnataka, Madhya Pradesh, Orissa, Rajasthan and West Bengal. Figure 15.1 shows the statewise distribution of key mineral reserves in India.

The contribution of the mining and quarrying sector is higher in some states when compared to the national average (depicted by a vertical line in Figure 15.2). In states such as Chhattisgarh and Jharkhand, the contribution of minerals in the state domestic product (SDP) is next only to agriculture and manufacturing.

Further, income from mineral royalties is a significant contributor to revenue in some of these states, it being the single most important contributor to nontax revenue (Figure 15.2). It is seen that coal accounts for 65–90 per cent of the royalty revenue in Chhattisgarh, Jharkhand, Orissa and Madhya Pradesh. Other important minerals in terms of their contribution to royalty in these states are limestone, iron ore, bauxite and chromite.

Despite their mineral wealth, these states are economically weak. Figure 15.3 highlights that the leading mineral-producing

Figure 15.1

Statewise Distribution of Select Mineral Reserves in the Country (as in 2005)

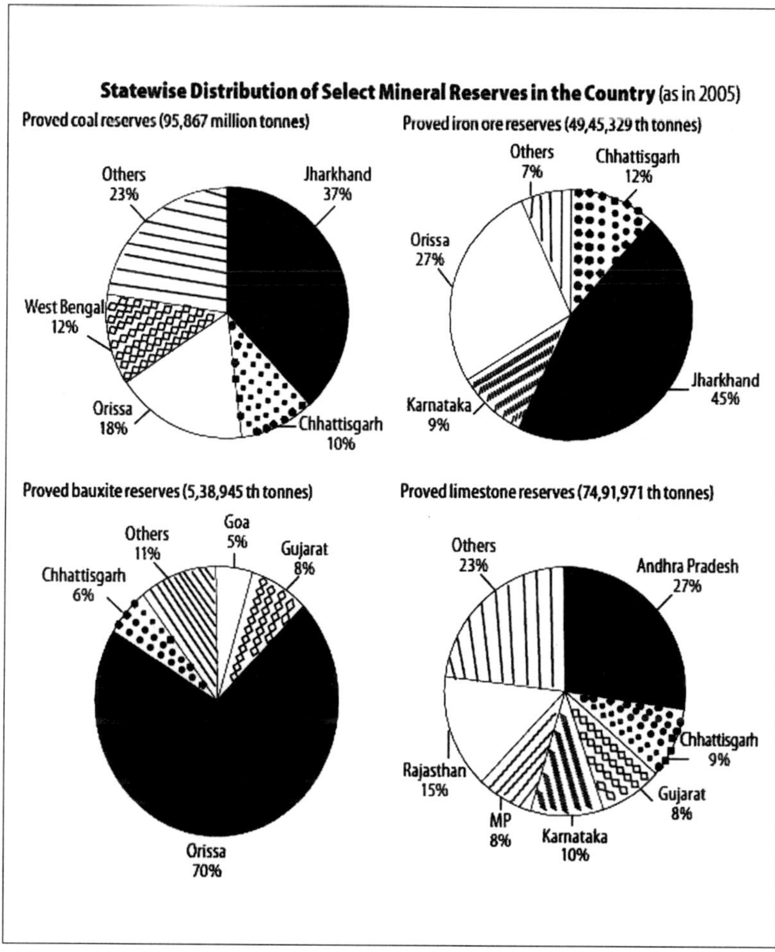

states of the country have per capita incomes lower than the national average. Looking at fiscal indicators, mineral-rich states present a mixed picture – some newly formed states such as Chhattisgarh are better than national average performers on most indicators, while much older states such as West Bengal do not fare well. On the other hand, newly formed Jharkhand falls short of national averages. Clearly the size of the mining industry is only one of the factors influencing fiscal performance.

Figure 15.2

Importance of Mining in Select States: Some Indicators (2005–2006)

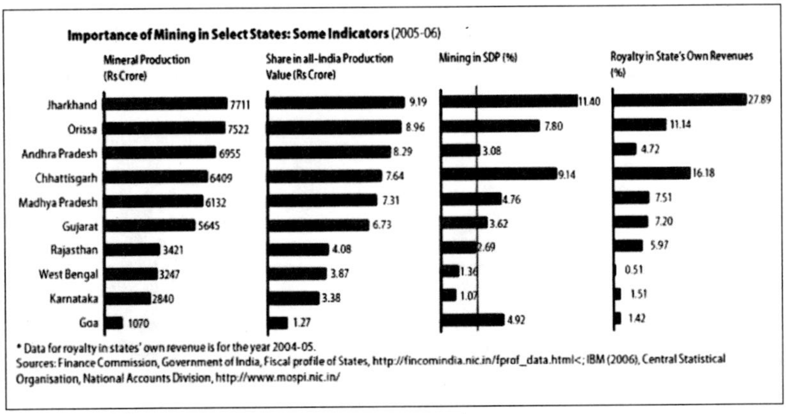

Figure 15.3

Fiscal and Economic Indicators for Select Resource Rich States (2005–2006)

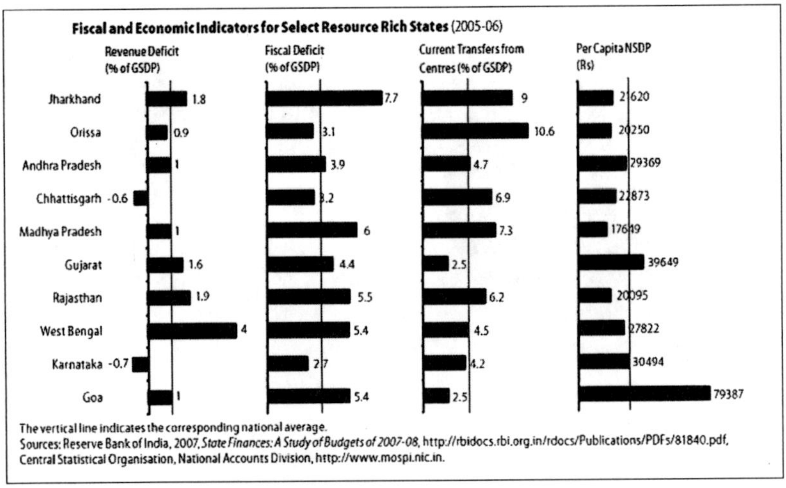

With growing expenditures and rising fiscal deficits, states are increasingly looking to augment their revenues. In resource-bearing states, the focus is on ways in which they can benefit from mineral royalties, which are nontax revenues. The memos submitted by them to the Twelfth Finance Commission suggest that these states see the potential for income and revenue generation by the resource sector as a key policy option to increasing their fiscal capacity. The memos also demand more control over minerals development.[6] Analysing these demands requires us to examine the provisions and the distribution of powers and rights over natural resources in the federal set-up of the country.

Assignment of Powers with Respect to Natural Resources

The Constitution of India has assigned functions, legislative competence and fiscal powers to both the centre and states with respect to different subjects.[7] Different aspects of natural resources are administered by either the central or a state government depending on where they are in Schedule VII of the Constitution. This aspect can be clarified by a discussion on how mineral resources and land (a key factor in minerals development) are dealt with in the Constitution.

Minerals

In India, the proprietary title to onshore minerals vests in the federating states. However, this ownership is subject to legislation governing regulation and control of mining enacted by the Parliament.[8] Minerals within the maritime jurisdiction of the country are owned by the central government. The Mines and Mineral Development and Regulation (MMDR) Act confers the right to allow exploitation of minerals by granting licences and leases on the state governments, but in accordance with the MMDR Act and its rules, as enacted and notified by the central government. With respect to Schedule I minerals, states have little powers except possession, receiving royalty and a few other payments. Neither can they determine the rates of royalty, the most important nontax revenue from minerals. With respect to minor minerals,[9] the states can make their own rules and regulations, a provision they have taken advantage of. Taxes on mineral rights are the prerogative of the state in which they are located. However, this power is not absolute and is subject to any limitations imposed by any law enacted by the Parliament. In 1992, when certain West Bengal laws[10] levying cess on coal were challenged, they were held ultra vires by the high court. However, the Supreme Court upheld the legislation on the ground that states were competent to levy cess as long as the cess was on coal-bearing land. It was further held that 'So long as a tax or fee on mineral rights remains in pith and substance a tax for augmenting the revenue resources of the State or a fee for rendering services by the State and it does not impinge upon regulation of mines and mineral development or upon control of industry by the central government, it is not unconstitutional'.[11] Box 1 summarizes how legislative powers over mineral resources are shared by the central and state governments.

To sum up, while states own the mineral resources located within their territory, the centre has jurisdiction over the regulation of mines and mineral development. At the same time, states are empowered to legislate on regulation and development of mines and mineral development, but subject to the powers of the centre under List I. So, even though states may own mineral resources, legislative control over them effectively lies with the centre.

Box 1

Sharing of Legislative Powers over Mineral Resources

	State	*Centre*
Regulation of mines and mineral development	?*	?
Safety in mines	–	?
Minor minerals	?	–
Tax on land	?	–
Tax on mineral right	?*	–
Tax on Producation	–	?
Tax on sale	?	–
Fees on respective subjects	?	?

* Subject to law made by Parliament, that is, the MMDR.

Land

Land is a particularly contentious issue with regard to minerals development, especially in areas with tribal populations, and it is important to understand the constitutional provisions here. The Constitution of India provides specific protection to tribal rights over their customary resources, particularly in Schedule V and Schedule VI areas. Under the framework of the Constitution and, in line with the spirit of the Government of India Act, 1935, which categorized 'Tribal Areas' as excluded areas, special provisions were made in Schedule VI of the Constitution for administration with special powers. Other tribal tracts, categorized as 'Partially Excluded Areas', were christened Scheduled Areas and placed under Schedule V of the Constitution.[12] The object of Schedule V and Schedule VI is to ensure that tribals remain in possession and enjoyment of the lands in Scheduled Areas for their economic empowerment, social status and dignity. Equally, exploitation of mineral resources is for the development of the nation. The competing rights of tribals, or adivasis, and the state have to be adjusted without defeating the rights of either.[13] The National Forest Policy, 1988, has a separate section on 'Tribal people and forests'.

Most of the geographical areas rich in minerals and other natural resources fall under Schedule V of the Constitution.[14] In these areas, the governor is empowered to make regulations, repeal or amend any law of Parliament to prohibit or restrict the transfer of land by or among members of the scheduled tribes, or regulate the allotment of land to members of the scheduled tribes in such area.[15] This power vested in the governor is subject to only the condition that it does not affect the basic structure of the Constitution. Relying on Schedule V provisions empowering the governor to restrict or prohibit transfer of land in Scheduled Areas, the Supreme Court in the landmark Samatha judgement ruled that government lands, tribal lands and forest lands in Scheduled Areas cannot be leased out to nontribals or to private companies for mining or industrial operations. Although this case was specific to the state of Andhra Pradesh, the court categorically ruled that land in Schedule V areas could not be so transferred. It was held that the executive, while exercising the constitutional power to dispose of its property,[16] 'should equally be cognisant to the constitutional duty to protect and empower the tribals. Therefore, the court is required to give effect to the constitutional mandate and legislative policy of total prohibition on the transfer of the land in Scheduled area to non-tribals'.[17]

Environmental and Livelihood Protection

Environmental protection is clearly provided for in the Constitution of India and judicial interpretation has strengthened this mandate. In recent cases, the courts have recognized the right to a wholesome environment as being implicit in the fundamental right to life, guaranteed in Article 21 of the Constitution (Rosencranz et al. 1991).

In the national interest and in certain special circumstances, the Constitution enables the Parliament to legislate with respect to matters in the State List under Articles 249 and 252. The Government of India has enacted several acts on the environment. The Water (Prevention and Control of Pollution) Act 1974 was promulgated under Article 252,[18] as water is a state subject. On the other hand, the Air (Prevention and Control of Pollution) Act 1981 and the Environment Protection Act 1986 were promulgated under Article 253. The Forest Conservation Act of 1980, enacted primarily for conservation of forests and checking the de-reservation of protected areas, governs the diversion of forest lands for nonforest activities. As per the act, development activities are not prohibited in forest areas but restricted and subject to clearance from the central government. The juridical principles included in the National Environment Policy 2006 include the polluter pays principle, right to life, intergenerational equity and the precautionary principle.[19]

Loss of habitat and livelihood are one of the earliest and most direct impacts of development activities. The Constitution of India does not explicitly recognize any right to be protected from losing one's habitat and livelihood. However, as in the case of environmental jurisprudence, using the fundamental rights and directive principles under the Constitution, the courts have often dealt with the problem of dislocation. Article 21, which confers the right to life, is undoubtedly one of the most read into provisions of the Constitution. It is up to the states to determine the extent to which the communities that are dislocated and suffer loss of habitat and livelihood can have a say in the matter of being compensated for livelihood losses. Since relief and rehabilitation policies should have adequate local participation and a decentralized approach, some states such as Orissa have also come up with their own rehabilitation policies besides the National Relief and Rehabilitation Policy.[20]

An analysis of the assignments of powers and the way they have functioned suggests that even though the centre may be empowered by the Constitution to take mines and mineral development under its control, there is encroachment on the states' domain because the MMDR Act does not sufficiently recognize their ownership rights. Despite states being the owners, important matters such as fixing royalties and revision and approval for Schedule I minerals are all under the centre's control. The encroachment, or the need to encroach, is to ensure that mineral resources are used in the national interest. While this is reflected in the fact that regulation and control over the major minerals is vested in the centre, the controls over decisions that relate to revenue augmentation for the states ought to be decided by an independent body, such as the Finance Commission or some other third-party mechanism that is neither linked to the centre nor the states.

Decentralization and Resource Development

With the 73rd and 74th Amendments, local governance bodies received constitutional recognition. It paved the way for a 'multi level federation with elected local bodies at district and below'[21] in a polity earlier governed by the centre and the states. Local government being a state subject,[22] the power to legislate for local government, including village administration, rests with the states. Earlier the states were mandated to take steps to organize village panchayats and 'endow them with such powers and authority' so as to enable them to function as units of self-government. After the insertion of Part IX in the Constitution, establishment of panchayats for rural areas at three levels – village, intermediate and district – was envisaged.[23] The Constitution states that a gram sabha or village assembly may exercise such powers and perform such functions as the legislature of the state may by law provide.[24] Hence, states are not bound to devolve powers on panchayats but they may endow these units of local governance with power to prepare and implement plans for economic development and social justice, levy, collect and appropriate taxes, duties, tolls and fees in matters as they may find appropriate.

Parts IX and IX A of the Constitution, which embody the principles of self-governance, did not include the Scheduled Areas in its application till as late as 1996 except for the power given to the Parliament and state legislatures to extend provisions of this part with necessary modification and exception.[25] Based on the recommendations of the Bhuria Committee,[26] the Parliament, in 1996, passed a separate legislation as an annexure to the 73rd Amendment laying down provisions for panchayats in Schedule V areas.[27] The Panchayat Extension to Scheduled Areas (PESA) Act was enacted giving special powers to gram sabhas in Scheduled Areas, which were a little different from the powers given to gram sabhas in non-Scheduled Areas. Here, not only the elected panchayat but also the gram sabha has been made the core of decentralized administration. One of the important features of the PESA is that it acknowledges the competence of gram sabhas, the formal manifestation of village communities, to 'safeguard and preserve the traditions and customs of the people, their cultural identity, community resources'.[28] It mandates that there should be consultation before land acquisition for development projects and before resettling or rehabilitating persons affected by such projects. The PESA further provides that every panchayat at the village level shall obtain from the gram sabha a certification of utilization of funds for these plans, programmes and projects. In the case of minor minerals, it is mandatory to obtain the recommendations of the gram sabha before granting any lease or concession.

Under the PESA Act, all the states were given one year to amend their panchayat legislations to bring them in conformity with the new law. By now all the states have made necessary enactments and amendments but 'a closer look establishes that almost all powers have been made subject to rules/further orders by the State

Box 2: Functions and Functionaries

Key Functions/ Responsibilities	*Centre*	*State*	*Local Government*
Land issues: access, Compensation for damage		*DoRev, Agriculture*	
			Missing/ weak link
Post-closure issue	*IBM*	*DoMines*	
Oversight of environment impacts, including forests	*MoEF*	*SPCB, DoEF*	
Mining clearances	*IBM/MoM /MoEF*	*DoMines*	
Rehabilitations of Projects-affected people	*MoRD*	*DoRev/RD*	
Social investment programmes			

IBM: Indian Bureau of Mines; MoEF: Ministry of Environement and Forests; MoM: Ministry of Mines; MoRD: Ministry of Rural Development; SPCBs: State Pollution Control Boards; DoRev: Department of Revenue.

Governments'[29]. It is not just the panchayat law that has to be consistent with the PESA. There are other laws as well that have a bearing on the rights and powers of gram sabhas and therefore need to be looked into. To summarize, the steps taken by the states for the purposes of the PESA have not been adequate in strengthening the concept of self-governance as envisaged by it.

Drawing from the assignment of powers and functions in the context of minerals, the Box 2 shows the organizations across various levels of government that are charged with some key functions and responsibilities. These relate to land, to post closure of mining, oversight of environmental (including forests) impacts, rehabilitation of project-affected people (PAP) and social investment programmes. It is evident that local governments have not so far been assigned some of the functions that are key to improved governance. Moreover, resource revenue related social investment programmes are left to mining companies.

Fiscal Decentralization

Fiscal decentralization involves 'the devolution of taxing and spending powers to lower levels of government'[30] while revenue sharing refers to the mechanism through which revenue collected by one or more parts of the government is distributed across various levels of government. Both fiscal decentralization and revenue sharing are crucial concepts in intergovernmental fiscal relations. The 73rd and 74th Amendments to the Constitution demarcated the functions and sources of finance between the centre, states and local governments. Schedules XI and XII specify roles and responsibilities for rural and urban local bodies, but leave the actual devolution and the assignment of revenues and expenditures to the states. Fiscal transfers in India tend to be independent of the financial contribution by a region for the development of its natural resource activities and the revenue so generated is generally used for broad social and infrastructure needs. Fiscal decentralization, however, has met with different degrees of success in different parts of the country.

A key fiscal issue in the context of minerals development is the timeliness of resource flows: the flow of funds from resource development and the actual time of need in producer areas do not match. State and local government units require large amounts of funds in the initial stages of resource development to address the needs of the

Figure 15.4

Public Costs and Tax Revenues across Life Cycle of Resource Development

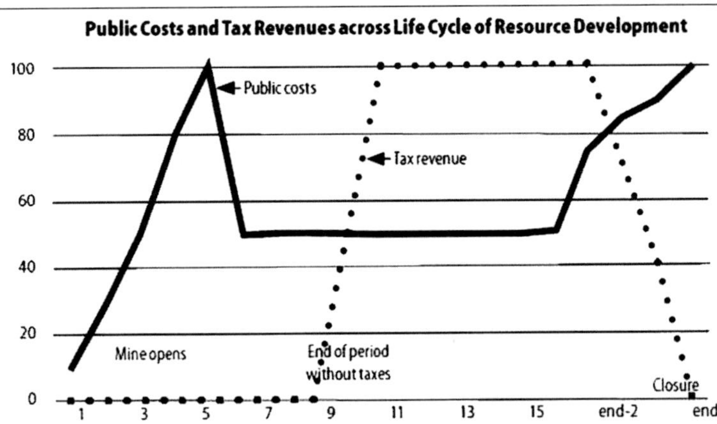

Source: Olle Östensson, Presentation at the RIIA workshop on Sustainable Relationships: Financing and Monitoring Responsibilities.

local people affected, but resource rent flow gradually increases only with production. Funds are also needed at the time a mine is closed to take care of its environmental and social impacts. Moreover, the initial phases are often declared 'tax-free' to attract investors. Figure 15.4 captures this fiscal challenge.

Existing Revenue Assignments and Sharing in the Mineral Sector

Both the centre and states in India collect revenue through different taxes and levies imposed on minerals under different legislations. States collect revenue through royalty, dead rent, cess, sales tax, environmental protection fees, prospecting and mining lease fees and so on. The centre collects revenue in the form of excise duty, forest conservation charges, corporate taxes and so on. Apart from these taxes, some states such as West Bengal impose a cess on minerals. Box 3 summarizes the main payments in the case of minerals and Table 15.1 points out the levies across government levels at different stages of mining.

Research by the authors based on some limited data sets from the minerals and coal sector seems to suggest that resource revenue distribution between the centre and states is very much linked to the

Box 3: Key Payments

Royalty and dead rent
Compensatory afforestation and NPV (forest lands)
Fees
R&R payment
Income taxes
Environmental Fees
Water cess
General Sales tax
Local taxes
Labour welfare cess
Cess on local bearing lands (some states)

amount of profits that companies are making. So in the case of coal development, the distribution across a select group of profit-making coal companies suggests a 50 per cent share of revenues between the centre and the states. An analysis of the balance sheets of two iron ore companies for 2005–2006 (one each in the public and private sectors) reveals that the share of state taxes (royalty and sales tax) in total revenues is in the range 17–23 per cent while the centre's share (mainly income tax and dividend tax) accounts for the balance. This is because large profits are made by iron ore companies due to increased demand, high prices and very low royalty payments that they make to states.[31]

The royalty system in India is a mix of unit-based and *ad valorem*-based approaches. For 39 minerals, the royalty is based on an *ad valorem* system (ranging from as low as 1% of sale price in the case of manganese concentrates to as high as 20% in the case of gypsum) while for 18 others, including iron ore, coal and lignite, it is a fixed amount per tonne of dispatch. There is currently a move in the direction of *ad valorem* rates, as the specific rates yield very low revenues to states in a time of buoyant commodity markets. While this move may be in conformity with international practice, the issue of determining the 'value' on which royalty is charged needs to be resolved. Comparing unit-based rates, it appears that with a few exceptions like iron ore, the royalty rates in India are higher than international rates (Table 15.2). This could be due to several factors, including mining conditions and costs.

Table 15.1
Charges Levied by Various Tiers of Government as Different Stages of Mining

Instrument	*Remarks*
Pre-production stage Central government Compensatory Afforestation charges and net present value (NPV0 of diverted forestland	All money paid by user agencies towards Compensatory Afforestation and NPV of diverted forestland is required to be put into a Compensatory Afforestaton Fund established under the new Compensatory Afforestation Management and Planning Authority (CAMPA)
State government	
Reconnaissance permit fee	
Prospecting fee	
Application fee for reconnaissance permit	
Application fee for mining lease	
Security deposits for reconaisance permit, prospecting licence and mining lease	
Consent to establish fees paid to the state pollution control board	
Production stage	
Central government Labour welfare cess	Applicable to mines of iron ore mangamese ore, chrome are, mica, limestone, and dolomite
Customs duty	Certain concessional rates available for mining
Excise duty	Minerals, except coal, exempted, however beneficiated/intermediate products subjects to duty. Intermediate products include mineral concentrates, cement clinkers, etc.
Income tax State government Royalty	Levied on a per-unit of weight basis or an ad valorem basis on sale price. Rates laid down by the central government
Dead rent	Uniform rate for the country, varies by lease area, period of idleness of lease, value of mineral and whether the lease is captive or not. The holder of the lease is liable to pay either royalty and dead rent, whichever is greater.

Cont'd...

Cont'd...

Surface rent	Paid on surface area used for mining operations at a rate not exceeding the land revenue
Water rent/rate/cess/tax	For the use of water for mining operations
Development charges	Some state governments levy charges for construction of road, bridges, etc.
Tax on land use	Some state governments levy tax on the land used for mining purposes
Stamp duty	On the instruments of transaction
Forest produce tax and forest passes	
Consent to operate fees paid to the State Pollution Control Board	
Local government taxes	
Property/house/municipal tax	On the basis on the asset value of property
Local government body taxes (village panchayat levies	
Post production/marketing stage Central government Central sales tax	
Export duty	
State government	
General sales tax	For availing of the government provided road infrastructure
Non-agricultural land assessment	May be levied on diversion of land for non-agricultural purposes like mining
Local government body tax	
Toll tax. Octrol/entry tax	
jurisdiction for Other charges	Levied on a good entering the local sale or consumption on tonnage or on a lumsum basis or on the basis of the mineral
Port charges	Levied by the port authorities for various services offered. For handling of cargo. landing and shipping fee, plot charges for stacking and other technical services like towing, varies by port and mineral

Table 15.2

Royalty Rates for Select Minerals in Some Countries of Asia

	Coal	*Iron Ore*	*Limestone*	*Copper*	*Bauxite*
Indonesia	13.5% fob or of sales revenue	<100.000 Tonnes. $2.7 /Tonne;> 100.000 tonees, $2.9/tonne	<500.000 tonnes, $0.14/tonne; > 500.000 tonnes, #0.16 tonne	<80.000 tonnes, $45/tonne; > 80.000 tonnes. $5/tonne	<200.000 tonnes 50.40/tonne; >=200.000 50.50/tonne
Philippines	10 pesos/tonne	2% and valorem on market value	2% ad valorem on market value	2% ad valorem on market value	Not available
China	1%of sales revenue (add resource tax 0.3–5 yuan/tonne)	2% of sales revenue (add resource tax 2–30 yuan/tonne)	2% of sales revenue (add resource tax 0.5–20 yuan/tonne	2% of sales revenue (add resource tax 0.4–30 yaan/tonne	2% of sales revenue (add resource tax 0.4–30 yaan/tonne
India	Coking coal; Rs 115–250/tonne; Non-coking coal; Rs 65–165/tonne	Rs 4/tonne (10% Fe or less) to Rs 27/tonne (65% Fe content or more)	Rs 55/tonne	3.2% of London Metal Exchange Copper metal price chargeable on the contained copper metal in ore produced	(a) 0.40% of London Metal Exchange Aluminium metal price chargeable on the contained aluminium metal in ore produced for those despatched for use in alumina and aluminium metal extraction. (b) 20% of sale price on ad valorem basis for those despateched for use other than alumina and aluminium metal extraction and for export

Source: Otto et al. (2006) and Otto and Cordes (2003).

As a percentage of price, the current royalty rates of noncoking coal in India translate into about 8–16 per cent of the pithead price,[32] which is much higher than the *ad valorem* rates charged internationally (2–8%), though strictly speaking it may not be relevant to compare rates, given the differences in the quality of Indian coal and the lack of clarity on what the value basis used internationally is. In the case of iron ore, Indonesia follows specific rates that are much higher than Indian rates (in rupee terms). Further, the specific rates for iron ore were in the range of 1–2 per cent of the sale price in 2004–2005, which is comparable or lower than the rates internationally. However, a meaningful comparison is difficult without clearly understanding the base on which *ad valorem* rates are applied.

States have argued for royalty rates to be revised more frequently than what has been done in the past because they claim to have lost out on revenue even in real terms. In the case of coal, for instance, which accounts for the largest share of royalty revenue, rates have been revised only four times since the nationalization of the industry between 1971 and 1973. Second, it is argued that royalty should set on an *ad valorem* basis so as to provide greater buoyancy to revenues in line with the rise in price of minerals,[33] a demand that was recommended by the Hoda Committee in 2006[34] but is not get reflected in the National Mineral Policy of 2008.[35] The Hoda Committee highlights the loss to mineral-bearing states from using specific rates of royalty for iron ore (Table 15.3).

Table 15.3

Comparison of Current Royalty Revenue versus One Based on Ad Valorem Rates for Iron Ore (2005–2005) (Rs. Crore)

State	*Specific Rate*	*Assuming a 7.5% Ad Valorem Rate*
Chhattisgarh	42	260
Jharkhand	23	180
Orissa	72	456
Karnataka	79.75	418
Country (142 mt)		1600
		Assuming a Price of Rs 1500/mt

Source: Planning Commission (2006), pp. 152–53.

Voices from States and Local People

Resource-bearing states have become increasingly dissatisfied with centre–state relations, both fiscal and administrative, and the space that is occupied by the centre. The government of Chhattisgarh, for example, had the following to say in its memo to the Twelfth Finance Commission.[36]

> Extraction of minerals is governed by the policy of the Union Government which also lays down the rates of royalty to be charged on minerals. Perhaps since the Central Government undertakings have been the biggest consumers of these minerals, the revision of the rates of schedule have never been timely. Even the belated revision in the rates has been guided more by commercial interests of these undertakings rather than market trends.

Further it says,

> For major minerals, the Government of India fixes royalty rates, which are supposed to be revised every three years.[37] There is always a delay in revising these rates. These delays are obviously of benefit to the Union, at the expense of States. As a major mineral producer, Chhattisgarh has been particularly hard-hit, with the non-revision of rates resulting in revenue stagnation on this account and a potential loss to the State. Non-revision of rates in a regular and transparent manner amounts to a discrimination against the States, which rely heavily on mineral resources, which also happen to be the backward States.

At the state level, a summary of the major demands would include the following:

- Move to an *ad valorem* system of royalty;
- Minimize central government intervention and control; and
- Provide a more stable fiscal regime.

At the local level, antimining protests in some states and difficulties in starting new mines in others are pointers to poor management of the local impacts of mineral development and a fast eroding social licence to operate. Most often this hostility is due to decisions taken by governments without consulting the local people. Negative environmental and social outcomes in mining regions are a result of inadequate oversight by regulatory bodies at various levels of government and poor rule enforcement. Our earlier studies in the mining regions of Goa suggest that oversight bodies fail to deliver not only because they are captured by mining interests in the region, but also because these institutions lack the capacity and the knowledge to carry out their responsibilities. This lack of capacity is compounded by a shortage of human and financial resources (TERI 2002, 2006).

Conclusions

This chapter sought to address the following questions: How are the powers and functions over resources and resource development assigned among various levels of government? Do governments at different levels respect the constitutional assignment of powers and functions or is there an encroachment into each other's domains? Does the functioning of the institutions of federalism in the context of resource development ensure the goals of economic efficiency, political participation and protection of rights? How can federalism be strengthened, given the current developments in the area of natural resource development? In this concluding section we bring together our observations on what we have learnt from this study and make some suggestions to strengthen resource federalism.

Our key observations can be summarized as follows:

1. The Constitution while recognizing the rights of states to regulate mines and mineral development does so with a rider – that it has to be in conformity with the centre's power to do exactly the same through legislation. While states have the right to allow exploitation of minerals, they have to have the prior approval of the centre in the case of some major minerals specified by central legislation.
2. There is an encroachment into the states' domain in the working of resource federalism through the MMDR Act. The sources of disagreement between the centre and states revolve around the following points:
    - The manner of royalty fixation.
    - Delays in revising royalty rates for coal
    - Control over minerals development by the centre that does not reflect states' need for new investments
    - Matters of cess and other charges on mines and other minerals under Entries 49–50 of List II
    - Under the Indian Constitution, decentralization until the level of the gram sabha is recognized. But most of this decentralization is left to be defined by the states. All the

> powers, whether regulatory, administrative, or fiscal 'may' be provided for by the states in their laws on panchayats. This is especially problematic in Schedule V areas (key to the mineral-rich states) where there are provisions under the PESA Act giving special powers to the gram sabhas in Scheduled Areas, The steps taken by the states have not been adequate in strengthening the concept of self-governance as envisaged by this legislation.

In general, the focus of institutions has been on pursuing economic efficiency goals, not the other goals of government such as ensuring greater political participation among the local people and protecting their rights. Mineral resource endowments are sources of wealth but also sources of social disruption, displacement, environmental degradation, health impacts and potential sources of conflict and violence. Therefore, the distribution of benefits and costs of such development across and within states should become key to the discussion on resource federalism.[38]

Resource federalism, we argue, can be strengthened through the creation of more independent bodies to determine issues related to centre–state interests, expanding the space for local governance; improved compensation and the sharing of resource revenues and enhanced local institutional capacity. Based on our analysis, we would argue that control over decisions that relate to revenue augmentation for the states should be exercised by an independent body, such as the Finance Commission or some other third-party mechanism that is neither linked to the centre nor the states. Alternatively, a cooperative arrangement can be set up by the states, or collectives of states, for the purpose of setting common royalty rates across states, which better reflect their interests and needs.

Compensation payments, however, need to go beyond being just for resource use and for incremental costs created by resource development and should include both a share in economic rents and project benefits.[39] Such payments cannot be just for restoring what is lost, but to create stakes in the project for those who contribute to it through loss of socio-cultural assets, livelihoods and land. We would argue that local people in mining regions should get a share of royalty payments, not directly, but through special dedicated expenditure programmes run on this share, that are aimed at teaching them new skills. The resource development process involves profound changes in the lives of people. A whole generation unlearns its skills and becomes dependent on the resource development. At the time of closing a project, if adequate planning has not been put in place, locals are left with few opportunities now that their key resource is depleted, and what were their traditional occupations before the resource development are lost. This cannot be acceptable in a true federation. It is important for federations to recognize that the finiteness of mineral resources and the profound changes they create in lives of local people during their development cycle give local people a moral right to a share in the depletion component of the royalty payment.

Institutional strengthening is key to addressing externalities at the local level. It is true that states being the owners of minerals should have the power to manage their resources according to their needs and that includes raising revenue from them. However, it is equally important that the revenue so generated is put to use in a judicious manner. The states and local governments should be enjoined to have adequate mechanisms in place and the capacity to use the funds to deal with the adverse impacts of mining on both the environment and the people. Management of such revenues may often be inadequate, either because of corruption, low accountability and/or inadequate implementation capacity. The negative aspects associated with resource development suggest that demands by resource-bearing states cannot be seen as just a centre–state issue, but one involving the substate and local level, where various groups have interests in the development of resources or their nondevelopment. Resource federalism will need to reflect this inclusive governance.

Notes

1. See the discussion in 'Rethinking Federalism', Inman and Rubinfeld, 1997, *Journal of Economic Perspectives*, Vol. 11, No. 4. Fall, 43–64, where they argue that the institutions of federalism need to balance competing goals of government: economic efficiency, political participation and protection of rights; also Bagchi 2003, 37–38, for a discussion in the Indian context.
2. Impacts from minerals development include land alienation and deterioration, loss of access to common property and services, loss of traditional

livelihoods, the crowding out of agriculture, increased morbidity and mortality from environmental health impacts, human rights infringements and displacement. MERN Working Paper series, G. McMahon, ed. (1998); Cernea (2000) and IIED and WBCSD (2002).

3. Baviskar depicts the multiple affiliations well, 'The adivasi fighting against displacement in the Narmada valley is simultaneously a tribal, a farmer, a collector of forest produce, a woman, a mother, a consumer of manufactured goods like fertilizers and saris, a worker on state drought-relief projects …' (2003: 5052).
4. Ministry of Mines, Annual Report 2009–2010; http://mines.nic.in/index.aspx?lid=346&level=2&chk=24dfe45y5edf5e3
5. Data source: Ministry of Mines; web site: http://mines.nic.in/writereaddata/Contentlinks/749ebe57043244788110501263142941.pdf
6. http://fincomindia.nic.in/pubsugg/memo_ori.pdf, http://fincomindia.nic.in/pubsugg/memo_jkhand.pdf and http://fincomindia.nic.in/pubsugg/memo_chattis.pdf *The web link is no longer operational. It was a memorandum submitted by the State for the twelfth Finance Commission and the authors had accessed it last some time in 2009.*
7. Schedule VII of the Constitution of India, read with Article 246, in its three lists, union, state and concurrent, deals with this assignment. Broadly, List I or the Union list covers subjects that serve at a national level and List II or the State List comprises those areas which are limited to a state's jurisdiction, subject to other clauses. With regard to List III, both the Parliament and state legislatures can make laws but in the case of a conflict there is no scope for a harmonious reading of the provisions, the law made by the Parliament prevails. Only the Parliament has the residuary power to make laws on matters that are not included in any of the three lists.
8. Regulation and development of minerals is a state subject, but it has to be in conformity with the central legislation.
9. Minor minerals refer to building stones, gravel, ordinary clay, ordinary sand other than sand used for prescribed purposes and any other mineral which the central government may, by notification in the official gazette, declare to be a minor mineral. See MMDR Act sec 3 (e). They comprised 11 per cent of the total value of mineral production in the country in 2005–2006.
10. Cess Act 1880, West Bengal Rural Employment and Production Act, 1976, West Bengal Primary Education Act, 1973.
11. *State of West Bengal vs Kesoram Industries Ltd* 1532–1533 of 1993.
12. P.A. Chacko et al., 'Enquiry Report – PUCL Dumka, Jharkhand Unit', September 2003. Available at http://www.pucl.org/Topics/Industries-envirn-resettlement/2003/pachwara.htm

13. *Samatha vs State of Andhra Pradesh* (1997) 8 SCC 191.
14. Scheduled Areas in Andhra Pradesh, Jharkhand, Gujarat, Himachal Pradesh, Madhya Pradesh, Chhattisgarh, Maharashtra, Orissa and Rajasthan.
15. Para 5 (2) of Schedule V, Constitution of India.
16. Article 298, Constitution of India.
17. *Samatha vs State of Andhra Pradesh* (1997) 8 SCC 191.
18. The power of Parliament to legislate for two or more states by consent and adoption of such legislation by any other state.
19. http://envfor.nic.in/sites/default/files/introduction-nep2006e.pdf
20. http://www.dolr.nic.in/NRRP2007.pdf
21. George Mathew, 'Institutions of Self-Government in India: Towards a Multilevel Federalism', *Review of Development and Change*, Vol. II, No. 2, 1997, Chennai.
22. Entry 5, List II.
23. Article 243.
24. Article 243 A.
25. Article 243M (4) and Article 243ZC (3).
26. Committee to make recommendations on the salient features of the law for extending provisions of the Constitution 73rd Amendment Act, 1992, to Scheduled Areas.
27. States with districts in Schedule V areas: Andhra Pradesh, Jharkhand, Gujarat, Himachal Pradesh, Madhya Pradesh, Chhattisgarh, Maharashtra, Orissa and Rajasthan.
28. S 4 (d) of PESA.
29. Sanjay Upadhyay, 'Tribal Self-Rule Law and Common Property Resources in Scheduled Areas of India – A New Paradigm Shift or Another Ineffective Sop?' International Association for the Study of Common Property (IASCP) (2004).
30. Odd-Helge Fjeldstad, 'Intergovernmental Fiscal Relations in Developing Countries: A Review of Issues', CMI Working Paper WP 2001: 11.
31. However, these shares do not take into account the shares of states in the central tax pool and the redistribution that occurs to address vertical and horizontal fiscal imbalances.
32. Pit mouth value in case of coal in India as declared by the coal companies covers costs of production, depreciation and return on investment. In many ways it approximates the Gross Sales Value minus transport, handling and insurance valuation basis used in other countries. But a full parity is difficult to establish.
33. In the case of iron ore, dramatic price increases in the last few years have meant that the *ad valorem* incidence of specific rates fell to 1–2 per cent in 2004–2005 compared to 5–10 per cent in the two preceding years.

34. Planning Commission. 2006. Report of the High Level Committee (Hoda Committee)
35. http://mines.nic.in/NMP2008.pdf
36. http://fincomindia.nic.in/pubsugg/memo_chattis.pdf; see also the views of Jharkhand and Orissa, http://fincomindia.nic.in/pubsugg/memo_jkhand.pdf; http://fincomindia.nic.in/pubsugg/memo_ori.pdf
37. Section 9 (3) of the MMDR Act, however, stipulates that the central government shall not enhance the rates of royalty with respect to any mineral more than once during any period of three years. An expert group appointed for the purpose recommends the rates to the central government.
38. This is especially the case for hydropower projects.
39. See Cernea (2007) for a detailed discussion on this issue.

References

Bagchi, A. 2003. 'Rethinking Federalism: Changing Power Relations between the Centre and the States', *Publius: The Journal of Federalism,* 33 (4), pp. 21–42.

Baviskar, A. 2003. 'For a Cultural Politics of Natural Resources', *Economic & Political Weekly,* Vol. XXXVIII, No. 48, pp. 5051–5056.

Cernea, M. 2000. 'Impoverishment or Social Justice? A Model for Planning Resettlement', in H. Mathur and D. Mardsen (eds.), *Development Projects and Impoverishment Risks: Resettling Project Affected People in India,* New Delhi: Oxford University Press.

——. 2007. 'Financing for Development: Benefit Sharing Mechanisms in Population Resettlement', *Economic and Political Weekly,* Vol. 42, No. 12, 24 March, pp. 1033–1046.

Chacko, P.A. et al. 2003. 'Enquiry Report—PUCL Dumka, Jharkhand Unit', September. http://www.pucl.org/Topics/Industries-envirn-resettlement/2003/pachwara.htm

Finance Commission. http://fincomindia.nic.in/pubsugg/memo_ori.pdf; http://fincomindia.nic.in/pubsugg/memo_jkhand.Pdf; http://fincomindia.nic.in/pubsugg/memo_chattis.pdf

IIED and WBCSD. 2002. *Breaking New Ground: Mining, Minerals and Sustainable Development,* London: Earthscan.

Inman, R.P. and Daniel L. Rubinfeld. 1997. 'Rethinking Federalism', *Journal of Economic Perspectives,* 11 (4), pp. 43–64.

Mathew, George. 1997. 'Institutions of Self-Government in India: Towards a Multilevel Federalism', *Review of Development and Change,* Vol. II, No. 2, Chennai.

McMahon, G. (ed.). 1998. *Mining and the Community: Results of the Quito Conference,* Washington: World Bank.

Ministry of Environment and Forests. http://envfor.nic.in/sites/default/files/annual_report/nep2006e.pdf (Reference for endnote no. xix)

Ministry of Statistics and Programme Implementation. http://www.mospi.nic.in/Odd-Helge, F. 2001. *Intergovernmental Fiscal Relations in Developing Countries: A Review of Issues,* Working paper No. 11 (Reference source for figure 15.2 and endnote no. xxx).

Östensson, O. (n.d.). 'Revenue Sharing and Distribution', presentation at the RIIA workshop on Sustainable Relationships: Financing and Monitoring Responsibilities (Reference source for Figure 15.4).

Otto, J.M. and J. Cordes. 2002. *The Regulation of Mineral Enterprises: A Global Perspective on Economics, Law and Policy,* Westminster, Colorado: Rocky Mountain Mineral Law Foundation (Reference source for Table 15.2).

Otto, J.M., C. Andrews, F.T. Cawood and M. Doggett. 2006. *Mining Royalties: A Global Study of their Impact on Investors,* Government and Civil Society, Washington: The World Bank Group (Reference source for Table 15.2)

Planning Commission. 2006. *Report of the High Level Committee (Hoda Committee) to Review the National Mineral Policy and to Recommend Possible Amendments to the Mines and Minerals (Development and Regulation) Act, 1957,* New Delhi: Planning Commission, Government of India (Reference for endnote no. xxxiv).

Reserve Bank of India. 2007. 'State Finances: A Study of Budgets of 2007–08', http://rbidocs.rbi.org.in/rdocs/Publications/PDFs/81840.pdf (Reference source for Figure 15.3).

Rosencranz, A., S. Divan and M.L. Noble. 1991. *Environmental Law and Policy in India: Cases, Materials and Statutes,* Bombay: Tripathi.

TERI. 2002, 2006. *Environmental/Social Performance Indicators (ESPIs) and Sustainability Markers in Minerals Development: Reporting Progress Towards Improved Health and Human Well-being: Phases II and III*. Report submitted to IDRC, Canada.

——. 2007, 2008. *Study on Compensation to Resource-Bearing States Submitted to Inter-State Council Secretariat, Ministry of Home Affairs*, New Delhi (Project Report No. 2006RD21).

Upadhyay, S. 2004. *Tribal Self-Rule Law and Common Property Resources in Scheduled Areas of India: A New Paradigm Shift or Another Ineffective Sop*, International Association for the Study of Common Property (IASCP) (Reference source for end note no. xxix).

List of Cases

State of West Bengal vs Kesoram Industries Ltd, 1532–1533 of 1993

Synthetics and Chemicals Ltd. & Ors vs State of UP & Ors (1990) 1 SCC 109

Samatha vs State of Andhra Pradesh (1997) 8 SCC 191

List of Acts

Cess Act 1880

Land Acquisition Act of 1894

West Bengal Rural Employment and Production Act, 1976

West Bengal Primary Education Act, 1973.

16

Internal Security

Pretext for More Central Control or Genuine Urge to Counter Terror

Dhananjay Tripathi

Following the Indian Constitution, the very first article is, 'India, that is Bharat, shall be a union of states' and the very next article elucidates that 'Parliament may by law admit into the Union, or establish, new States on such terms and conditions as it thinks fit'. With just a cursory look at these two articles, one can justify the comment of the constitutional expert, Granville Austin, that India is a 'Quasi-Federal' state. Architects of the Indian Constitution had their explanations for keeping the basic structure of the Constitution more in favour of the centre in terms of enjoying more power than the states and many scholars justify this unique feature of Indian federalism. For the adherent supporters of Indian federalism, legacy of partition and the weight of history cannot be ignored while discussing the question of Indian federalism (Arora 2007). Indian Constitution, which came into existence following independence from the British Raj, faced several challenges – the foremost among them being the maintenance of unity and integrity of the country. In view of various pulls and pressures from different sides under the aegis of princely states, the Constitution kept foreign policy, national security and monetary policies on the Union list. Interestingly, internal security was also brought under the control of the centre with several powers vested with it to keep a check on states. The founding fathers of the Indian Constitution offered a justification for a strong centre, as reflected in the debates of the Constituent Assembly.

> Now that the partition is a settled fact, we are unanimously of the view that it would be injurious to the interests of the country to provide for a weak central authority which would be incapable of ensuring peace, of coordinating vital matters of common concern and of effectively for the whole country in the international sphere.[1]

In brief, a strong centre was the need of the time, but today the appropriate question is, should we rethink Indian federalism, particularly with respect to the issue of internal security. A skewed distribution of powers, once legitimized on certain grounds, needs a proper discussion in the light of security threats being posed to India from across the border.

Security Situation of India

India, as a country, has been confronted with several security threats since long both from the external and internal sources. India is faced with unreceptive and hostile neighbours such as China and Pakistan and also other bordering countries with which it does not share very cordial relationships. The issue of Kashmir between India and Pakistan continues to be the main source of hostility between the two countries; in fact a few other conflicts in the post-World War II era (with the possible exception of Arab–Israel dispute) have proved as much intractable (Gunguly 2001). Infiltrations from Pakistan are yet to be fully controlled, while threats from cross-border infiltration cannot be ignored. There exist similar problems in Punjab and Assam as also in Tripura, Meghalaya, Manipur and Nagaland, which need to be fully solved. Different groups operating from foreign soils are covertly or overtly aiding some of these activities.

India has not only faced problems pertaining to security abetted from other countries but also from many internal conflicts. Religious extremism, violence and riots are part of the bigger problems, and at times, it requires interventions from the centre. In the past, as there are evidences to show, whenever the state governments failed to maintain proper law and order situation, either they requested for the central forces or the centre itself took charge. Recently, the communal violence in Assam has left no choice for the state government, but to request the involvement of the central forces. In fact, the Chief Minister of Assam even went public, criticizing the delay in the deployment of central forces to bring normalcy in the riot-hit areas. These are evidences enough to substantiate the bigger role of the centre in keeping the law and order intact in the country.

While discussing security threats to India, one cannot overlook the left-wing extremism that lately has become a major cause for worry, with Prime Minister acknowledging it as the biggest threat to internal security. In one of the speeches, while addressing the Chief Minister's meet on Naxalism, India's Prime Minister Dr Manmohan Singh had said,

> I came here with the primary purpose of listening to your views and the strategies you are adopting to face the challenges of Naxalism. It would not be an exaggeration to say that the problem of Naxalism is the single biggest internal security challenge ever faced by our country.[2]

The assertion of Prime Minister has been ever authenticated by the government reports. As per the recent report of the Ministry of Home Affairs (MHA), nine states are worst affected by Naxal violence. Although the total number of deaths due to Naxal violence has declined, in some states, these figures are on the rise (see Table 16.1). In brief, Naxalism has become a major threat to India's internal security and the government is duty bound to take all necessary measures to keep the unity and the integrity of the country intact.

Table 16.1

Statewise Left-Wing Extremism Report (2009–2011)

States	*2009*		*2010*		*2011*	
	Incidents	*Deaths*	*Incidents*	*Deaths*	*Incidents*	*Deaths*
Andhra Pradesh	66	18	100	24	54	09
Bihar	232	72	307	97	314	62
Chhattisgarh	529	290	625	343	465	204
Jharkhand	724	208	501	157	517	182
Madhya Pradesh	1	—	7	1	08	00
Maharashtra	154	93	94	45	109	54
Odhisa	266	67	218	79	192	53
Uttar Pradesh	8	2	6	1	01	00
West Bengal	255	158	350	258	90	41

Source: Annual Report 2011–2012; MHA, Government of India.

The discussion on security situation in India will remain incomplete without a proper reference on terrorism. As a matter of fact, India is in the forefront among those countries that have suffered immensely because of terrorism over the last several decades, while varying only in degree, terrorism has struck India's every corner (Chandra 2004). As per the report of MHA 2011–2012, there is an improvement and the terrorist activities have gone down, 'terrorism in the hinterland has been by and large under control except for the serial bomb blasts in Mumbai in July, 2011 and the bomb blast in Delhi High Court in September, 2011'. The numbers of terrorist activities in the recent years have declined, but the threats are real and very much present. Under these circumstances, the exercise of vigilance on the part of centre is critical and it is difficult to argue for the curtailment of its role in counter terror activities.

From a security perspective, India is faced with a number of problems and those scholars arguing for a strong centre cannot be completely ignored. Still, it is important to debate the intention of the centre when it comes up with proposals such as National Counter Terrorism Centre (NCTC). Analytical political questions are justified when a proposal is floated, which ultimately gives an extra power to the central agencies, while ignoring the role of state agencies in dealing with issues pertaining to security threats.

Internal Security and the Question of Federalism

Is internal security a subject of the centre or of states? There is a degree of ambiguity with respect to this subject. It is disappointing to note that despite several regional problems, issues of terrorism and disturbances and riots, we still shy away from discussing these issues in detail. Regarding many of these situations, the role of states is critical, but it is always considered limited to law and order. This is where lies the root of problems. On important matters of security, the role of state is neither recognized nor involved in the decision-making process at the macro level.

We somehow miss the point that the problem of internal security embraces aspects of social, economic and political life. The larger socio-economic and political questions emanating from indigenous sources are often of more immediate concerns (Mathur 1994). The political differences between the centre and states also sometimes lead to problems and can become a source of internal security threat, but these are somehow brushed aside. Hence, we cannot deny the fact that caste and religion do also play a critical role in the Indian polity and sometimes rifts between different castes and communities take on the shape of a serious security threat. It will also not be wrong to assert that we, as a nation, have yet to get out of our colonial past and failed to rewrite our future. One can understand that the Constituent Assembly was overly conscious of security issues and posed equal threat to internal and external security by giving more unitary powers to the centre to override its constituent units at its sweet will (Prakash 2005). The wisdom of the Constituent Assembly was impeccable considering the fragile situation prevailing at the time of independence, but it would be wrong to assume that the contemporary problems related to internal security are of similar nature. Hence, there is a need to rethink the sharing of power between the centre and states so that the issue of internal security is not presumed as a seed of political contention in the Indian federal structure.

Before coming to the specific debate, it is worth noting that maintaining security (internal/external) is considered an obligation on the part of a state. This is the reason why some political theorists defended the application of all possible means to preserve the authority of a state. Interestingly, social contract theorists such as Thomas Hobbes argued vehemently for an all-powerful 'Monarch' in his classical work Leviathan. Protecting the state is the foremost responsibility of the 'Monarch', he argued. Since democratic governments have displaced monarchy in the modern times, one can also interpret Hobbes in a different way. For the supporters of Hobbesian thesis, an elected government must apply stringent policies for maintaining law and order. This is a hawkish viewpoint as it gives complete freedom to the state leaving ample of scope for the misuse of power. The scare of insecurity always strengthens the state apparatus and this is evident from the developments following the terrorist attacks on the United States.

On the contrary, another social contract theorist Jacques Rousseau contends that government is a result of social contract and, thus, remains legitimized by the people. In the contemporary political theory, the use of excessive force or coercive tactics by the state for maintaining law and order is questioned. 'Coercion and force may be important but that does not mean they are more important than anything else. A political order, which may not hold together without force, may also collapse if numerous other factors are not present. Even tyrannical regimes require something more than force to remain in place; they cannot maintain themselves only with force' (Morris 2004: 201). Thus, there are other ways of maintaining security and the state need not be always centralized and coercive in its acts. Hence, it is wrong to argue that India as a state survived only because of a strong centre. There are several other factors and one must not forget the immense role of democracy in this country. In the light of this, we should look at the new debate on internal security and Indian federalism.

In this regard, the example of Naxal violence is of paramount importance considering the fact that how significant is the role of state when it comes ensuring to internal security. From paradigm of security, Naxalism is an antistate armed movement and it should be dealt with an iron hand. This is one side of the story; and by adhering to this position, we are ignoring the primary cause of Naxalism. No doubt left-wing extremism is an ideological war being waged against the Indian state, but its supporters/cadres are mainly the ones who are at the receiving end of this parliamentary democracy. Even after more than 60 years of independence, Indian state has failed to solve the problems of poverty, hunger, homelessness, illiteracy and, above all, the problem of social discrimination in the name of caste. The urge to resort to violence finds a fertile ground precisely in such a situation (Raja 2008: 2). Therefore, a complete security approach and bulwark from the top, ignoring the political role of other constituent units, is bound to fail in the case of Naxal violence. There is an issue of development, which can be dealt with properly at the local level, where the role of state governments is important. In short, some of the internal security challenges can be resolved through a proper coordination between the centre and states. A deviation from this has different political implications. It can be interpreted as a well-thought out plan of the centre to tighten its grip on states.

NCTC – Critical Debate in Right Direction

From time to time, debates on internal security and federalism are raised in India and this time it is on the issue of NCTC. In the past several terrorist attacks, particularly 26/11 Mumbai terror strike had shaken the country even as fingers are being raised towards our preparation to counter terror. Many scholars dubbed 26/11 Mumbai terror attack as a complete failure of intelligence, which, however, was countered by the centre. Not only in the case of Mumbai terror attack but also with respect to other such incidents, the centre and states blame each other for not acting on time. The centre generally accuses state governments of not taking intelligence inputs seriously, while the state governments refute these charges and many a time a war of words between the centre and states becomes unpleasant. To resolve these differences, the centre has proposed a federal agency to counter the terror threat on the lines of the United States – NCTC, but with different provisions, which have been advised especially for the Indian context. This idea of NCTC has not been received well by several states. There is a perception that NCTC will ultimately destroy the federal structure. However, it is not that everyone is opposed to NCTC and that there is even a strong section within the national security establishment which is of the view that tough acts and unitary control are the only credible deterrence to the menace of terrorism. For them, the opposition to NCTC is politically motivated and lacks substance (Chowdhary 2012). In this regard, we have to critically examine the relevance of NCTC.

The very first question is, do we really need NCTC? Interestingly, NCTC is an idea, taken from the United States, but is very different from the version adopted in India. The NCTC of the United States is undoubtedly a strong body, but it does not have similar powers, as proposed in its 'Indian version'. American NCTC comes under the Directorate of National intelligence, with specialists from Pentagon, FBI and CIA. The American NCTC also has experts from other such agencies empowered to access databases of all the specialized security agencies. In brief, the NCTC of the United States is only entitled to collect, collate and assess terrorism-related information. It does not enjoy the powers to conduct any covert or overt operations (Chari 2012). This is a major point of difference between the Indian NCTC and American NCTC.

In the case of India, NCTC is not only responsible for intelligence gathering but also entrusted with the power to conduct operations including raids, searches and arrests. India already has had several agencies both at the central and state levels for intelligence gathering as also to conduct operations to deter terrorism. In this regard, the government needs to justify one extra agency for almost similar objectives. There are already lots of criticisms about the lack of coordination between these agencies and it is considered a problem by itself. The other significant point is that NCTC will function under the Intelligence Bureau (IB), which in itself is a problematic connotation. As a well-known fact, IB in the past was used for political purposes and sometimes for gathering information for the ruling parties for hatching political strategies. The lack of coordination between Research and Analysis Wing (RAW) and IB has also come to be noticed. Keeping NCTC under IB will not only raise questions regarding the political motives of the centre, but also it will widen the wedge between IB and RAW. Thus, whatever the intentions, the end results might be very different.

There are central and state intelligence agencies other than IB such as National Intelligence Agency (NIA), National Intelligence Grid (NATGRID) and National Technical Research Organisation (NTRO). It is important to note that NIA Act 2008 came into force after the 26/11 Mumbai attacks. The NIA Act empowers the central agency to arrest individuals, search premises and seize material evidences for the trail of offences in NIA special courts. According to Chapter II, Article 3 (2) of the NIA Act, 'officer of the agency shall have throughout India in relation to the investigation of Scheduled Offences and arrest of persons concerned in such offences, all the powers, duties and privileges and liabilities which police officers have in connection with the investigation of offences committed therein'. This itself amounts to violating the basic federal principles (Chakma 2012). Apart from setting up NIA, it was also approved that the government would establish regional hubs of the National Security Guard (NSG) in Mumbai, Chennai, Hyderabad and Kolkata. These regional NSG hubs are to assist help in counter terror operations. With a new NIA Act of 2008 and regional NSG hubs, one can even question why in such a short span, the government has become so interested in setting up another intelligence agency under the direct control of the centre.

Internal security always has been a critical issue for the Indian state but it remains unrecognized officially. Many a time, security experts have suggested that India have a Ministry of Internal Security for appropriately dealing with these problems. This has never been given a proper hearing by the establishment and inferences can be drawn from these instances. The prime question here is, is internal security really an issue for the Indian state or it is an old presumption that anything related to security should exclusively be treated under the union list of our constitution. Therefore, the question on the intention of the central government is valid and the practicability of NCTC has come under the scanner. The doubts and objections of the state governments on the draft of NCTC is not a chimera based on some unwarranted worry. There is a justified issue of federal principle linked with the NCTC. The central government must take into confidence all the constituent units, before taking a final decision on NCTC. It is good that a debate on federalism and internal security has come to the forefront due to NCTC, but it should not remain limited to a specific issue. This is the time to rethink Indian federalism from the perspective of internal security.

Conclusions

Indian federalism has always been under discussion with respect to several subjects and there are adherent critiques of the present power sharing arrangements. The unitary bias of the Indian Constitution was defensible at the time of independence. Even now, India is among the countries that have witnessed several secessionist movements and especially in the present context, Naxalism, as a potential threat. In these circumstances, no one can evade the question of security, particularly internal security, but the question is how to respond to these intriguing developments? Should we continue with our age-old policy of strong centre with everything kept strictly under the union list or should we openly deliberate on the role of states for long lasting solutions. A number of problems associated with internal security are consequence of our denial to accept that socio-economic issues have their own role to play. The persisting internal security complications cannot be solved only by a tough and technical implementation of rules and procedures. The government needs to go beyond the conventional thinking and the role of states should be duly recognized. Without a proper consent of the constituent units, any effort towards enhancing security apparatus will only be perceived as a ploy of the union to have more control on states. The genuine urge to deter terrorism can only be possible through a genuine involvement of states and the centre in accordance with the correct principles of federalism.

Notes

1. See, the debate in the Constituent Assembly. This is part of the report of the union powers committee presented by Pt. Nehru. Available at: http://parliamentofindia.nic.in/ls/debates/vol5p3b.htm

2. For the complete speech, visit http://www.pmindia.gov.in/speech-details.php?nodeid=302

References

Arora, B. 2007. 'India's Experience with Federalism: Lessons Learnt and Unlearnt', paper presented in Seminar on *Constitutionalism and Diversity in Nepal,* organized by Centre for Nepal and Asia Studies, Kathmandu, 22–24 August. 2007.

Chakma, S. 2012. 'India Does Not Need NCTC', *The Pioneer*, 2 May. Accessed on 15 August 2012, http://www.dailypioneer.com/columnists/item/51542-india-does-not-need-nctc.html.

Chandra, R. 2004. *Global Terrorism: A Threat to Humanity*, New Delhi: Kalpaz Publications.

Chari, P.R. 2012. 'National Counter Terrorism Centre for India Understanding the Debate', *IPCS Policy Brief*, No. 181, March.

Chowdhary, A. 2012. 'Why India Need a National Counter Terrorism Centre'. Accessed on 17 August 2012, http://www.rediff.com/news/slide-show/slide-show-1-the-upa-government-gets-stumped-again/20120222.htm.

Gunguly, S. 2001. *Conflict Unending: India-Pakistan Tension Since 1947*, New York: Columbia University Press.

Mathur, M.K. 1994. *Police, Law and Internal Security,* New Delhi: Gyan Publisher.

Morris, W.C. 2004. 'The Modern State', in Gerald. F. Gaus and Chandran Kukathas (eds.), *Handbook of Political Theory*, London: Sage Publications.

Prakash, A. 2005. *Politics and Internal Security*, Mumbai: Popular Prakashan.

Raja, D. 2008. 'The Naxal Movement: A Realistic Approach', in P.V. Ramana (ed.), *The Naxal Challenge: Causes, Linkages and Policy Options*, New Delhi: Dorling Kindersley.

Contributors

Anil Kumar Vaddiraju, Centre for Political Institutions, Governance and Development, Institute for Social and Economic Change, Bangalore.

Anirudha Barik, Doctoral Scholar, Centre for Economic Studies and Planning (CESP), Jawaharlal Nehru University (JNU), New Delhi.

Balveer Arora, Chairman, Centre for Multilevel Federalism, Institute of Social Science, New Delhi and Former Professor of Political Science, Jawaharlal Nehru University (JNU), New Delhi.

Biswajit Mohapatra, Department of Political Science, North-Eastern Hill University, Shillong.

Dhananjay Tripathi, Department of International Relations, South Asian University, New Delhi.

Dinkar Nayak, Department of Business Economics, The M.S. University of Baroda, Vadodara.

Divya Datt, The Energy and Resources Institute (TERI), New Delhi.

Harihar Bhattacharyya, Professor of Political Science, University of Burdwan, Burdwan.

Jayesh Shah, Research Associate, Centre for Culture and Development, Vadodara.

Lancy Lobo, Director, Centre for Culture and Development, Vadodara.

Ligia Noronha, Executive Director, Research Coordination, The Energy and Resource Institute (TERI), New Delhi.

Mrutuyanjaya Sahu, Research Associate, Centre for Culture and Development, Vadodara

Nagindas Sanghavi, Political Analyst, Mumbai.

Nidhi Srivastava, The Energy and Resources Institute (TERI), New Delhi.

P.V. Sridharan, The Energy and Resources Institute (TERI), New Delhi.

Prakash C. Jha, Lecturer (Senior), Amity Law School, Amity University, Jaipur.

Priyavadan Patel, Professor and Head, Department of Political Science, Faculty of Arts, The M.S. University of Baroda, Vadodara.

S.N. Sangita, Professor and Head, Centre for Political Institutions, Governance and Development, Institute for Social and Economic Change, Bangalore.

Sajal Nag, Head, Department of History, Assam University, Silchar (Assam).

Sangita Agrawal, Department of Business Economics, The M.S. University of Baroda, Vadodara.

Subhash C. Kashyap, Former Secretary-General of Lok Sabha and former Honorary Constitutional Adviser to Government of India.

Tapas Sen, Senior Fellow, National Institute of Public Finance and Policy, New Delhi.

Index